The Economic Cold War

Cold War History Series

General Editor: **Saki Dockrill**, Senior Lecturer in War Studies, King's College, London

The Cold War History Series aims to make available to scholars and students the results of advanced research on the origins and the development of the Cold War and its impact on nations, alliances and regions at various levels of statecraft, and in areas such as diplomacy, security, economy, military and society. Volumes in the series range from detailed and original specialised studies, proceedings of conferences, to broader and more comprehensive accounts. Each work deals with individual themes and periods of the Cold War and each author or editor approaches the Cold War with a variety of narrative, analysis, explanation, interpretation and reassessments of recent scholarship. These studies are designed to encourage investigation and debate on important themes and events in the Cold War, as seen from both East and West, in an effort to deepen our understanding of this phenomenon and place it in its context in world history.

Titles include:

Günter Bischof
AUSTRIA IN THE FIRST COLD WAR, 1945–55
The Leverage of the Weak

Martin H. Folly
CHURCHILL, WHITEHALL AND THE SOVIET UNION, 1940–45

Ian Jackson
THE ECONOMIC COLD WAR
America, Britain and East–West Trade, 1948–63

Saul Kelly
COLD WAR IN THE DESERT
Britain, the United States and the Italian Colonies, 1945–52

Donette Murray
KENNEDY, MACMILLAN AND NUCLEAR WEAPONS

Kevin Ruane
THE RISE AND FALL OF THE EUROPEAN DEFENCE COMMUNITY
Anglo-American Relations and the Crisis of European Defence, 1950–55

Cold War History
Series Standing Order ISBN 0–333–79482–6
(*outside North America only*)

You can receive future titles in this series as they are published by placing a standing order. Please contact your bookseller or, in case of difficulty, write to us at the address below with your name and address, the title of the series and the ISBN quoted above.

Customer Services Department, Macmillan Distribution Ltd, Houndmills, Basingstoke, Hampshire RG21 6XS, England

The Economic Cold War

America, Britain and East–West Trade, 1948–63

Ian Jackson

Lecturer in International Relations and American Foreign Policy
De Montfort University
Leicester

First published 2001 by
PALGRAVE
Houndmills, Basingstoke, Hampshire RG21 6XS and
175 Fifth Avenue, New York, N. Y. 10010
Companies and representatives throughout the world

PALGRAVE is the new global academic imprint of
St. Martin's Press LLC Scholarly and Reference Division and
Palgrave Publishers Ltd (formerly Macmillan Press Ltd).

ISBN 0–333–92031–7

This book is printed on paper suitable for recycling and made from fully managed and sustained forest sources.

A catalogue record for this book is available from the British Library.

Library of Congress Cataloging-in-Publication Data
Jackson, Ian, 1973–
    The economic Cold War : America, Britain and East–West trade, 1948–63 / Ian Jackson.
        p. cm. — (Cold War history series)
    Includes bibliographical references and index.
    ISBN 0–333–92031–7
        1. United States—Commerce—Communist countries—History.
        2. Communist countries—Commerce—United States—History.
        3. Great Britain—Commerce—Communist countries—History.
        4. Communist countries—Commerce—Great Britain—History.
    I. Title. II. Series.
    HF1456.5.C65 J32 2000
    382'.0973'01717—dc21
                                                            00–055680

10 9 8 7 6 5 4 3 2 1
10 09 08 07 06 05 04 03 02 01

Printed and bound in Great Britain by
Antony Rowe Ltd, Chippenham, Wiltshire

For my mother

Contents

List of Abbreviations

CFEP	Council for Foreign Economic Policy
ChinCom	China Committee
CoCom	Coordinating Committee
ECA	European Cooperation Administration
ECRB	Export Control Review Board
EDC	European Defence Community
EPC	Economic Policy Committee
ERP	European Recovery Programme
ESC	Economic Steering Committee
JWPC	Joint War Production Committee
NSC	National Security Council
OEEC	Organisation for European Economic Co-operation
PPS	Policy Planning Staff
PRC	People's Republic of China

Acknowledgements

When writing this book I received valuable assistance from a number of individuals and institutions. My greatest academic debt is to Dr Klaus Larres. Not only did he patiently supervise the thesis on which the present work is based, he continues to provide welcome support and encouragement in the formative stage of my professional career. I would also like to extend my appreciation to Professor Michael Cox and Dr Ann Lane for their advice, help and encouragement during the four years I have been working on this project. Gratitude is also due to Frank Cain, Yoko Kato and Tor Egil Førland for sharing the fruits of their fine research on Anglo-American East–West trade policy. In the United States two outstanding scholars, Professor Thomas McCormick of the University of Wisconsin-Madison and Professor Melvyn Leffler of the University of Virginia, encouraged my research from the outset. I cannot overemphasise the importance of Professor Alan Dobson's contribution to the improvement of my work. As the examiner of the original doctoral thesis he made many incisive comments that enabled me to write more confidently about a complex topic.

The research for this book was based on government documents in four archives in two countries. I am indebted to the staff of the Public Record Office in the UK and the National Archives, College Park, Maryland, the Harry S. Truman Library, Independence, Missouri, and the Dwight D. Eisenhower Library, Abilene, Kansas, in the United States for making my research trips a pleasurable experience. I acknowledge crown copyright on material cited from documents held at the Public Record Office. I also wish to acknowledge the enthusiastic reception of this project by the general editor of the *Cold War History* series, Dr Saki Dockrill.

I have dedicated this book to my mother in recognition of her generous support for my work and her faith in my academic ability during difficult times. I am most fortunate.

IAN JACKSON

Introduction

In recent years historians of post-war international relations have begun to focus on Anglo-American trade policy towards the Soviet Union and the People's Republic of China (PRC) in the early decades of the Cold War. This research has been stimulated by the declassification of thousands of government documents on East–West trade controls in the United States and Britain during the 1980s and 1990s. While this scholarship has cast a new light on the economic dimension of Western containment policies towards communist nations during the Cold War, research on the multilateral East–West trade coordinating committee on security export controls (CG-CoCom) is still in its formative stages. Although Western economic defence policy has been the subject of many articles and has been documented in several monographs, a comprehensive treatment of Anglo-American economic strategy during the Cold War has yet to appear. This study attempts to fill that gap in the historiography of the Cold War.

There are three main themes in the present work. First, this book synthesises previous writing on Western security export control policy. It discerns two schools of thought in scholarship on CoCom: the 'traditionalist' and 'revisionist' schools. Second, it examines Anglo-American perceptions of economic defence or containment strategy towards the Sino-Soviet bloc. This study concludes that Western governments instituted a strategic embargo and not a policy of economic warfare against communist nations from 1948–63, contrary to the findings of some scholars. Finally, this work analyses the cooperation and conflict between the United States and Britain over trade and strategic objectives in the early Cold War.

The historiography of CoCom: 'traditionalism' versus 'revisionism'

For the purposes of discussion, the historiographical debate on the origins and development of CoCom will be explained through an examination of two research schools, termed 'traditionalism' and 'revisionism'. It should be noted that these two schools do not bear resemblance to the traditionalist and revisionist paradigms that have dominated research on the origins of the Cold War. In this case, traditionalism refers to scholarly works that have been strongly influenced by the pioneering work of the political economist Gunnar Adler-Karlsson. The findings of revisionist research contradict the main conclusions of Adler-Karlsson's thesis, which argues that the United States, through economic coercion, forced its Western European allies to apply stringent controls on trade with communist nations. By contrast revisionists have contended that the United States did not dominate policy making in CoCom. In fact some Western European governments, notably Britain and France, were able to moderate the United States' economic defence demands through their influence on Washington's overall global security policy.

While there are different variants within the two schools, it is possible to identify the main characteristics that distinguish traditional and revisionist scholarship on CoCom. With respect to traditionalism, research has generally confirmed the findings of Adler-Karlsson's book, *Western Economic Warfare, 1947–67: A Case Study of Foreign Economic Policy*, published in 1968.[1] Historians Yoko Yasuhara and Vibeke Sørensen agree with Adler-Karlsson's conclusion that the United States drew on economic coercion – through the denial of economic and military assistance – to compel the European members of CoCom to support a policy of economic warfare against the Soviet bloc.[2] Although Yasuhara and Sørensen emphasise the important contribution and influence of Britain in the formulation of economic defence policy, as far as they are concerned the United States was the dominant nation in CoCom by virtue of its hegemony and leadership of the Western alliance. For traditionalists, then, any analysis of the origins and development of the strategic embargo during the late 1940s and early 1950s must involve an evaluation of American power and dominance over the Western European governments in CoCom. According to the traditional perspective, the military dependence of Western Europe on Washington, in the face of a Soviet strategic threat, accounted for the decision of these nations to capitulate to American embargo demands, despite the importance of East–West trade to the economic recovery programmes of these nations.

The opening of government archives in the 1980s led some scholars to challenge the main tenets of the traditional thesis. In particular historians Alan P. Dobson and Tor Egil Førland, through exhaustive research in American and British archives, began to dispute the traditionalist claim that successive administrations in the United States resorted to economic coercion in an attempt to secure Western European compliance for a strategic embargo on trade with the Soviet Union.[3] Supported by the theoretical observations of the political scientist Michael Mastanduno, they suggested that, despite pressure from Congress, policy makers in the United States were reluctant to apply sanctions against Western European nations that were failing to comply with American embargo demands, as such action would be detrimental to mutual security cooperation.[4] Instead they proposed a revisionist interpretation of US–Western European relations in CoCom. According to these scholars, a full understanding of policy making in CoCom was only possible through an evaluation of the response of Western European governments to American embargo proposals. By focusing on the influential presence of Britain in the multilateral export control group, they began the paradigm shift in research on Western economic defence policies during the early Cold War years.

The present work draws and builds on the new interpretation promulgated by the research of the revisionist school. Anglo-American relations in CoCom are an omnipresent feature in the chapters that follow. As well as pursuing the development of multilateral export control policy beyond 1954, this study revisits the much-debated history of the origins of economic containment through the eyes of American and British policy planners. Significantly, the conclusions of this book, while refuting traditionalist arguments, question revisionist findings. One theme that emerges from this study, for example, was the efforts of successive American presidents and senior policy makers in the State Department to limit the embargo to goods of a strictly military nature, thus allowing the Western European nations to maintain valuable non-strategic trading links with Eastern Europe. Consequently a fresh interpretation of American motivations and policy goals from 1947–63 is presented in the following pages. As such, the book deals with policy divisions between departments within American administrations, executive–legislative friction and Anglo-American differences over the structure and scope of the strategic embargo.

Economic containment: theory and practice

There has been considerable discussion in the literature on CoCom about the type of economic strategy utilised by the Western alliance to curb the growth of Soviet military power. Whereas some scholars have argued that American and British government officials favoured a policy of economic warfare against the Soviet bloc, others have demonstrated that during the early Cold War years the CoCom members employed a strategic embargo on trade with communist nations. The lack of consensus amongst advocates of the economic warfare and strategic embargo approaches has called into question the applicability of a theoretical analysis to the history of international East–West trade controls during 1948–63. Most strikingly, American and British government policy papers and telegrams rarely mention the terms 'economic warfare' or 'strategic embargo' with respect to CoCom and East–West trade. In light of this conceptual problem, it is necessary to elucidate the contrasting definitions that researchers have applied to these terms in relation to CoCom before proposing an alternative explanation of Western trade strategy towards the Soviet bloc.

Theorists have agreed on a general definition of the concepts of economic warfare and strategic embargo. Two leading experts on CoCom, Michael Mastanduno and Tor Egil Førland, have provided a similar explication of the meaning of these concepts. For Mastanduno and Førland, economic warfare can be viewed as a strategic instrument employed by an aggressor nation or nations aimed at weakening the strategic and industrial base of a target state.[5] Typically, governments utilising a strategy of economic warfare will not only attempt to delay the military build-up of the target state, but will also endeavour to weaken the civilian economy and industrial complex of the adversarial power. Thus economic warfare will be used in conjunction with other conventional warfare techniques to destroy or severely incapacitate the military–industrial base of an enemy state.

Both Mastanduno and Førland, drawing on the work of the political scientist David Baldwin, assert that during the 1940s and 1950s Western governments applied a strategy of economic warfare against the Soviet bloc and other communist states in the context of the East–West global conflict. Yet they differ markedly over the extent and intensity to which economic warfare was deployed by the CoCom member. According to Mastanduno the United States drew on economic warfare as a strategic weapon during the period 1948–54. By contrast he believes that CoCom only instituted this strategy as a united body at the height of the Korean War in 1950–51. He estimates that economic warfare was no longer the preferred policy of the Eisenhower administration or the Western European governments after the August 1954 international list revisions. From the mid 1950s to the late 1960s, in Mastanduno's opinion, CoCom applied a strategic embargo on East–West trade.

Førland offers a conflicting assessment of Western economic warfare policies in 1948–54. To his mind economic warfare and strategic embargo cannot be viewed as two distinct strategies. Throughout the formative years of the Western multilateral export control programme the United States and its allies consistently pursued a strategy of economic warfare against the Soviet bloc. He submits that the intensity to which economic warfare was employed was dependent on Western perceptions of the Soviet military threat at a given point in time. Hence he concludes that upon the establishment of CoCom in 1950 the members pursued a policy of limited economic warfare. The outbreak of hostilities in Southeast Asia and the commencement of Western European rearmament programmes in 1950–51, moreover, forced CoCom to intensify its economic warfare against Moscow. Førland points out that even though the multilateral export control lists were substantially reduced in 1954, Western governments did not dispense with economic warfare as a continuing Cold War strategy.

Inherent in the theoretical analysis of both Mastanduno and Førland is the concept of strategic embargo. This trade strategy is also mentioned in the work of Sørensen and Dobson, but not developed within a rigid conceptual framework. Each of these scholars has concluded that Western governments implemented an embargo on strategic goods in trade with the Soviet Union and Eastern Europe during the early stages of the Cold War. The purpose of this policy was to prohibit the exportation of items of strategic value that would be beneficial to Soviet military production. Policy planners in CoCom believed that if key military and technological items were restricted in East–West trade the West would be able to maintain its strategic superiority over the Soviet bloc. A strategic embargo, moreover, would allow the CoCom governments to contain the Soviet threat through economic statecraft over the long run, thus narrowing the potential risk of conventional and nuclear conflict between East and West.

Mastanduno and Førland, while sharing the same definition of the term strategic embargo, clash over the application of the concept to Western export control policy in the 1940s and 1950s. Mastanduno views the strategy of economic warfare as distinct from a strategic embargo. It is his assertion that the CoCom governments only instituted a strategic embargo when the strategy of economic warfare was deemed to be obsolete in August 1954. With the abatement of East–West tensions in the mid 1950s the Western governments developed a new approach to economic containment, which they pursued until the late 1960s. On the other hand Førland argues that the concepts of strategic embargo and economic warfare must be juxtaposed when examining Western export control policy towards the Soviet bloc. From Førland's perspective, economic warfare was the strategy pursued by CoCom and a strategic embargo was the means to execute this policy. Thus while the Western governments persistently followed a strategy of economic warfare throughout the Cold War era, the intensity of this policy was regulated by increasing or reducing the number of embargoed goods contained on the three international lists.

The evidence presented in this study demonstrates that the Western governments in CoCom did not implement a strategy of economic warfare against the Soviet bloc during 1948–63. While this strategy was the subject of much debate within successive American administrations and CoCom, the international export control programme that materialised in the late 1940s and early 1950s can be clearly seen as a strategic embargo on East–West trade. Although the Western European governments were concerned that the United States would press for a policy of economic warfare in CoCom, policy planners in the State Department ensured that calls by the American defence community for a complete cessation of trade were not reciprocated at the international level. Likewise they succeeded in circumventing the efforts of Congress to force the Western Europeans to comply with a strategy of economic warfare by granting waivers to the Kem Amendment and the Battle Act. Realising the importance of civilian trade to the European members of CoCom, State Department officials were anxious to limit trade controls to items of military importance. Thus contemporary policy documents, which only mention 'economic warfare' and 'strategic embargo' on an infrequent basis, do not dovetail with the theoretical observations of Mastanduno and Førland.

This work argues that Western export control policy in the Cold War years must be viewed as 'economic containment' or 'economic defence'. Mastanduno mentions economic containment in his work, but surprisingly he does not develop this concept.[6] Economic containment and economic defence – the term used by American officials to describe the strategic embargo on East–West trade – are constantly mentioned in the chapters that follow. In effect these terms, which are used interchangeably in this study, follow the definition of 'strategic embargo' as outlined above. From the available evidence it can be argued that at no time during the history of the Western export control programme from 1948–63 did policy makers implement a strategy of economic warfare against the Soviet bloc. Rather they sought to prevent Soviet military build-up by restricting exports in strategic goods. Conflict between the United States and Britain arose not over economic warfare, but over the definition of strategic goods, in particular 'dual-purpose' items. Whereas Washington wanted to embargo industrial items of dual benefit to Soviet military and civilian production, London pushed for a limited export control programme containing only items of primary strategic significance to Moscow. This clash is a major theme of the present study.

Anglo-American strategic and economic objectives and the Cold War

Another central theme of this book is Anglo-American collaboration and conflict over strategic and economic goals during the Cold War. For the most part American and British policy makers shared similar outlooks towards post-war security. By the early 1950s both nations were committed to the global containment of communism. While disagreements surfaced over policy towards certain regions, notably the Middle East and Southeast Asia, the two countries had forged a firm partnership that became the bedrock of the Atlantic alliance. Although reluctant to tie itself to an exclusive 'special relationship' with London, Washington drew on Britain's global presence in waging a cold war against the Soviet Union and the PRC. By 1949 the Attlee government, with the decline of the British Empire and rejection of a prominent role in a supranational Western Europe, had begun to define its foreign policy in terms of an intimate working relationship with the Truman administration.

In the 1950s and 1960s the Conservative governments under Churchill, Eden and Macmillan continued to emphasise the importance of an Anglo-American 'special relationship' in British foreign policy. But notwithstanding Britain's influential presence in the Atlantic alliance, the Eisenhower administration was not disposed to attribute exclusivity to its relationship with Britain at the expense of other Western European powers. Although the two governments continued to work closely on matters of mutual security, conflict occurred over regional issues. Most significantly the Eisenhower and Eden governments clashed over the Suez Crisis in 1956. In many ways Suez marked a watershed in Anglo-American relations. From the late 1950s to the early 1960s the new government, led by Harold Macmillan, sought to redefine British foreign policy. With the decline of the Empire, Macmillan began to reorient policy towards Western Europe, culminating in Britain's first application for membership of the European Economic Community in the summer of 1961. The Macmillan government also strove to build fences with the Eisenhower administration in an effort to preserve Britain's status as a key member of the Western alliance. With the exception of a major stand-off over nuclear collaboration, Macmillan and Eisenhower's successor, John F. Kennedy, fostered a close personal working relationship. Kennedy actively supported Britain's application to join the EEC and Macmillan provided counsel to the president during the Cuban missile crisis.

Yet the economic dimension of the Anglo-American partnership was fraught with friction. By 1945 the United States had become the largest military and economic power in the world. By contrast, involvement in the Second World War had virtually bankrupted the British economy. As a result of this weakened financial position, Britain developed an economic dependency on the United States. From 1941–46 the United States, through assistance in the form of Lend-Lease aid and a low interest loan of $3.75 billion, attempted to force Britain to remove discriminatory imperial trade practices. The burgeoning 'dollar gap' crisis, however, further weakened Britain's economic condition, leading to the failed efforts of the British Treasury to make sterling a convertible currency in 1947.

The precarious state of the Western European economies, devastated by the war and severe harvest failures in 1946–47, necessitated an immediate response from the Truman administration. No longer able to sustain a multilateral world order, the United States adopted a regionalist approach to Western Europe. Through the European Recovery Programme (ERP) American policy planners sought not only to rebuild the Western European trading system into an integrated, supranational bloc, but also to bolster the continent against Soviet expansionism from the east.[7] Washington expected London to play a key role in the newly emerging European political and economic community. Yet by 1948 Whitehall had rejected this proposal on the grounds that it would undermine British imperial interests and restrict London's ability to provide meaningful support to the United States in the Cold War struggle. Thus strategic considerations dictated that the Truman administration accept the continuing existence of the Imperial

Preference trading system and Britain's decision to remain outside an economically and politically integrated Western Europe.

The realities of British post-war economic decline impelled the governments of the 1950s and 1960s to reduce Britain's imperial and global commitments. Even so Whitehall maintained strong economic ties with the Commonwealth countries and endeavoured to expand trade with the fiscally conservative Eisenhower administration. In 1958 sterling became fully convertible as the Macmillan government pressed for the removal of international tariffs on trade during the Dillon Round of the General Agreement on Trade and Tariffs (GATT). Macmillan also cast a worried glance towards the EEC in the late 1950s, fearing that protectionism would curtail valuable British trading links with the six members. While he was instrumental in creating a rival trading bloc, the European Free Trade Area (EFTA), the prime minister reached the conclusion in 1960 that Britain's economic future would be better served through membership of the EEC, a view held by policy makers in Washington since the Truman administration.[8]

It was against this background, then, that Anglo-American trade policy towards the Soviet Union and Eastern Europe in the Cold War was established. Trade with the Soviet bloc had both strategic and economic implications for the Anglo-American relationship. From the perspective of mutual security, both nations believed that a strategic embargo on East–West trade was necessary in light of the Soviet military build-up in the 1940s and 1950s. They hoped to delay the Soviet Union's capacity to produce nuclear and conventional weapons by restricting shipments of strategic materials to the Soviet bloc. But policy planners in London and Washington disagreed over the scope and content of this trade embargo. British ministers and officials were keen to ensure that export controls would be applied only to items of military value. As Britain required imports of essential raw materials from non-dollar sources, it did not want the embargo to jeopardise non-strategic trading links with Eastern Europe. In negotiations with successive American governments, Britain persistently declared its opposition to the institution of trade controls on non-military items and a large number of industrial commodities.

American officials, however, perceived the strategic embargo on East–West trade differently. While policy makers in the United States were divided on the length and complexion of the strategic export control programme to be implemented against the Soviet bloc, they clearly desired a more extensive embargo than their counterparts in London. Thus Anglo-American discussions on economic defence matters were often views on whether industrial items should be included in the embargo. British negotiators, stressing economic recovery concerns, argued that a large number of industrial exports could not contribute to Soviet military production. They claimed, moreover, that the expansion of industrial trade with Eastern Europe would be beneficial to the economic strength of the Western alliance in the long run. American diplomats demurred. According to Washington the wholesale shipment of industrial commodities would contribute to the Soviet war economy in the long run. If these exports were not prohibited in East–West trade the Western alliance's strategic superiority over the Soviet Union would be greatly diminished in the event of a future military conflict. In the 1950s and 1960s the Eisenhower and Kennedy administrations also sought to prevent advanced technology transfer in electronic items from West to East. Once again Britain was opposed to such trade controls on the basis that these exports were of considerable commercial value to Western industrial nations. It pointed out, moreover, that since the Soviet Union was a technologically sophisticated industrial power, trade controls on electronic items would have little effect on Moscow's military development.

These issues are discussed in the chapters that follow. Emphasis is placed on the context in which the East–West trade embargo was created and developed. The first five chapters describe the origins of Anglo-American economic defence policy during the Truman administration. Careful attention is paid to the formation of CoCom and disputes between the United States and Britain over embargo policy. The final four chapters examine the conflicting efforts of British and American officials to adjust the economic containment strategy for the 'long haul' during the Eisenhower and Kennedy years.

1
The Origins of Economic Containment, 1947–48

In March 1948 the Truman administration implemented domestic restrictions on exports to the Soviet Union. This marked a change in policy from economic cooperation with Moscow through the Lend-Lease Programme in the Second World War to a strategy of economic containment, which was ultimately transformed into an economic cold war against the Kremlin. There are several reasons why American government officials initiated this policy reversal.

First, at the end of the Second World War the Soviet Union embarked on an ambitious programme of expansionism in Eastern and Central Europe. Fearing Soviet domination of the Eurasian heartlands, the United States intervened in the Near East and Western European regions through two major foreign policy initiatives: the Truman Doctrine and the Marshall Plan. The resulting clash between the two powers over the control of Europe, and in particular Germany, led to the Cold War between the United States and the Soviet Union. Second, officials in the Commerce and State Departments, under pressure from an increasingly anticommunist Congress, began to examine the merits of a strategic embargo on East–West trade aimed at preventing Soviet military build-up. Finally, the State Department feared that Moscow, which had not been included in the European Recovery Programme (ERP), would attempt to acquire strategic items through third-party trade under the Marshall Plan. It was thus imperative for the ERP governments to participate in a common export control policy with the United States to ensure that American assistance in the form of military supplies was not re-exported from Western Europe to the Soviet bloc.

The onset of the Cold War

Despite their contrasting political and economic systems, the threat of Nazi Germany brought the United States and the Soviet Union together in a close alliance during the Second World War. During the conflict the American president, Franklin D. Roosevelt, offered Moscow unrestricted aid through the framework of the Lend Lease Act of March 1941. From November 1941 to the final defeat of Germany in May 1945 the Soviet Union obtained approximately $11 billion of assistance from the United States.[1] When the war ended Roosevelt sought to continue his close personal contact with the Soviet leader, Joseph Stalin, even though American foreign policy objectives clearly clashed with those of the Soviet Union. While appalled by Stalin's seizure of Latvia, Lithuania and Estonia, and concerned by Soviet aggression towards Poland and Finland, Roosevelt hoped that Moscow would play a constructive role in the post-war order. In fact, at the Yalta Conference in February 1945 the president revealed that he was prepared to tolerate the Soviet Union's domination of Eastern Europe in return for Moscow's participation in the creation of a collective security organisation.[2]

Upon Roosevelt's death two months after Yalta his successor, Harry S. Truman, unschooled in foreign affairs, continued the policy of accommodation towards the Soviet Union. But Stalin's expansionist plans in Eastern and Central Europe gave the new president grave cause for concern. Truman feared that the Stalin would seek to capitalise on the economic and political weakness of Western Europe in an attempt to take over the continent. If Stalin co-opted the Western European nations into his sphere of influence, Truman was convinced that this would have severe consequences for American national security. Control of European economic and military resources would provide the Soviet Union with enough power to challenge the United States for leadership in the international system; it might also allow Stalin to plan a military attack on American territory. With these considerations in mind Truman began to take a stronger stance towards the Soviet Union.

Truman's change of attitude was tempered by several factors. First, Stalin's continued policy of expansionism in Central and Eastern Europe and his refusal to adhere rigidly to the Yalta Accords forced Truman to withdraw American economic assistance to the Soviet Union. Once Germany had been defeated in June 1945 all Lend Lease aid shipments ceased. The Soviet Union requested a $6 billion loan from the United States, but the State Department never processed the application. This in contrast to the low-interest loan received by Washington's other Second World War ally, Britain, in 1946. The Soviet Union's failure to participate in the establishment of international economic organisations such as the International Monetary Fund (IMF) and the World Bank further exacerbated tensions between the two powers. Although the Soviet Union participated in the newly founded United Nations (UN) in 1945, its foreign policy objectives in Eastern Europe, as far as the Truman administration was concerned, could not be reconciled with the American conception of a liberal and democratic capitalist world order.[3]

Another source of tension between the two countries concerned the future of Germany. Both Truman and Stalin were anxious to ensure that a fully rejuvenated Germany would not prove a future military threat. The division of the country into fours zones occupied by the four victorious allies – the United States, the Soviet Union, Britain and France – in the immediate aftermath of the war only prolonged friction over the future of Germany.[4] While Truman slowly began to mistrust Stalin and Soviet diplomatic aims in Europe, British policy makers were convinced that the Soviet Union had grander designs than the protection of its territorial borders. The foreign secretary, Ernest Bevin, urged his American counterpart, James F. Byrnes, to be mindful of Soviet motives in Europe and Asia. More explicitly Winston S. Churchill, the leader of the British Conservative Party, warned the United States of an impending cold war between East and West in a speech delivered in Truman's home state of Missouri in early 1946.[5]

Perhaps the most profound influence on Truman's decision to confront the Soviet threat in Europe and Asia was a telegram drafted by George F. Kennan, an American diplomat stationed in the US embassy in Moscow. Kennan painted a rather bleak picture of the Stalinist system, which he compared to the Russian Empire of the seventeenth and eighteenth centuries: the overriding objective of Soviet foreign policy was territorial expansionism. He recommended that the Truman administration take a firm Stand against the Soviet Union through a policy of containment.[6] During 1946 Truman heeded these warnings but remained cautious and uncommitted to any direct action against the Soviet Union in Europe. The doctrine of containment, which came to characterise American foreign policy for more than forty years, was implemented in an incremental or, in the words of historian Wilson D. Miscamble, 'piecemeal' fashion.[7] Even Stalin's attempt to extend his sphere of influence into the Near East region in 1946–47 brought a circumspect response from Truman. While the president pledged $400 million of limited economic and military aid to Turkey and Greece, this was ostensibly to share the financial burden of Britain, a key power in the region. His enunciation of the so-called 'Truman Doctrine' to help free peoples everywhere to combat communism was a clever political device to gain support for assistance to the Near East from an increasingly isolationist Congress. It is important to note that Truman had no intention of committing ground troops to the region. Nevertheless the Truman Doctrine did mark a turning point in American policy towards the Soviet Union in 1947.

Thus the containment strategy that began to take shape from 1947–50 in Europe and Asia was premised on the belief that the United States needed to build strong power centres in Western Europe and Japan to resist communist aggression from both the Soviet Union and, after 1949, the People's Republic of China (PRC).[8] It could be argued that containment was largely a reactive policy. American policy makers in the late 1940s did not want to become embroiled in political and military struggles in Eurasia; but the threat of Soviet aggression together with the economic weakness of Western Europe and Japan did provoke a response from Washington. It was against this background, then, that the Truman administration began to reexamine American trade policy towards the Soviet Union. Like political containment, economic containment emerged as the defining framework through which the United States formulated its East–West trade policy. As we shall see, the strategy of economic containment evolved in an incremental manner after much debate within the Truman administration. First, in order to understand the origins of the American trade policy towards the Soviet Union it is necessary to examine the views of leading conservative isolationist politicians in Congress.

Congress and East–West trade

During and after the Second World War the Roosevelt and Truman administrations faced strong opposition to their foreign policy objectives from an increasingly vocal isolationist wing in Congress. The isolationists not only protested against involvement in the war in 1941, but also opposed an American role in the building of a new world order in 1945. Although the isolationists shared the same ideological objection to the intervention by the United States in world affairs, they came from diverse backgrounds and geographical locations throughout the United States and had different motives.[9] The ensuing Cold War struggle between the United States and the Soviet Union was a source of great concern to conservative isolationists. On the one hand they were adamantly opposed to Stalinism, which they viewed with great trepidation, but on the other they tried constantly to block the Truman administration's containment policy in the late 1940s and early 1950s. The issue of economic and military assistance to Western Europe was a particular bone of contention as far as these representatives were concerned. It is not surprising, therefore, that American trade with Eastern Europe was the subject of protracted discussion in both houses of Congress.

By and large the congressional isolationists were against any form of commercial relationship with the Soviet Union in the years after the war. Once cooperation between the two countries had broken down at the beginning of the Cold War, they began to press the Truman administration to sever trading links with Eastern Europe. Many congressmen believed that the United States could use trade as a lever to extract concessions from the Soviet Union. If applied effectively, economic sanctions, they thought, might force the Soviet leaders to change the aggressive nature of their policy towards Europe. More significantly, however, representatives in the Senate and House of Representatives called on the administration to place restrictions on strategic exports to the Soviet Union. They feared that military shipments from American ports to Eastern Europe would allow Stalin to stockpile arms and ammunition in anticipation of a future war with the West. But some congressional representatives and senators did not limit their attack to weapons; they also sought to prevent trade in industrial commodities and items that could be used in military production. Anxious that the United States should not repeat the mistake of trading with the enemy, as in the case of Japan during the Second World War, the isolationists bombarded the Commerce and State Departments with letters from angry constituents.

Much of the congressional opposition to East–West trade in the early years of the Cold War derived from anticommunist public opinion on the issue. Members of the public did not shrink from expressing their dissatisfaction with American trade policy towards Eastern Europe. To cite one example, Senator Guy Cordon of Oregon was inundated with letters of protest from his constituents. One such letter, which was sent to the State Department, seemed to reflect the concerns of the average voter. Referring to the adverse consequences of exporting heavy machinery to Russia, one individual invoked the analogy of Pearl Harbour to illustrate his point:

We are shipping them [the Soviets] steel, machinery and other industrial goods that not only can, but will be converted to war purposes against us. For years before Pearl Harbour every morning that I drove down from my office, I saw trucks taking junk to the waterfront via Frisco [sic] and Seattle, mostly, to Japan. Our boys got much of that steel in their bodies in the late unpleasantness, and, like the saps we are, we are repeating history, this time to Russia instead of Japan.[10]

Congressman John F. Kennedy, who later became an advocate of increased trade with Moscow, informed Charles E. Bohlen of the State Department that the Shamrock Club of Boston had passed a motion to lobby the government to 'establish an embargo against shipping to Russia any materials that may be used as war materials'.[11]

Protest against trade with the Soviet Union was not targeted exclusively at members of Congress. Undersecretary of State Robert A. Lovett received a very pointed letter from a former colleague at Brown Brothers Harriman and Co., a distinguished Wall Street bank. Critical of the Truman administration's East–West trade policy, the letter suggested that:

The present policy is as bad as our shipping to Japan in 1941, and conceivably has more harmful results. Here is Russia fighting us on every diplomatic front and yet we treat her as a most favoured nation, though our dread of her keeps us awake nights.[12]

Another angry response came from the Consolidated War Veterans Councils of Michigan, which claimed that veterans of the Second World War were 'greatly alarmed over the attitude of our government towards Russia and want to go on record as vigorously opposing the shipment of anything to Russia'.[13] While most public disgruntlement was levelled at shipments bound for Soviet ports, some members of the business community complained to the Commerce Department that they had incurred a financial loss as a result of the restrictions imposed on trading licences to Eastern Europe.[14] What these examples, chosen from different parts of the United States, demonstrate is the degree of public concern about the potential ramifications for American security of providing strategic exports to the Soviet Union.

As the Cold War between the United States and the Soviet Union raged on in 1947–48, congressional representatives continued their onslaught against the Truman administration's plan to provide economic and military assistance to Western Europe. Congressman Robert T. Ross of New York echoed the sentiments of many in the House of Representatives when he asserted that:

> either we are engaged in a cold war against communism or we are not engaged in one – unless we use every weapon at our command to win this cold war, we are likely to find some of these materials coming back to us in the form of shrapnel in the event we have a hot war. It seems the height of foolishness to furnish Western European materials necessary to combat communism and at the same time continue to ship materials to Russia-dominated nations.[15]

Ross, like many representatives, could not understand the wisdom behind the Truman administration's decision to provide aid to Western Europe under the Marshall Plan for the purposes of counteracting communism, while at the some time continuing a normal trading relationship with the Soviet Union. It was this feeling of unease about the motives behind the administration's foreign economic policy that provoked a response from Congressman Karl E. Mundt, a conservative Republican from South Dakota.

  Mundt proposed an amendment to the legislation governing the Marshall Plan that would prevent participating European governments from exporting to the Soviet Union strategic materials obtained under the Foreign Assistance Act of 1948. The amendment, which was inserted into the Economic Co-operation Act as Section 117(d), called for the administrator of Marshall aid to:

> Refuse delivery insofar as practicable to participating countries of commodities or products which go into the production of any commodity for delivery to any non-participating European country which commodities or products would be refused export licences to those countries by the United States in the interests of national security.

While the amendment did not refer specifically to the Soviet Union or its satellite states in Eastern Europe, the Soviet Union's exclusion from the Marshall Plan made it a direct target of the legislation. In a speech introducing his amendment to the House, Mundt stressed that the legislation did not seek to disrupt 'peaceful channels of trade' in Europe; it was aimed, he pointed out, at prohibiting the shipment of strategic exports to the Soviet Union.[16] When Congress passed the

European Co-operation Act in April 1948 the 'Mundt Amendment' became an integral component of the Marshall Plan. It would also play an influential role in the Truman administration's efforts to establish an international security export control programme in respect of East–West trade during 1948–50.

The Truman administration and economic containment

The Truman administration's decision to implement an embargo on East–West trade in December 1947 was motivated by three factors. First, Cold War tensions between the United States and the Soviet Union reached new heights during 1947 with the continuing failure of both countries to agree a final political settlement on the future of Germany. Matters worsened, moreover, with the Soviet Union's refusal to participate in the Marshall Plan – to the relief of the State Department – and Stalin's ongoing obsession with consolidating Soviet power in Eastern Europe.[17] Second, congressional pressure on the Commerce Department to prohibit trade licences on exports deemed to be of strategic value to the Soviet Union impelled the administration to take steps towards regulating international economic policy. Finally, the existence of wartime legislation on export controls on goods in short supply provided policy makers with a relatively inexpensive of means of pursuing a national security policy of preventing the shipment of military items to Eastern Europe.[18] This way the Truman administration could add an economic dimension to the containment strategy proposed by Kennan in an effort to counter Soviet aggression throughout the globe.

In autumn 1947 the Commerce Department, under the leadership of former Wall Street banker and ambassador to the Soviet Union, W. Averrell Harriman, started to review trade policy towards Eastern Europe. National security considerations coupled with congressional pressure prodded Harriman and senior officials in the department to change the United States' commercial relationship with the Soviet Union. The results of this review led Harriman, in a paper to the National Security Council (NSC), to advocate the virtual cessation of trade with the Soviet Union and Eastern Europe. Premised on the belief that the Truman administration's main objective in foreign policy was the maintenance of peace based on the 'revival of a working world economy', Harriman argued that the Soviet Union's refusal to participate in the Marshall Plan represented 'a threat to world peace, and in turn US security'. He considered Stalin's decision to opt out of the American economic assistance programme to be a declaration of Soviet intent to sabotage the Marshall Plan. He therefore proposed that the NSC take all necessary measures to prohibit the exportation of strategic commodities to the Soviet Union, in order to restrict its ability to acquire materials for military production. In effect Harriman was encouraging the United States to pursue a policy of economic warfare against the Soviet Union.[19]

At an NSC meeting on 17 December Truman approved the Harriman initiative and ordered the Commerce Department to monitor trade with Eastern Europe through a strict licensing policy to be known as the 'R' procedure. The new policy was to take effect in March 1948 with the implementation of domestic restrictions on strategic East–West trade.[20] Significantly, the Harriman initiative did not address the issue of Western European trade with the Soviet Union. This particular subject would be a constant thorn in the administration's side as it tried to formulate an effective export control policy on East–West trade. From the perspective of the Commerce Department, it was expected that the European participants in the Marshall Plan would automatically follow the lead of the United States on export policy towards the Soviet Union and Eastern Europe. The State Department, which had studied the East–West trade question in some detail, disagreed.[21]

First, the Policy Planning Staff (PPS), a policy unit with the task of assisting the secretary of state, George C. Marshall, concluded that as trade with the Soviet Union was minimal, a strategic embargo would not delay Soviet military build-up.[22] The PPS, under the directorship of George Kennan, also argued that American national security objectives would be better served by creating a liberal world economic order without trade barriers and protectionism. Nonetheless, in concurrence with Harriman, Kennan and his staff recommended that executive action be taken to prevent the flow of strategic materials to Eastern Europe.[23]

Secretary Marshall, strongly influenced by Kennan's recommendation, also opposed a policy of economic warfare against the Soviet Union.[24] Instead Marshall examined East–West trade from the viewpoint of Western Europe. Since the United States required European participation to make economic containment effective, it was necessary to consider the requirements of American allies. In a discussion paper forwarded to members of Truman's cabinet, Marshall outlined the economic plight of the Western European nations devastated by the Second World War. These nations, he remarked, required trade with Eastern Europe as part of their economic reconstruction programmes to stimulate production and increase exports. Most importantly they needed to obtain supplies of raw materials from the Soviet bloc region without expending vital dollars, given the growing currency gap between Washington and its allies. With these considerations in mind the United States should, Marshall stated, implement a limited policy of economic containment. This policy would take the form of 'selective control' of exports that official experts judged would contribute substantially to Russian military production: items of a strictly strategic nature and industrial commodities used in military production. Crucially, Marshall estimated that a limited embargo would not disrupt essential non-strategic trade channels between Western and Eastern European governments.[25]

Marshall's proposal was accepted as official policy at the cabinet meeting of 26 March 1948, thus adding a new dimension to the strategy of economic containment. A series of turf battles occurred, however, between the Commerce and State Departments as each bureaucracy tried to outmanoeuvre the other for control of policy direction.[26] Under the 'R' Procedure the Commerce Department had full responsibility for licensing policy on exports bound for Western and Eastern European ports. Yet a report prepared by an ad hoc subcommittee, consisting of officials from Commerce and State, set up to advise the secretary of commerce on East–West trade appeared to reflect the concerns of both Harriman and Marshall. The report listed three objectives with respect to American trade policy towards the Soviet Union. First, the United States should endeavour to assist Western European governments to obtain imports necessary for economic recovery. Second, as part of national security policy the Truman administration should seek to restrict the build-up of Soviet military potential through a strategic embargo. Finally, this strategic embargo should be of a limited nature so that the United States could continue to obtain valuable supplies of platinum, chrome and manganese from Eastern European sources. Moreover, the subcommittee, recommended that exports to the Soviet bloc be divided into four classes, with strategic and semistrategic items in the first two classes and items of little or strategic value in the third and fourth classes.[27]

While Marshall and Harriman's successor, Charles W. Sawyer, generally approved the report, the State and Commerce Departments again came into conflict over the participation of Western European governments in the embargo programme. Sawyer, a diehard anticommunist, complained to Marshall that since domestic export controls had been put into operation, Western European nations had continued normal trading relations with Eastern Europe, rendering the American restrictions ineffectual. He asserted that Washington should call upon these nations to implement similar controls on East–West trade immediately.[28] Marshall disagreed. He suggested to Sawyer that he view the problem from the perspective of European governments struggling to rebuild their war-torn economies. It was essential, from the standpoint of national security, for the United States to encourage the Western Europeans to increase production and stimulate trade in order to build a strong balance of power on the continent to withstand Soviet aggression. In a letter to the secretary of commerce he wrote that:

> I believe we are all agreed that export controls should be so exercised as to maximise for the US and for Western European countries friendly to us the net benefits in terms of economic strength and progress, of trade between the US and Western Europe on the one hand and the Soviet orbit on the other. As a matter of the national interest we should certainly want to feel that our efforts are securing for the US and her friends from this trade at least as great benefits, preferably greater, than are accruing to the USSR and her allies.[29]

It would take several months to work out a compromise between the positions of Marshall and Sawyer. In fact the views of the State and Commerce Departments would never be truly reconciled during the period under study here.

In the summer of 1948 a technical steering committee composed of representatives from the State, Commerce and Agriculture Departments, the Pentagon and the Central Intelligence Agency (CIA) finally resolved the dispute between Marshall and the Commerce Department. The technical steering committee reduced the four classes of exports in East–West trade to two to be known as Class 1-A and Class 1-B.[30] Class 1-A contained items of a purely strategic or military nature, for example arms, ammunition, atomic production material and advanced industrial technology. Class 1-B was composed of commodities deemed to have less strategic value than items on List 1-A. List 1-B items were considered to be of primary strategic value when exported in large quantities to Eastern Europe, and included merchant ships, machine tools and chemicals.[31] A tug-of-war over the length of the two lists ensued between the State Department and the European Co-operation Administration (ECA) on the one side and the Commerce

Department and the military establishment on the other. But by July the State Department and the ECA had managed to persuade the Commerce Department to shorten the lists before the next stage of economic containment: selling the strategic embargo to Western Europe.[32]

Exporting economic containment: the Marshall Plan and East–West trade

The task of convincing Western Europe to participate in a strategic embargo against the Soviet Union was entrusted to the American special representative to the ECA in Paris, Averrell Harriman.[33] Harriman, a former secretary of commerce, was a leading proponent of restrictions on strategic trade with Eastern Europe. In August 1948, under the instruction of Marshall and the ECA administrator, Paul G. Hoffman, he was charged with the delicate task of gaining support from Washington's European allies for a common export control strategy. Through the framework of the Marshall Plan, which had been passed by Congress in April, Harriman spent several months attempting to convince key European governments that Western security would be better served if trade in strategic exports to the Soviet bloc was curtailed.

The Marshall Plan was perhaps the most ambitious and creative foreign policy initiative ever undertaken in the history of American diplomacy. When the programme was completed in 1952 some $14 billion of assistance had been provided to the economies of Western Europe. Historians have long debated the motives behind Marshall Aid; and despite a variety of different interpretations it is possible to discern from this research three main objectives behind the European Recovery Programme (ERP). First, American policy makers wanted to build a strong and independent power centre in Western Europe to withstand Soviet aggression. Economic assistance to the governments participating in the Marshall Plan would help them to rebuild their war-torn economies by stimulating production and encouraging intra-European trade. Second, the Truman administration became wedded to the idea that Western Europe could become a powerful and dynamic region if leading governments took measures to integrate politically and economically with each other. The resulting continental arrangement would not only provide the United States with an important trading partner, but would also allow Western Europe to derive the economic benefits of a revitalised Germany while creating a balance of power to contain the Soviet Union. Finally, the Marshall Plan, the State Department reasoned, would deter Stalin from capitalising on the economic and political weakness in Europe. Through economic aid the United States could help to dissuade the rise of indigenous communist parties, supported by Moscow, by improving living standards and bringing prosperity to the region.[34]

Yet for the Marshall Plan to fulfil these aims, the State Department and the ECA administrator concluded, an effective export control programme was required to ensure that the Soviet Union did not acquire strategic exports from Western Europe through third-party trade. They realised that economic assistance to the region would be counterproductive if the Soviet Union managed to obtain military and industrial items for potential use in a future war against the United States. It was with this concern in mind that they forwarded a telegram on East–West trade to Harriman on 27 August.

The State Department–ECA telegram provided Harriman with a comprehensive list of instructions on how to initiate discussions with the Western European governments. It outlined the most pertinent principles underlying American export control policy. Harriman was to stress the necessity of denying strategic materials to the Soviet bloc in order 'to hold down the war potential of the East'. By prohibiting the exportation of military and heavy industrial items to the Soviet Union the West would be able to increase 'its strength relative to that of the East'. Thus the special representative was to sell economic containment to the Western Europeans as a crucial defence measure. Both Marshall and Hoffman hoped that the threat of Soviet aggression would spur the ERP nations to rethink their trade policies towards Eastern Europe from the perspective of mutual security.

The telegram, adhering strictly to Marshall's recommendations, ordered Harriman to limit the European export control programme to trade in strategic materials and industrial commodities that Washington deemed could contribute to Soviet military production. The embargo should not disrupt civilian trade between Western and Eastern Europe. The dispatch recognised that the success of the Marshall Plan depended on substantial European East–West trade; moreover, it acknowledged that if commercial links were completely severed between the ERP nations and Eastern Europe, Western European governments would lose vital raw material supplies from traditional sources. These imports, which included coal, timber, foodstuffs and potash, were required to expedite European economic recovery. Finally, the Class 1-A and 1-B lists currently in operation in the United

States were to be used by the ECA in Paris as a basis for constructing a Western European export control programme. The telegram stated that, given the significance of East–West trade to European economic recovery, Harriman should adopt a flexible approach in talks on the 1-A and 1-B lists. His primary aim was to secure voluntary support from the European governments for a common export control programme, but he should be prepared to encounter opposition to some items contained on the American domestic lists. Nonetheless Harriman was instructed to obtain full support in principle for the denial of Class 1-A goods to the Soviet Union.

The State Department–ECA telegram concluded with the approach to be taken by Harriman in his negotiations with the Western European governments. He was to contact governments on a bilateral basis rather than collectively; an approach was to be made to each ERP nation through the ECA diplomatic mission station stationed in that country. As a consequence of Washington's close ties with London, Harriman was directed to commence informal discussions with Britain and officials in bizonal Germany.[35] In fact the history of the East–West trade embargo from 1948–63 would be dominated by American attempts to harmonise British export control policy with that of the United States. Once agreement had been reached in principle with the Attlee government, the ECA was to open talks with France, the Benelux countries, Denmark, Austria and Norway. As far as the State Department was concerned, Harriman would have little trouble convincing Italy, Greece and Turkey to follow Washington's line. Other ERP nations such as Ireland, Iceland and Portugal did not have substantial trade with Eastern Europe and would not be invited to participate in the strategic embargo.

Marshall and Hoffman reasoned that by working bilaterally with each of the participating governments the ECA could determine which exports the Western European nations valued in trade with Eastern Europe. This would reduce potential conflicts over items to be prohibited to the Soviet bloc when Washington and its allies implemented a multilateral embargo on East–West trade. With the exception of Britain, the ECA was not to divulge the contents of the 1-A and 1-B lists to the participating ERP governments. As full disclosure of the American domestic lists would provoke more reticent governments to oppose wholesale restrictions on East–West trade, Harriman's most pressing task was to obtain voluntary support, in principle, for a strategic embargo. Once a majority of ERP nations had agreed to a common export control programme the United States would seek to design an embargo that would not only prevent the Soviet Union from acquiring strategic goods, but would also allow the ERP nations to continue unhindered in non-strategic trade. The telegram concluded by suggesting that the items on the 1-B List be considered for embargo only when common European acquiescence for an export control programme had been reached.[36]

Conclusion

In an illuminating account of the origins and development of the Western strategic embargo on East–West trade, one scholar has written that the economic containment policy implemented by the United States in 1948 can best be described as a strategy of economic warfare.[37] It could be argued, however, that this approach misinterprets the motives and objectives of the Truman administration when formulating its export control policy towards the Soviet Union. While American policy makers certainly wanted to disrupt the Soviet Union's trading channels with the West from a security standpoint, the economic sanctions were limited to items of a solely strategic nature. Any use of the term 'economic warfare' would imply that the United States sought not only to prevent the Soviet Union from acquiring strategic materials for military production, but also to incapacitate the civilian economy through a comprehensive trade embargo. This was clearly not the case. As shown by the evidence provided in this chapter, the State Department–ECA telegram to Averrell Harriman in August 1948 did not mention economic warfare. The strategy of economic containment that materialised in 1947–48 was developed strictly with a view to constraining the Soviet Union's ability to procure military and strategic items from the Western bloc for use in a future war against the United States.

Economic containment, then, did not mean economic warfare. In pursuing economic containment the Truman administration was attempting, in a subtle manner, to maintain its military ascendancy over the Kremlin. A strategic embargo on East–West trade, officials thought, would yield much in the way of strategic advantage to the United States and its allies in the short term. But in the long term a successful export control programme would limit the Soviet Union's ability to obtain materials necessary for military production. If conflict should break out in the future between the Western and Soviet blocs, Washington and its European allies would be better prepared militarily than Moscow.

2
The Response: Britain, Western Europe and East–West Trade, 1948–49

On 27 August 1948 Averrell Harriman and the ECA began to negotiate a common strategic embargo with Western Europe on East–West trade. The assignment would take an arduous fourteen months. Although the ECA would report in November 1949 that the instructions listed in the State Department–ECA telegram had been carried out, the embargo would look somewhat different from the Class 1-A list forwarded to Harriman by the State Department as a basis for obtaining European cooperation.

Conscious of the close relationship that existed between Washington and London, the telegram had directed Harriman and his team to draw on the support of the Attlee government in their discussions with the Western European nations. After the Second World War Britain was the first Western nation to perceive a potential military and political threat from the Soviet Union. During the late 1940s, as the United States began to implement its containment doctrine, London proved a reliable partner in the struggle against the forces of international communism. Thus when approached by the ECA in autumn 1948 to lead the Western European response to economic containment, the Attlee government willingly obliged. In doing so it sought to moderate the American proposal: it wanted to shape the embargo to reflect British security and trade interests. The main purpose of this chapter is to chart Britain's uneasy attempt to balance the strategic considerations of economic containment against the economic recovery aspirations of Western Europe.

Britain and the Cold War

Despite the relative decline in British global influence after the Second World War, Britain was the world's third largest power after the United States and the Soviet Union. Politically and economically it was still Western Europe's strongest nation, ahead of France and Germany. Yet this seemingly potent international presence masked an underlying economic weakness that was to plague Clement Attlee's government in the post-war years. In financing the successful war effort against Nazi Germany, Britain had spent one quarter of its wealth, accumulated £14 billion of sterling debts and suffered a sharp decline in the value of exports to one third of the 1939 figure.[1] A low-interest loan of $3.75 billion from the United States, while much welcomed by the Treasury, did little to replenish Britain's dwindling dollar supply. In fact by 1947 the British exchequer was close to bankruptcy in its external accounts and efforts to reestablish sterling as a major international currency through convertibility merely plunged the economy further into crisis.[2]

However this precarious economic position did not prevent the Attlee government from playing an instrumental role in the Western alliance against Soviet communism in the formative years of the Cold War. The United States and Britain forged a firm partnership based on shared democratic values and the common objective of containing communism in Europe and Asia. It was not, however, a partnership of equals: Washington was clearly the dominant power.[3] But that is not to suggest that London deferred completely to the Truman administration's demands and policy initiatives. As the last chapter argued, the United States established its containment doctrine towards the Soviet Union in a cautious and incremental manner, with factors outside Washington acting as crucial determinants of Truman's response in 1947. Britain's economic weakness was perhaps the most important factor behind the president's decision to involve the United States in European affairs. Attlee and Foreign Secretary Ernest Bevin decisively seized the opportunity presented to them by Truman to organise the Western European response to Soviet aggression in Europe. Thus while the United States provided economic and military support to the continent through the Truman Doctrine, the Marshall Plan and the North Atlantic Treaty Organisation (NATO), Britain acted as the unofficial leader of Western Europe.

Britain had become aware of a potential Soviet threat long before the Truman administration launched its containment strategy in 1947. In 1943 the British Joint Chiefs of Staff, in a series of position papers on national security, had predicted grimly that the next great adversarial power to challenge the international order would be the Soviet Union. On assuming office in 1945 the Labour government had approached relations with Moscow very warily. Attlee and Bevin, both hard-line anticommunists, had been most concerned by Stalin's actions in Eastern and Central Europe and had therefore sought to build a position of strength in Western Europe to counteract Soviet aggression.[4] Bevin had effectively excluded the Soviet Union from any participation in the Marshall Plan and had foreseen the division of Europe into two blocs well before the breakdown of the talks with Moscow over the future of Germany in November 1947. During the late 1940s he was the most vocal supporter of an Atlantic alliance that would tie Washington to the defence of Western Europe in the event of a Soviet invasion.[5] Ironically, despite being strongly committed to the political and military containment of the Soviet Union, the Attlee government was to pursue an ambivalent economic policy towards Moscow.

Economic containment versus economic recovery

Britain's response to the Truman administration's economic containment strategy was mixed. While London could see the merits of a strategic embargo on military shipments for the Soviet Union, it was reluctant to participate in an export control programme that would disrupt Britain's traditional trading links with Eastern Europe. In the years preceding the Second World War the markets of the Soviet Union, Poland and Czechoslovakia had yielded some 6 per cent of total British exports and imports respectively. These predominantly agricultural economies were still an important source of raw material imports such as grain, timber and coal. Furthermore, given the Soviet Union's growing demand for capital equipment and manufactured consumer goods, exports from Britain to Eastern Europe had grown steadily in the 1930s. In 1932, for example, the Soviet Union had imported 80 per cent of its metalworking tools from Britain. Thus in the midst the growing currency crisis with Washington in the 1940s, the Attlee government had turned to Eastern Europe as a vital non-dollar region in which to procure the raw materials necessary for economic recovery. Imports of coarse grain for livestock and timber for housing had become essential components of the British economic reconstruction programme as policy makers in Whitehall fought to preserve the dwindling dollar supplies. Despite the emergence of Cold War tensions between Moscow and London, the value of British imports from Eastern Europe had grown threefold in 1946–47 from approximately £6 million to £18 million, the bulk of this trade being with the Soviet Union.[6]

The Attlee government had first become aware of American plans to restrict trade with the Soviet Union in April 1948. As a participant in the Marshall Plan, Britain was obliged to terminate shipments of strategic goods to the Soviet bloc under Section 117(d) of the European Co-operation Act. In general, those officials at the Foreign Office who were responsible for dealing with economic recovery were most perturbed by the implications of the Mundt Amendment on British East–West trade policy. They were particularly concerned that the ERP administrator would have the power to grant or deny export licences to British firms trading with Eastern Europe. This issue was raised at a meeting between Roger Makins, a senior Foreign Office official, and Don Bliss of the American embassy in London. In registering the British government's dissatisfaction with Section 117(d), Makins pointed out to Bliss that it was Whitehall's impression that the Marshall Plan was designed to stimulate the growth of European East–West trade to the high levels attained before the war. With this notion in mind the Board of Trade had encouraged British manufacturers to sign trade agreements with Eastern European governments. Makins concluded the meeting, however, by assuring Bliss that Britain would cooperate with the United States in a policy of restricting strategic exports in East–West trade.[7]

Uncertain about American motives, the Attlee government proceeded cautiously in trade policy towards Eastern Europe. It continued to prohibit military shipments to the Soviet Union under Group 17 of the Export of Goods Order Act 1948. Yet due to the vagueness of Section 117(d) the Board of Trade was unable to establish firm guidelines for manufacturers trading with Eastern Europe. A letter from A. E. Welch of the Board of Trade to Makins highlights this dilemma:

> So long as this uncertainty continues UK manufactures will be shy of accepting orders which involve them in outlay which may be frustrated, while Eastern European governments will be driven to formulate their economic programmes on the assumption that they look elsewhere for their supplies – with consequent detriment to our prospect of getting food and raw materials from the East.[8]

Dogged by the Truman administration's failure to clarify its position on East–West trade policy, Britain could not continue to trade freely with the Soviet bloc. Cold War concerns, moreover, forced the Attlee government closely to monitor strategic shipments to the Soviet Union. But as far as officials in the Foreign Office and the Board of

Trade were concerned, Britain could ill afford to lose valuable imports of raw materials from Eastern European markets. At a meeting at the Foreign Office on 10 August, senior civil servants seriously considered the suggestion that London should accept a reduced allocation of Marshall aid rather than sacrifice non-strategic East–West trade.[9]

The United States finally revealed its economic containment strategy to Britain on 2 September. Harriman contacted the Foreign Office through the ECA mission in London, as instructed by the State Department–ECA telegram. Copies of the American Class 1-A and Class 1-B lists were enclosed, with a request on behalf of President Truman for the Attlee government actively to participate in a common export control programme against the Soviet Union. Acknowledging Britain's influential position in Western Europe, Washington was anxious to persuade London to lead the European response to economic containment. By obtaining the support of its closest ally for a strategic embargo, the United States hoped to work closely with Britain towards the formation of an effective international export control programme. Thus, during the autumn of 1948 Harriman and Thomas Finletter of the ECA Mission in London ensured that the Foreign Office was fully briefed on the objectives of economic containment.

Upon receipt of the two lists and a briefing from the ECA on economic containment, British ministers carefully considered the implications of a potential embargo for Britain's national security and international trade policies. While the Ministry of Defence and Foreign Office were receptive to security controls on trade with the Soviet bloc, the Board of Trade tended to view the problem from the perspective of Britain's dollar gap with the United States. Nonetheless there was general agreement among the departments that the American lists were too restrictive. Even the hard-line Cabinet Defence Committee believed that to include all items of military potential in Group 17 of the Export Goods Order Act would be detrimental to British East–West trade. Acting in response to Stalin's blockade of Berlin in June 1948 and with the spectre of Soviet aggression looming on the horizon, Attlee and his cabinet decided to cooperate with the United States in creating an international strategic trade embargo. But Attlee was not prepared to accept the American export control lists in their present form. He ordered the Ministry of Defence and the Board of Trade to draw-up a new Class 1-A list that reflected British security concerns and economic needs. This new list could then be used as a bargaining lever in negotiations with the ECA and other Western European nations. Forwarded to the ECA for inspection in January 1949, the British 1-A list was approximately two thirds the length of its American counterpart.[10]

London took another significant step towards active participation in economic containment in December 1948 when the cabinet approved the Economic Policy Committee's (EPC) recommendation that Britain lead negotiations with its European partners.[11] Sensing that British controls would be largely ineffectual if other European nations did not participate in the embargo, the EPC had concluded that agreement on a common approach could be achieved through the Organisation for European Economic Co-operation (OEEC). Furthermore the newly created British 1-A list could be used as a basis for negotiating a European strategic embargo on East–West trade. From a tactical standpoint, if London could gain support for the new 1-A list from the OEEC members, Western Europe's bargaining position *vis-à-vis* the American lists would be greatly improved. Thus any future Western embargo would be composed only of items of military value and would not contain items listed in trade agreements between the OEEC governments and Eastern Europe.[12]

First steps: Britain, France and the development of the multilateral embargo, January–April 1949

As the Cold War entered its most dangerous phase at the height of the Berlin Blockade, Britain initiated negotiations with other Western European governments on East–West trade policy. On 17 January Britain led a discussion on the American embargo proposal during a meeting of the OEEC nations in Paris. Seizing the opportunity to present the Attlee government's thinking on the security aspects of trade with the Soviet Union, British diplomats outlined the case for a limited export control programme. Given the strategic climate in Europe and the potential military threat posed to the continent by the Soviet Union, they asserted that it was imperative for the OEEC to follow Washington's lead. The British delegation further stated that a selective embargo on strategic shipments to the Soviet bloc, if implemented effectively, could delay the build-up of Soviet military power.

Several delegations reacted negatively to the British delegation's calls for a limited strategic embargo. In particular Sweden and Switzerland were opposed to any restrictions whatsoever on trade with Eastern Europe. This had become apparent to ECA officials in bilateral talks with the two countries in the latter months of 1948. Essentially Sweden, Switzerland and other members of the OEEC could not understand the logic behind the American embargo proposal, which seemed to them to contradict the objectives of the Marshall Plan. During the January OEEC meeting, moreover, they informed the British delegates that any prohibition of exports to Eastern Europe by their governments would have severe domestic political repercussions. While acknowledging that mutual security considerations required the control of military exports to the Soviet Union, they were not prepared to risk losing supplies of raw materials and foodstuffs during the period of economic readjustment.[13]

By contrast the French delegation favoured the British initiative. France had abandoned its hope of close cooperation with the Soviet Union at the end of the war and by 1947 had become Britain's closest security partner in Europe.[14] As well as leading the European response to the Marshall Plan, Britain and France were founding members of the Brussels Pact of March 1948. Both governments shared a common concern for a strong defence alliance in Western Europe with American involvement to counteract the Soviet threat.[15] Thus Paris was keen to implement a strategic embargo on East–West trade, but it sought several assurances from London. First, French participation was conditional on full support in principle from the other OEEC governments. Second, the government wanted to ensure that the embargo would be limited to strategic exports and would not involve the loss to France of imports of essential raw materials from Eastern Europe. Finally, commodities contained in trade agreements with Soviet bloc governments signed by Paris would not be subject to export control.[16]

A series of discussions between British and French diplomats during January finally paved the way for an Anglo-French partnership in East–West trade. On 26 January, France approved in principle the contents of the British 1-A list. Although they objected to twelve items, the French delegation was willing to accept the list as the basis for negotiating a Western European export control programme with the other OEEC governments. Once cooperation between the two countries had been achieved, a new list reflecting the security and trade concerns of London and Paris was drawn up. Both delegations consented to circulate the Anglo-French list to the OEEC membership for consideration at the multilateral level.[17]

Now that France had agreed to cooperate closely with Britain in export control policy, the Attlee government's bargaining position with respect to the United States improved substantially in three respects. First, with French support, as had been the case with the Marshall Plan and Brussels Pact, London's task of convincing the other

OEEC governments to support a multilateral embargo was made much easier. As the two largest powers in Western Europe, France and Britain were the main architects of economic recovery and security on the continent.[18] They could therefore expect cooperation from their Western European Union (WEU) partners and Italy, a loyal ally of the United States. Second, if the OEEC membership could be persuaded to accept the Anglo-French list as a basis for negotiating a multilateral European embargo, policy makers predicted that London's ability to moderate the scope and contents of the ECA lists would be greatly enhanced. The Truman administration, in the interests of Western unity, would be forced to limit a common embargo to exports of a strictly strategic nature; commodities of economic importance to Western Europe would not be affected. Finally, by heading the European export control effort with Paris, London sought to ensure that the British economy did not suffer from trade discrimination in Eastern European markets. In other words, should the Attlee government apply restrictions on East–West trade it would have some guarantee that other OEEC governments would follow suit.

On 3 February, at a meeting in Paris, the Anglo-French list was duly circulated amongst the OEEC members for close examination. This list, which contained 125 items, was considerably shorter than the American 1-A list, which consisted of 163 commodities. When the OEEC reconvened on 14 February the general response to the Anglo-French initiative was more favourable. This was due to two factors. First, the uncertain strategic climate in Europe with the ongoing Berlin blockade by the Soviet Union convinced the Western European governments that a strategic embargo on East–West trade was desirable. Second, the Anglo-French list was more in line with European trade and security interests: it had removed from the ECA 1-A list items of economic value. Notwithstanding the continued resistance of Sweden and Switzerland to export controls, the OEEC membership moved in principle to adopt a multilateral embargo on strategic exports to the Soviet bloc.[19] In summing up the mood of British diplomats, Eric Berthoud of the Foreign Office remarked guardedly that 'there will be a substantial measure of agreement in the end although this may take some time'.[20]

Yet despite some measure of agreement with its continental allies, London had to contend with the ECA's dissatisfaction with Britain's handling of the Western European negotiations. Still in dispute with Britain over the exclusion of 31 Class 1-A items from the British list, American diplomats charged the Attlee government with placing economic interests above strategic considerations. Although the ECA had encouraged Britain to commence multilateral talks with other European governments, it was concerned that London's attempt to modify the 1-A list would undermine American bilateral negotiations with individual countries. Ambassador Jefferson Caffery commented in Paris that:

> This 'arms length' dealing is obviously highly unsatisfactory and we foresee that the other participating countries will probably utilise the existence of two 1-A Lists, with differences due to a complex of economic and strategic factors, to delay adherence to either list.

Continuing his attack on the Anglo-French initiative Caffery argued that:

> [A] further danger is that discussion of [a] joint Anglo-French 1-A List with [the] other participating countries may well lead, even if adherence should be finally obtained from all, to a list which is merely [the] least common denominator and omits many items considered by us to be of important security significance.[21]

Paul Hoffman of the ECA, who believed that Britain had acted 'prematurely' in creating a joint list with France, shared Caffery's concerns. He believed that formal multilateral discussions within the framework of the OEEC should not commence until agreement had been reached between Washington on London on the contents of the ECA's 1-A list.[22] The Foreign Office, however, was not prepared to compromise on the 31 items in dispute with the ECA and decided to act independently of the United States.

By March 1949 Britain was clearly playing a pivotal role in international East–West trade policy. It found itself in the unenviable position of trying to balance American security objectives against Western European trade concerns. Paul Gore-Booth of the Foreign Office succinctly described the Attlee government's dilemma:

> altogether we are acutely aware of what might to called the rival desirabilities in this matter – the desirability of going as far as we can with the Europeans without committing ourselves to the Americans and the desirability of giving the Americans as much help as possible with Congress.[23]

While this situation presented a considerable diplomatic challenge to London, it could use the absence of agreement between Washington and the Western Europeans to the advantage of British trade and security interests. If a consensus could be fostered between the ECA and the OEEC on a limited strategic embargo, Britain would be able to achieve its dual objectives: the denial of strategic exports to the Soviet Union and the preservation of civilian trade with Eastern Europe. Nevertheless the Attlee government stood to lose most should this tactic fail to yield the desired result.

In March the cabinet approved a policy paper prepared by the EPC recommending that export restrictions on trade with Eastern Europe be instituted 'without delay'. Exports to the United States, the Commonwealth and the OEEC nations were to continue to flow freely in order to minimise the effect of the East–West trade restrictions on Britain's balance of payments position.[24] The decision to implement the embargo in April was due to a number of reasons. First, concern about the threat of a Soviet invasion of Western Europe had led Bevin to lobby the Truman administration to extend its security commitment to Western Europe through a formal alliance. After signing the North Atlantic Treaty (NAT) on 4 April with the United States and ten other nations, Britain decided to prohibit strategic exports to the Soviet bloc as part of the common defence effort. Second, pressure from Hoffman and Congress to adhere to Section 117(d) of the ECA Act forced the cabinet to control the export of strategic materials to Eastern Europe or risk losing Marshall aid. Finally, the Ministry of Defence and the Foreign Office were of the opinion that the other OEEC governments would follow Britain's lead in restricting East–West trade. The wisdom of this bold manoeuvre would become apparent upon the publication of an export control list of 153 items on 8 April by the president of the Board of Trade, Harold Wilson.[25]

A difficult task: negotiations between Britain and the OEEC

Once the Attlee government had instituted domestic controls on trade with Eastern Europe it began a concerted campaign to encourage its OEEC partners to do likewise.[26] In the short term this tactic failed. Britain's OEEC partners elected to maintain their existing trade contacts with the Soviet bloc governments, deciding that economic recovery outweighed mutual security. Although several of these nations had joined the North Atlantic Treaty Organisation (NATO) in response to the Soviet threat, they were not prepared to make economic sacrifices in East–West trade.[27] This inaction by the Western European governments did not bode well for London. From the perspective of security, British domestic controls on strategic shipments to the Soviet Union were largely nullified as these exports were readily available from other OEEC nations. Nor did the failure of its continental allies to institute a strategic embargo help Britain's economic condition. As recently declassified documents prepared by the Foreign Office and Ministry of Defence illustrate, officials were not only distressed by the loss of trade through export controls, they were particularly disturbed by reports that OEEC governments were benefiting from Britain's withdrawal from Eastern European markets.[28] Thus by the summer of 1949 the Attlee government's bold initiative to lead the Western European embargo negotiations was clearly floundering. As early as March, John Coulson of the British OEEC delegation had remarked that: 'The net result of this is that we are not much further forward and I think we will require a charge of dynamite to be applied in due course if we are to get get anything like a real agreement.'[29] In fact, given the adverse effect of the embargo on Britain's balance of payments figures, some officials were of the opinion that the East–West trade control system should be dismantled.

In a report on the efficacy of the British trade embargo the Economic Intelligence Department of the Foreign Office painted a very bleak picture. It estimated that Britain would continue to lose key imports contained in trade agreements with the Eastern European governments as long as the restrictions were maintained. As $125 million worth of these imports would have to be acquired from alternative sources, Britain's currency gap crisis with the United States would continue to spiral, causing a 'crisis of first class dimension' in the latter months of 1949. In blunt terms the report concluded that this was an exorbitantly high price to pay for a security measure that was being rendered ineffectual by the refusal of the other OEEC nations to impose similar restrictions on trade.[30]

More worrying for the Board of Trade was the dire effect of the embargo on small traditional firms who relied solely on the Eastern European market. Since a substantial amount of heavy industrial equipment was subject to export control, many of these firms had continued to lose business to Western European competitors who were unencumbered by trade restrictions. Likewise manufacturing companies that relied on raw materials from the Soviet bloc region also suffered as Eastern European governments retaliated against British trade controls by imposing their own restrictions. Thus with the inability of exporters and manufacturers to trade with any degree of certainty a large number of businesses were forced to close, bringing unemployment to many regions throughout Britain.

It should be noted, however, that East–West trade was only 6 per cent of Britain's total world trade. Of course trade with the United States, the Commonwealth and Western Europe was of more concern to the Board of Trade and the Treasury. But as the largest European trading nation with Eastern Europe, the loss to Britain of Soviet bloc markets was, as one official at the Ministry of Defence put it, 'significant in amount in kind and may be permanent in some cases'.[31] The Board of Trade calculated that more than £10 million of export trade had been lost during the first three months of the embargo (April to June).[32] The economic implications of this lost trade concerned the 117D Working Party, composed of officials from the Foreign Office and the Ministry of Defence, and they concluded that export controls were 'increasingly difficult to justify as their security value is frustrated'.[33] They were aware that if an agreement between Britain and the OEEC on a common embargo did not materialise in the near future the Attlee government would have to abandon its domestic restrictions on East–West trade.[34] This was a scenario that defence officials in Britain wanted to avoid in the context of growing Soviet military power.

Anglo-American conflict

The Attlee government was presented with yet another obstacle to its ostensibly elusive quest to establish a European strategic embargo on East–West trade: American intransigence about the 1-A list.[35] As noted above, London and Washington had been in dispute over 31 items on the 1-A list since February 1949. Most of these items were civil industrial exports and included commodities relating to metalworking machinery. Officials were reluctant to place restrictions on these exports because Eastern Europe continued to be a significant importer of British machine tools.[36]

In a series of exchanges with the ECA during the spring and summer, the Foreign Office argued forcefully that these exports were of little strategic value to the Soviet Union. The matter was further raised at a meeting on 22 July between American and British technical experts in London. The British delegation emphasised that the Attlee government could not afford to prohibit trade in civil industrial exports as parliament and public opinion would oppose export controls on non-military items. After some debate and careful scrutiny of trade statistics, the American delegation found that the strategic significance of these items had been 'exaggerated' and that Britain actually exported only 'very small quantities' of these commodities to Eastern Europe. When pressed to impose quantitative restrictions on 27 of these items, the British delegation responded by suggesting that ministers would only consider controls if other Western European countries did likewise.[37] The net effect of these discussions was that the issue renamed unresolved; the debate on quantitative controls would be resumed when Britain and the United States discussed the 1-B list in early 1950.

There was also disagreement between London and Washington over the insistence by the Truman administration that the embargo be linked formally to the American military assistance programme. The United States believed that it could use military assistance as a lever with which to force the Western Europeans to accept an embargo on East–West trade. Such an approach, British officials surmised, would undermine London's bargaining position with the OEEC nations. Worse still, Britain would be unable to prevent the ECA from making unanimous acceptance of the 1-A and 1-B lists a condition for receiving military aid. Clearly the Europeans would have little choice but to follow Washington's lead.[38] Yet for the most part Britain succeeded in stalling the efforts of Hoffman and the ECA to tie export controls to military aid. It was not until the congressional investigation into Western European trade with the Soviet bloc during the Korean War that the issue of trade versus aid became a considerable bone of contention between the United States and its allies. In the short term, however, the Foreign Office managed to keep negotiations with the OEEC a 'European affair'.[39]

Progress

After months of deadlock the negotiations between Britain and the OEEC were given a new lease of life by the decision of the French government on 29 August to publish a list of exports to be controlled in trade with Eastern Europe. This was to prove a significant turning point.[40] The French initiative was taken in light of the increasing likelihood of Soviet aggression in Europe after reports indicated that the Soviet Union in the process of testing an atomic bomb. With the indication by France that it would participate in a strategic embargo, the

British delegation to the OEEC met French government officials in Paris in late September. Averse to American involvement in European East–West trade talks, French representatives objected to John Coulson's suggestion that the ECA be allowed participate in the negotiations with the OEEC members. Although Coulson stressed that America's embargo aims would coincide with those of Western Europe, the French delegation remained resolute.[41] The available evidence suggests that France refused to endorse American participation on the ground that Washington would endeavour to press the OEEC into full acceptance of the 1-A list.

While the role of the United States in talks with the other OEEC governments was left unresolved, Britain and France moved swiftly to construct a new A-F list as a basis for negotiations with their continental allies. The new list, which was accepted without reservation by both countries, omitted from the 1-A list 48 items that were deemed vital to Western European trade with the Soviet bloc. The new Anglo-French list thus offered the best opportunity for Britain and France to reach agreement with the OEEC. Encouraged by the successful outcome of the Anglo-French meeting of 11 October, C. B. Duke of the Foreign Office optimistically wrote that 'these developments in Paris suggest that more effective cooperation from other Western European countries may be forthcoming in the reasonably near future'.[42]

Yet the issue of American participation had to be resolved. In an effort to overcome French obduracy on this matter the Foreign Office contacted the British embassies in Rome and the Benelux countries to arrange a meeting on East–West trade. All six nations agreed to attend discussions on the revised Anglo-French list, and the Italian and Dutch governments insisted that the United States be represented at the talks. Sensing that it would be alienated from the negotiations, France, in the interests of Anglo-French harmony, withdrew its objection to American representation.

On 12 October a meeting was held in Paris to discuss the Anglo-French proposal. Attended by delegates from Britain, France, Italy, the Benelux countries and the United States, the meeting, while not yielding 'any tangible progress', was conducted in a 'friendly and co-operative' atmosphere. Although Sweden and Switzerland did not formally participate in the meeting, delegates from both nations kept a watchful eye on the proceedings. Significantly, security considerations during the summer and autumn months had forced the Benelux governments to rethink trade policy towards the Soviet

Union and Eastern Europe. While still not disposed to institute a wide-ranging embargo on East–West trade, the delegates from the Benelux countries recommended that their governments implement restrictions on a large proportion of the items on the Anglo-French list. In order to enable the Benelux delegations to brief their governments on the Anglo-French proposal, a further meeting was convened in late November to explore the possibility of establishing a multilateral East–West trade group.[43]

In response to the moderately successful outcome of this meeting the ECA decided to change its tactics in respect of negotiations with the Western European nations. Convinced that the only way to accomplish significant progress on a common embargo was through a multilateral framework, American diplomats abandoned the bilateral approach outlined by the State Department to Harriman in August 1948.[44] Thus in the intervening weeks before the November meeting in Paris the ECA special missions in London, Paris, Brussels, The Hague and Copenhagen urged the respective governments to support the Anglo-French initiative. The Commerce Department, however, did not endorse this view. In a telegram to Harriman, James Webb of the State Department alerted the special representative to Commerce officials' demands that the ECA seek Western European compliance on 'as much as possible' of the 1-A list.[45] It would appear that Harriman and the State Department largely ignored this request. American diplomats in Europe generally felt that real progress towards a common export control policy was in the offing, and therefore believed that it would be unwise to press the OEEC governments for full acceptance of the 1-A list at such a delicate moment in the negotiations. If a consensus could be reached on the revised Anglo-French list, Harriman thought, the United States would achieve its aim of establishing an international embargo on East–West trade.[46]

The creation of CoCom: towards limited economic containment

Negotiations in Paris between the United States, Britain, France, Italy, the Benelux countries and Denmark began in earnest on 14 November 1949.[47] Having reviewed the Anglo-French proposal the Benelux governments were now willing to implement prohibitions on strategic trade with the Soviet bloc. Drawing on the Anglo-French list as a framework for establishing a multilateral embargo, the group divided exports for control in East–West trade into three categories, each of which contained a list of items to be placed under embargo. International List I contained 129 military and strategic exports; International List II was composed of one semistrategic and a number of industrial commodities to be restricted quantitatively; and International List III included twelve items that would be reserved pending further discussion. In the spirit of unity each nation agreed unanimously to institute controls on the items specified in the three international lists.[48]

A further step was taken to facilitate the implementation of the new embargo lists. The participating countries and Norway formed an informal regime to monitor East–West trade. The regime consisted of a Consultative Group, responsible for policy making and policy execution, and a permanent Coordinating Committee (CoCom), staffed by technical experts, to scrutinise Western trade with the Soviet bloc. The work of both bodies was to be kept secret. Hervé Alphand, a senior French Foreign Ministry official, was appointed to chair the CG and Giovanni d'Orlandi of the Italian Foreign Ministry was selected to head CoCom.[49] The inaugural meeting of CoCom would take place in January 1950.

Both the United States and Britain viewed these developments in a positive light. After 14 months of protracted negotiations the ECA could at last report that the State Department–ECA objectives had been fulfilled. In a congratulatory telegram to Harriman, Secretary of State Dean Acheson remarked that 'solid progress' had been achieved.[50] But not all government departments were satisfied with the outcome of the November talks.[51] Predictably the Commerce Department felt that the new international lists did not reflect American national security interests. Moreover, Charles Sawyer complained to Acheson that the new lists did not contain 48 of the items on the original 1-A list. Sawyer blamed the State Department for this state of affairs, accusing Acheson of allowing Britain to dominate the negotiations with the OEEC.[52]

Some scholars have tended to exaggerate the Truman administration's diplomatic success.[53] While the ECA and the State Department certainly triumphed in their attempt to secure Western European participation in a common export control programme, the OEEC managed to tailor the embargo to the economic interests of its members. The Attlee government was the driving force behind Western European attempts to modify the American 1-A list. In partnership with France, London could claim to be the *de facto* leader of the Western European embargo effort. A comparison of the Anglo-French list with the three international lists produced in November 1949 demonstrates the extent to which Britain and France ensured that items of Western European trade interest were not embargoed. Thus the international export control programme that materialised in January 1950 can be termed a *limited* strategy of economic containment.

Conclusion

As this chapter has illustrated, the Truman administration was confronted with considerable opposition when it tried to negotiate an international export control programme with Western Europe. Even cooperation with Britain, its closest European ally, led to disagreement and discord between the two powers. For the most part, however, Britain was a firm supporter of a strategic embargo on East–West trade. The Attlee government shared America's concerns about Soviet communism and believed that a strategy of economic containment would play a decisive role in stunting the growth of Soviet military power. Throughout 1949 British diplomats tried to impress upon the OEEC governments the necessity of controlling trade with Eastern Europe in the context of the Cold War. In conjunction with France, Britain was responsible for encouraging several Western European countries to move from a position of staunch opposition to a strategic embargo to active participation in the formation of CoCom.

Yet Britain emerged as the chief guardian of Western European East–West trade interests. Upon receipt of the American export control lists in September 1948 the Attlee government took immediate steps to modify the ECA's proposed embargo. The Board of Trade and Ministry of Defence were instructed by the cabinet to construct a new Class 1-A list that mirrored Britain's strategic and trade interests. This list, which omitted many items proposed for control by Washington, was used as a basis for the OEEC embargo negotiations. While infuriating some American officials, this approach allowed Britain, with French cooperation, to make export controls more palatable to its continental partners. In the short term this tactic failed; in the long run it helped to remove the obstacles to the establishment of a multilateral export control programme in January 1950.

3
Divergent Strategies: American and British Economic Defence Policies in 1950

At the inaugural meeting of CoCom in January 1950 the members agreed to implement export controls on the items on the three international lists. As the Cold War entered its most dangerous phase, however, the United States took the lead in urging the participant nations to broaden the East–West trade embargo to include items on the 1-B list. The United States had already instituted domestic restrictions on this list and the Truman administration hoped that its allies would follow its example in the interests of mutual security. During 1950 the Western European governments took a firm stand against 1-B export controls. Emerging as the most forceful critic of the American proposals, Britain pointed to the economic value of industrial trade with Eastern Europe.

The confrontation that materialised between Washington and London is the subject of this chapter. First, the Truman administration's shift from a policy of political to military containment is discussed with special reference to East–West trade. Second, the Attlee government's perception of the 1-B list is analysed in detail. The chapter describes the points of departure of American and British policy. Finally, the influence of the Korean War on reversing London's standpoint on the 1-B list is examined in the context of recent studies of CoCom.

Building situations of strength

During 1947–49 the Truman administration, as we have seen, responded to Soviet expansionism in Europe and Asia by implementing a series of revolutionary foreign policy initiatives. The Truman Doctrine and the Marshall Plan sought to contain Moscow's influence in the Near East and Western Europe by economic means. In providing financial assistance to the war-torn economies of Western Europe, American policy makers hoped to create stability and strength on the continent as an effective counterweight to Soviet aggression. While these measures helped to rebuild the balance of power and aided economic recovery in Europe, several nations, under the leadership of Britain and France, endeavoured to secure American military commitment to the defence of the continent. The accentuation of Cold War tensions with the Soviet Union in 1948–49 over Berlin and Stalin's continuing drive to extend the Soviet Union's sphere of influence in Eastern Europe led to the formation of NATO in 1949. Once the Truman administration had signed the North Atlantic Treaty the United States was tied indefinitely to the security of Western Europe. Most significantly, the establishment of the Atlantic defence pact stimulated a change in American national security strategy from political to military containment of the Soviet Union.[1]

The shift from political to military containment was the result of new strategic thinking in the State Department. By appointing Dean Acheson to replace General Marshall as secretary of state in January 1949, President Truman signalled his intention to take a firm stand against Moscow. The new secretary had been involved in developing the Truman Doctrine and the Marshall Plan during his tenure as undersecretary of state. On assuming office, however, Acheson initiated a policy of power diplomacy against the Kremlin, favouring a massive rearmament programme to counter the spread of communism throughout the globe.[2] He believed that the United States needed to build 'situations of strength' in Europe and Asia lest Stalin co-opt these regions into the Soviet orbit. As far as Acheson was concerned, the loss of Western Europe and Japan to the Soviets would be catastrophic for American national security. A strategy of global containment was required that would bolster the European and Japanese economies, allow democracy to thrive and provide security guarantees against the Soviet threat to America's allies. In short, Acheson's interventionist approach to foreign policy committed Washington to seek 'preponderant power' in the international system.[3]

Indications that the Soviet Union had successfully tested an atomic bomb in late August 1949 led policy makers to believe that American global preponderance would be considerably undermined. No longer could the United States pursue its diplomatic goals behind the shield of nuclear superiority: Soviet possession of atomic bombs increased the threat of a 'hot' war with the United States. The ending of the Truman administration's nuclear monopoly coincided with another dramatic event that posed further problems for policy makers in the State and Defence Departments: the establishment of the People's Republic of China (PRC) by the communist victors of the Chinese civil war.[4]

Faced with global turmoil, Acheson, under the direction of Truman, ordered a review of the national security strategy. During the autumn and winter of 1949 the policy planning staff, headed by Paul Nitze, drew up a blueprint document that was to shape American foreign policy for the next 40 years. Titled NSC-68, Nitze's prescription for coping with the global menace of communism was a clarion call to arms.[5] Written in hyperbolic terms to grab the attention of top level policy makers, NSC-68 fleshed out Acheson's concept of a situation of strength, calling on the president to commit the United States to a world-wide containment policy to defend American interests and protect America's allies from Soviet aggression. The document recommended massive military build-up to a scale three times larger than the Truman administration's present defence budget of $13 billion. While Acheson and Nitze were convinced that military conflict with the Soviet Union was unlikely in the short run, they thought that possession of a nuclear arsenal would increase the Soviet Union's penchant for risk taking in Eurasia. Acheson maintained that if Stalin could gain control of the industrial infrastructure and raw materials of Western Europe and Japan, Soviet military and economic power might surpass that of the United States. It was therefore crucial for Washington to move swiftly to shore up the balance of power in key strategic areas through military, economic and psychological means. NSC-68 aimed to do this and more.[6]

There was not unified support for NSC-68 throughout the administration. At the State Department, George Kennan, Nitze's predecessor as director of the PPS, had many reservations about the objectives of the new policy. Although his perception of the Soviet threat mirrored that of Acheson, he was most disturbed by the document's main conclusion: the militarisation of containment. For Kennan a nuclear arms race with the Soviet Union would only lead to global destruction. What was needed, he suggested to Acheson, was continuance of the strategy of limited political containment that recognised separate spheres of influence. In essence Kennan believed that it would be futile to undertake a policy of global military containment of the Soviet Union; such an approach, he argued, would put America's interests and allies at risk from Soviet military power.[7] The secretary of defense, Louis Johnson, was initially opposed to NSC-68 on the ground that a substantial increase in military spending would create budgetary problems of substantial proportions for the administration. Johnson was further perturbed by the fact that Acheson and Nitze had left the Defence Department and the Joint Chiefs of Staff (JCS) out of the drafting process of NSC-68.[8] While proceeding cautiously with the new policy during the summer months, Truman finally endorsed his secretary of state's proposal in September 1950. The president's mind was finally made up in June, however, with the outbreak of the Korean War.

The State Department and export controls

In view of the Truman administration's decision to implement a global military containment policy towards the Soviet Union, policy planners in the State Department began to situate export control policy within the wider framework of American security objectives. Following reports from the US embassy in Moscow that the Kremlin was anxious to capitalise on the low price of Western European strategic exports for military production, officials now strove to institute comprehensive restrictions on East–West trade.[9] Although NSC-68 only mentioned trade with the Soviet Union in a brief paragraph, the document clearly suggested that policy makers should ensure that strategic exports from the Western bloc were denied to Moscow.[10] Now that Stalin had halted military cutbacks in the Soviet Union in favour of massive defence spending, a wide-ranging multilateral strategic embargo seemed consistent with national security goals. In fact some argued that economic containment should be linked intrinsically with the MDAP, the ERP and the American military programme in preparation for a future 'open conflict' with the Soviet Union.[11] Secretary of State Acheson certainly subscribed to this sentiment. In several keynote speeches to Congress, he elucidated the potential danger of a Soviet invasion and takeover of Western Europe. He argued that if the Soviet Union gained control of essential strategic raw materials these commodities would 'be put to use against us' in the event of a military conflict.[12] Thus by early 1950 the State Department was actively supporting an extension of export controls by the CoCom members: in effect the adoption by the Western European governments and Japan of Class 1-B items.[13]

Yet senior officials responsible for East–West trade were caught on the horns of a policy dilemma. An extension of the strategic embargo was desirable, but not at the expense of economic recovery. In adherence to the Marshall memorandum of 26 March 1948 they were careful to prioritise those European East–West trade interests that were deemed necessary for the continuing cohesion and strength of the Western alliance.[14] Estimates prepared by the State Department stressed that an extension of export restrictions by the Western European governments to the magnitude of the American 1-B list would reduce Eastern European trade by 48 per cent in some cases. These governments would then have no option but to obtain essential raw materials from dollar sources, weakening their balance of payments positions *vis-à-vis* the United States. A policy paper for the attention of the secretary of state concluded that a severe curtailment of East–West trade by the ERP countries would have enormous economic repercussions.[15] Not only would the dollar gap between Washington and its allies be widened, but also unemployment in industries involved in Soviet bloc trade would cause social and political unrest, playing directly into the hands of communist sympathisers. A weakened Western Europe would thus be vulnerable to Soviet military aggression, neutralising the balance of power on the continent and ultimately jeopardising American national security.[16]

With this in mind, Acheson was conscious of the need to reconcile security priorities, in the form of increased export controls, with the economic interests of the ERP nations. He reasoned that further controls would 'not be a practicable possibility' until the European governments participating in CoCom accepted these extensions voluntarily and multilaterally.[17] The secretary of state's primary aim since the beginning of his tenure in office in January 1949 had been the formation of a permanent Atlantic alliance with the leading powers of Western Europe against Moscow. He therefore did not wish to strain the Truman administration's close relationship with its allies by adopting a coercive approach to secure allied cooperation for a comprehensive embargo on East–West trade. In other words Acheson was not prepared to make acceptance of a substantial proportion of the 1-B list a prerequisite for economic and military aid. He thought that economic containment would be 'infinitely more effective' if based on the principles of cooperation and 'common recognition' of the grave Soviet military threat to the Western world.[18] The imposition of sanctions by Washington on countries that failed to observe the guidelines of American export control policy, Acheson argued, would lead to disgruntlement within the Atlantic alliance, increasing insecurity with respect to the Soviet threat. A strategic embargo based on mutual consent was required if the objectives of CoCom were to be achieved.[19] Acheson outlined his vision in an illuminating position paper presented to the National Security Council (NSC):

An effective programme of multilateral export controls depends upon voluntary agreement by the co-operating countries. We cannot expect that an agreement imposed by coercion would be enforced by those countries with the same vigour as one adopted voluntarily.[20]

This point was reiterated in a report to Truman on export control policy. Acheson once again spelt out the dangers for American national security should Washington decide to make aid to Western Europe conditional on the allies severing critical trading links with Eastern Europe. He explained to the president 'that considerations of political feasibility, military risk and economic cost make it undesirable to press for European controls completely parallel to those exercised by the US'.[21] Nonetheless the irrepressible Charles Sawyer of the Commerce Department accused Acheson and the State Department of being too accommodating to European economic interests.

Confrontation: Sawyer versus Acheson

The long-running dispute between Sawyer and the State Department over East–West trade reached its apogee in 1950. Since his appointment in May 1948 Sawyer had taken a most critical stance on Western European trade with the Soviet bloc. His views conflicted sharply with those of successive secretaries of state; first Marshall then Acheson. Adamant that the ERP governments' restriction on exports to Eastern Europe should match those of the United States, Sawyer believed that the containment of communism outweighed economic recovery in Western Europe. As an ardent anticommunist and conservative democrat, he was of the opinion that American national security dictated that Washington take a strong stand against Soviet expansionism throughout the world.[22] For Sawyer, economic sanctions directed against Moscow were an effective means to curb Soviet military power. Ironically, during the period covered by this book, the Commerce Department, a strong proponent of free trade, took a consistently protectionist view of trade with Eastern Europe.

As observed in the previous chapter, Sawyer had expressed considerable indignation about the ECA negotiations on a common embargo in 1948–49. In particular the international export control programme implemented by the CoCom members in January 1950 omitted too many of the commodities on the American lists. With such a wide divergence between American export controls and the international embargo, he charged, it was impossible adequately to restrict strategic shipments to the Soviet bloc. Worse still, Sawyer was dismayed by reports that some European countries were lax in instituting controls on exports to Eastern Europe. In characteristic fashion he asserted that due to the reluctance of the ERP governments to follow Washington's lead in CoCom, the 'beneficiaries have been Russia and manufacturers in Western Europe and the UK. The sufferers have been American manufacturers and anticommunist security.'[23] Sawyer, of course, was concerned that American corporations with links with Eastern European markets were losing valuable business to Western European counterparts that were unhindered by export prohibitions. But this was not the main reason for criticising the East–West trade policies of the OEEC governments.

In the interests of national security, Sawyer pressed the State Department to take a tougher stance against recalcitrant allies that refused to control the sale of strategic and industrial commodities to Eastern Europe. Arguing in NSC-69 that the volume of East–West trade required for economic recovery was much less than had been estimated, he called for a significant reduction in the gap of 'export control standards' between the United States and Western Europe. In view of the Soviet Union's acquisition of the atomic bomb and its militarisation policy, Sawyer pointed out that strategic preparedness should take precedence over economic recovery.[24] Thus in stark contrast to Acheson, Sawyer pushed for greater cohesion between the American and international embargo lists. He also favoured full acceptance by the Europeans of the 1-B list, commenting that 'it is possible to defend the position that practically all commodities in this era are strategic'.[25] It was this claim that led to confrontation between Sawyer and the State Department over international embargo policy.

The State Department responded critically to Sawyer's hard-line position on negotiations with the OEEC governments. The general consensus amongst senior officials was that any attempt to dictate export control policy to the Western Europeans would prove 'self-defeating'.[26] Responding to Sawyer, Acheson defended the economic concerns of the OEEC nations, stating that the United States should try to 'appeal to the common security interests of the Atlantic area rather than to threaten to carry out a denial of essential military or economic assistance'.[27] For Acheson, the creation of a strong, unified Western alliance was the bedrock of American national security. In London, US Ambassador Lewis E. Douglas shared the secretary of state's view. Demonstrating a good understanding of the international embargo problem, Douglas doubted 'whether there can ever be complete uniformity between US export controls and those of Western Europe because of [the] different local conditions' in each participating country.[28] The ambassador cautioned the State Department about the ramifications of a coercive approach to negotiations on expansion of the multilateral export control programme with Washington's allies. In Douglas' opinion:

> any attempt [to] dragoon [our] European partners into reluctantly paralleling US strategic trade controls would seriously jeopardise our efforts [to] attain real unity in [the] political, military [and] economic fields based upon [a] mutually agreed definition of aims and determination to reach them.[29]

Unlike Sawyer, both Acheson and Douglas tended to position East–West trade policy in the wider context of American strategic objectives. Whereas Sawyer campaigned unrelentingly for the harmonisation of international trade restrictions with those of the United States, the State Department was preoccupied with building a formidable alliance to counteract the Soviet threat. In effect Sawyer was anxious to prioritise the national economic interest, while Acheson's aspirations were avowedly geopolitical.

Officials at the State Department were greatly alarmed by Sawyer's criticism of CoCom. The general reaction to his views was disbelief. In particular, diplomats stationed in the OEEC countries feared that his condemnation of Western European East–West trade practices would undermine America's international embargo objectives and lead to friction within the Atlantic alliance. Confident that much progress had been made in negotiations with the allies on the formation of a multilateral embargo, they found Sawyer's comments disturbing. Although policy planners in the State Department shared the Commerce Department's contention that trade with the Soviet bloc should be curtailed for the purposes of Western security, they perceived coercive tactics to be counterproductive. As the OEEC governments required substantial non-strategic trade from Eastern Europe for economic recovery, they thought it a worthless endeavour to attempt to convince these nations that mutual security would be better served if traditional commercial links with the Soviet bloc were completely severed.[30]

The presence of Commerce Department officials in the negotiations, moreover, did little to help American representatives in CoCom to obtain European support for an embargo. It was reported that one

Commerce official 'became so tired of the refusals by the other governments to accept his position that he told them that he had never heard so many vetoes outside the United Nations. He wondered whether or not their word for no was "nyet".'[31]

In addition to the negative effect the Commerce Department was having on negotiations with the OEEC governments, Sawyer's proposal to tie economic aid to compliance with export restrictions on East–West trade worried the State Department. European recovery policy planners deduced that the United States would be obliged to locate new markets for Western Europe in the event that Sawyer's ideas were given credence by President Truman. Such a scenario, they predicted, would aggravate the dollar shortage between Washington and its allies, weakening Western Europe's economic position and rendering it vulnerable to Soviet aggression.[32]

In late summer 1950 the Commerce Department asserted its role in export control policy. With the failure of Austria, Sweden, Switzerland, Spain and Portugal to place restrictions on strategic items deemed to contribute to Soviet military potential, Sawyer refused shipment of Class 1-A items to these countries under Export Policy Determination No. 381. After much debate in the National Security Council this policy was approved as NSC Determination No. 347.[33] The reaction of the State Department was predictable. James Webb, the undersecretary of state, summed up the views of the Department by asserting that Sawyer's action would signal the 'abandonment' of 'a co-operative multilateral export control programme through CG-CoCom', and that the United States would provoke strong opposition from Western Europe if the strategic embargo were 'enforced through coercion'. If Washington unilaterally tried to force the Western Europeans to institute an extensive embargo, Webb argued, neither American nor allied security interests would be served effectively.[34] The American embassy in London overwhelmingly endorsed Webb's viewpoint. Embassy officials voiced their concern about the development of what they termed the 'Sawyer Programme', which appeared 'to contradict efforts to reach agreement through negotiation'.[35]

Although Sawyer could count on the support of Louis Johnson and the Defence Department for a coercive approach to international negotiations, Acheson and the ECA vehemently opposed him. A debate thus materialised over export control policy at the NSC level between the secretaries of state and commerce. At an NSC meeting on 24 August Acheson showed his clear understanding of international embargo policy by once more reiterating the importance of East–West trade to the creation of a strong power centre in Western Europe.[36] Yet Sawyer remained unconvinced. During several conversations with the secretary of commerce during October, Acheson further argued that the use of coercion to gain compliance for a strategic embargo would 'impair [the] ECA programme and jeopardise East–West trade negotiations with the Western Europeans'.[37]

The dispute remained unresolved, but Acheson was adamant that he could obtain the support of the president for his position. In a memorandum to Truman he set out his reservations about Sawyer's approach to East–West trade policy. While agreeing that it was in the best interests of American security to prevent the shipment of strategic items by Washington's allies to the Soviet bloc, he stated that the use of sanctions through aid denial against offending nations would be counterproductive.[38] Philip J. Funigiello has suggested that Acheson and Sawyer jointly supported NSC Determination No. 347.[39] It could be argued, however, that Acheson had no option but to support Sawyer's proposal given the NSC's approval of the policy. Certainly the evidence shows that Acheson had strong private reservations about the coercive nature of the executive policy decision. During the remaining years of Truman's term of office Acheson would have to draw on his considerable diplomatic skill to reassure the Western European governments that economic and military aid would not be denied to nations that failed to impose adequate restrictions on East–West trade. This task would not be easy. As the following chapters will illustrate, Acheson had to contend with congressional attempts to link economic and military assistance to East–West trade during 1950–51.

Britain and the 'special relationship', 1948–50

In order to understand the motives behind Britain's export control policy in 1950 it is necessary to examine the Attlee government's relationship with the United States.[40] Although Britain was undoubtedly the junior partner in the Anglo-American alliance against communism, London was not completely dependent on Washington. In many ways the Foreign Office was able to use American power to further British interests with great dexterity. Ironically the weakness of Britain's economic position ensured that American policy makers focused a good deal of attention on Anglo-American affairs.[41] Concerned that British and Western European vulnerability might entice Stalin to expand the Soviet sphere of influence westwards, they cooperated very closely with their counterparts in London. Thus during the late 1940s the Attlee government became an indispensable ally to Washington in the global containment of communism.

British policy makers exploited this 'special relationship' with the Truman administration. So much so that London also came to act as a constraining force on American foreign policy. While Britain was responsible, with France, for providing Western European leadership with respect to the Marshall Plan, the Attlee government was not favourable towards European integration. Efforts by the Economic Co-operation Administration (ECA) to nudge Britain in the direction of a political and economic union with its continental neighbours were to no avail. Instead London succeeded in maintaining the sterling area and close commercial ties with the Commonwealth; as a result the imperial preference remained and sterling was only partially convertible against the dollar. Not only were American plans for regional economic and political integration in Europe thwarted, but also the Truman administration's attempt to build a multilateral world order under the Bretton Woods Agreement was frustrated.[42]

Moreover, Britain exerted considerable influence over the United States on a global scale. As the most prominent power in the Middle East, Britain was able to draw on American economic and military support to safeguard its interests in the region. Friction characterised Anglo-American relations towards Asia. While Britain recognised the establishment of the People's Republic of China (PRC) in January 1950, the Truman administration refused to extend diplomatic status to Mao Zedong's communist government. Despite token support for the intervention of the United States in the Korean War, the Attlee government believed that Washington had exaggerated the threat of communism in Southeast Asia. During a visit to Washington in December 1950, the British prime minister was, moreover, instrumental in persuading Truman not to use nuclear weapons in the war.[43]

It was in this international context, then, that the United States and Britain addressed East–West trade in 1950. As the preceding narrative has suggested, the Attlee government had considerable influence on the making of American Cold War policy. The Truman administration realised the significance of the 'special relationship' with London, even though in public it constantly denied that an exclusive alliance existed with Britain. Nevertheless, as American documents show, Truman and the State Department drew on Britain's global presence when formulating their strategy of containing Soviet power in Europe, the Middle East and Asia.

Opposition: Britain and the 1-B list

With the inauguration of CoCom in January 1950 and acceptance by the members of export controls on the 1-A list, the State Department broached the contentious issue of extending the embargo to Class 1-B items. In general the European governments were reluctant to place restrictions on trade in 1-B exports to Eastern Europe. Unlike the high strategic content of the items on the 1-A list, the imposition of an embargo on 1-B exports would severely reduce the industrial and commercial East–West trade of the Western Europeans. Throughout 1950 relations between the United States and its allies in CoCom were strained as a result of the conflict over 1-B controls. The Attlee government, which had hitherto spearheaded the negotiations with its continental neighbours on embargo policy, became the leader of the Western European opposition to wholesale 1-B export controls.[44]

Since August 1948 the United States had looked to Britain to lead the Western European response to economic containment. It was a role that Whitehall was willing to play, once Washington was prepared to recognise the significance of East–West trade to British economic recovery. The decision by the State Department in the early months of 1950 to press its European allies to adopt a substantial proportion of the 1-B list altered Britain's attitude towards American policy making in CoCom. While Britain supported the strong military stance taken by the United States against Moscow, the Attlee government was alarmed by the Truman administration's commitment to an extensive embargo on exports to the Soviet bloc. Determined to prevent Washington from tabling restrictions on 1-B items in CoCom, the Foreign Office led a concerted campaign by the Western European governments to preserve industrial East–West trade. The clash that consequently ensued between Britain and the United States in the summer of 1950 centred on the shipment of dual-purpose items to the Soviet Union. In short, whereas American policy makers deemed industrial exports to have significant strategic value, British officials were of the opinion that dual-purpose items would not contribute substantially to Soviet military production.

The initial efforts by the American embassy in London to alert the Foreign Office to the necessity of instituting export restrictions on the 1-B list in April met little success. Although Foreign Office officials acknowledged the strategic importance of 1-B export controls, they objected to the inclusion of a large number of commodities on the list on the ground that these items were a valuable source of income for the

British economy. Most disturbed by this attitude, the American embassy declared in a telegram to the Foreign Office that Anglo-American relations in East–West trade policy had deteriorated considerably. The telegram claimed that this state of affairs was due to Whitehall's insistence on the primacy of trade interests above mutual security.[45] This view was strongly contested by the Mutual Aid Department of the Foreign Office, which accused the United States of 'throwing in a number of additional candidates for 1-A treatment and suggesting far-reaching changes in the treatment of 1-B items without previously concerting with us'.[46] While clearly troubled by Washington's 1-B proposal, the Foreign Office was prepared to adhere to present British export control policy of working with France 'to turn down any American suggestions which went beyond what was reasonable'.[47]

The main reason for this sudden breakdown in cooperation between Britain and the United States was not so much a question of policy but rather one of application. To be sure, the main cornerstone of British post-war foreign policy was the maintenance of a close alliance with the Truman administration against the Soviet Union. But the Attlee government could not afford to curtail East–West trade to the extent desired by Washington, as such a policy would have dire consequences for Britain's balance of payments during the period of economic recovery. Within the government, however, there was some disagreement over British export control policy. The Foreign Office and Ministry of Defence favoured an extension of restrictions on a number of non-strategic items on the 1-B list, while the Board of Trade was staunchly opposed to any expansion of the CoCom embargo.[48]

Moreover British representatives at the OEEC in Paris were concerned about the American method of introducing extensions to the international control lists negotiated in November 1949. Again, like their colleagues in the Foreign Office, they found American policy with respect to 1-B controls to be contrary to the multilateral spirit of the CoCom group. In contrast to the CoCom procedure of dividing items into strategic and non-strategic categories, representatives from the United States preferred to present a large number of 1-B items for control '*en masse*'.[49] Working under the principle that all industrial exports to Eastern Europe could be construed as contributing to Soviet military potential, American diplomats expected the European governments to embargo the vast majority of 1-B items. Herein lay the problem that was to plague Anglo-American unity in CoCom throughout 1950.

Britain's position on the 1-B list was explained in an *aide mémoire* to the State department on 1 August 1950. The British government underscored the ramifications for economic recovery in a succinct critique of the American 1-B proposals. Referring to the value of industrial exports to the British economy, the *aide mémoire* stated that 'any severe curtailment of that trade must necessarily weaken the position of the UK and impair its economic strength'.[50] The Attlee government further argued that if British East–West trade was reduced to the extent recommended by the United States the following would occur. First, trade with Eastern Europe would be brought to a complete standstill, at great cost to the British economy. This in turn would have a profound impact on Britain's contribution to the containment of Soviet influence. Second, a breakdown in cooperation would materialise over embargo policy, given the divergent views of the two countries on the strategic potential of industrial exports. This might lead to disharmony in Anglo-American relations. Finally, with the cessation of virtually all trade with the Soviet bloc, Britain would be forced to find new suppliers of traditional raw materials.[51] This would increase the dollar deficit between London and Washington, placing Britain's balance of payments in an even more precarious position.[52] In response to these grievances some American policy makers asserted that Western Europe was putting too much emphasis on the Soviet bloc as a reliable source of supply. In their opinion 'this argument had been greatly exaggerated'.[53]

The United States and Britain remained divided over the 1-B list in CoCom until a compromise was reached in a series of negotiations in New York and London in September and November. Although these talks will be the subject of the next chapter, it is necessary at this stage to assess the impact of the Korean War on Western European East–West trade policy in autumn 1950. This issue has been the subject of vigorous debate amongst scholars of the historiography of CoCom. In particular Tor Egil Førland and Vibeke Sørensen have argued extensively that the outbreak of hostilities in Southeast Asia did little to alter European opposition to 1-B export controls. In the opinion of Førland and Sørensen, there were numerous other reasons for the eventual acceptance by Britain and France of restrictions on industrial items in trade with Eastern Europe. While the strategic situation in Korea was important, other factors such as the threat of aid denial levelled by the US Congress and domestic pressure to take a firm stand against the spread of communism were equally crucial. In other words the Korean War played only an *indirect* role in changing Western European perceptions of East–West trade.[54] By contrast Michael Mastanduno contends that the decision by CoCom to extend the embargo to 1-B exports was a *direct* result of the outbreak of hostilities in Korea.[55]

Both of these interpretations correctly point to the Korean War as the major stimulus for the CoCom members' eventual acceptance of increased export controls in late 1950. British government documents show that the Attlee government was fearful of a potential Soviet invasion of Western Europe. London was concerned that the United States would become embroiled in the Korean conflict, leaving Western Europe vulnerable to aggression from Moscow.[56] The prohibition of some 1-B exports to the Soviet bloc was therefore deemed to be an appropriate national security measure. It should be noted that the British government adopted this course of action independently of Washington. Although pressure from Congress and the threat of aid denial influenced British thinking to a certain extent, security considerations were foremost in the minds of ministers when they decided to broaden the embargo to include industrial exports.[57] To understand Britain's reversal of policy on the 1-B list, the tripartite negotiations with the United States and France in 1950 must be examined in detail.

Conclusion

Despite close cooperation during the negotiations that led to the formation of the CoCom group in November 1949, the United States and Britain came into conflict over the 1-B list in early 1950. American policy makers held the view that the international embargo should be extended to 'dual purpose' or semistrategic exports. They believed that a comprehensive export control programme on East–West trade should be an essential component of military containment, as expounded in NSC-68. The Attlee government disagreed. While British officials supported restrictions on strategic exports to the Soviet bloc, they objected to wholesale controls on industrial and semistrategic commodities. As such London was not prepared to sacrifice trade with Eastern Europe that was vital for economic recovery solely to deny the Soviet Union exports that London did not believe would contribute to Soviet military power. It was not until the outbreak of the Korean War in June 1950 that ministers began to rethink Britain's trade policy towards Eastern Europe. Even though agreement was reached in CoCom to extend the embargo to some 1-B items, industrial exports of great importance to the economic welfare of the Western European members remained uncontrolled.

4
Compromise: America, CoCom and the Extension of the East–West Trade Embargo, 1950

Anglo-American relations in respect of East–West trade were characterised by conflict and compromise during 1950. From February to August the two governments clashed over the application of export controls on 1-B items. The United States insisted that restrictions on industrial trade with the Soviet bloc were now necessary in light of strategic developments in Eastern Europe and Southeast Asia. At first Britain was opposed to wholesale 1-B export controls. Ministers were concerned that an embargo on industrial or dual-purpose exports would severely damage Britain's essential trading links with Eastern Europe. It was not until the outbreak of war in Korea that the Attlee government began to view East–West trade in a more strategic light. Thus from September to November both powers, together with France, attempted to resolve the dispute over 1-B controls and devise an embargo programme that would deny strategic goods to Moscow without impinging on Western Europe's non-strategic trade with Eastern Europe.

The breakdown of Anglo-American cooperation

During the spring of 1950 the American secretary of state, Dean Acheson, embarked on a campaign to obtain British and French support for military containment. In light of the shift towards the militarisation of American national security policy as prescribed by NSC-68, Acheson hoped that key Western European allies would share the burdens of global containment. Yet the British foreign secretary, Ernest Bevin, and the French foreign minister, Robert Schuman, still harboured concerns about the future of West Germany's potential role in the Atlantic alliance.[1] Bevin and Schuman feared that the rearmament of Germany would significantly alter the balance of power on the continent. In particular Schuman was worried about the implications for French security of a militarily revitalised West Germany. At a series of tripartite meetings in London and Paris, Acheson sought to allay these fears. He would, however, encounter much difficulty in convincing both Britain and France of the necessity of placing mutual security interests above economic needs in order to prevent the expansion of Soviet influence in Southeast Asia and Western Europe.[2]

On the question of East–West trade Acheson received a similar response from Bevin and Schuman. Neither Britain nor France was in favour of broadening the international embargo to include semistrategic and industrial items. As the previous chapter has shown, the Attlee government was reluctant to sacrifice trade in dual-purpose commodities with the Soviet bloc governments, and this view was shared by most of the CoCom members. Given the slow and arduous process of economic recovery and reconstruction, Western European nations would not consider the restriction of items of indirect strategic value. In the early months of 1950, then, American calls for the incorporation of the 1-B list into the international East–West trade embargo fell on deaf ears.[3]

After an unsatisfactory meeting with Bevin and Schuman in London on East–West trade, Acheson once again raised the issue of the 1-B list in Paris during the tripartite meetings of 8–9 May. The Paris talks spanned a wide range of topics, including the Middle East, Schuman's plan for the integration of the French and West German coal and steel industries and German rearmament. Conducted in a decidedly prickly atmosphere, the meeting revealed serious disagreements between the United States and its allies over defence policy. Briefly, Washington wanted to adopt a firmer military posture against the Soviet Union, whereas London and Paris wished to move more cautiously and concentrate on economic recovery.[4] Acheson was also anxious for Britain and France to shoulder some of the burden of responsibility for the fate of Southeast Asia. Once again, both powers refused to make a firm commitment to the region, preferring to focus on the immediate threat to Western Europe from the Soviet Union.[5]

The meeting on export controls was no different. Acheson approached the East–West trade talks with a view to securing tacit approval for the 1-B list from Bevin and Schuman. In his presentation Acheson was careful to suggest that any extension of the international embargo lists would take into consideration the economic welfare of Europe. He stressed that although an expansion of the multilateral export control programme was necessary, the United States did recognise the value of East–West trade to Western Europe. Any extension of the strategic embargo, he stated, would ensure the continuation of trade in 'peaceful commodities' if 'so desired' by the governments participating in CoCom.[6] However Acheson warned his allies that the Soviet Union would benefit greatly from unrestricted strategic trade from Western Europe. It was therefore essential that an effective 'balance of collective forces' strategy on the continent be complemented by a comprehensive export control programme.[7] Although Acheson gave cognisance to the trading requirements of the OEEC countries, neither Bevin nor Schuman found his proposal to extend the embargo to industrial and dual-purpose items appealing. For them the 1-B list contained many items of significant economic value that were central to trade agreements with Eastern European countries. If these exports were prohibited in East–West trade, British and French manufacturing industries would suffer. Furthermore, imports of crucial raw materials would be lost it trade agreements with Eastern European governments broke down. Much of the conflict between Washington and its allies in Paris might have been avoided had the American representatives at CoCom consulted the British and French governments on the 1-B list. Instead the American delegation to the tripartite talks appeared to present Britain and France with a *fait accompli*. In effect the United States expected Britain and France to agree to the 1-B proposal to smooth the passage towards CoCom's acceptance of increased export controls.

The meeting ended in stalemate. Both the United States and Britain stuck rigidly to their respective positions. Acheson recounted the main argument of NSC-68: the Western alliance needed to prepare for a 'hot war' with the Soviet Union, which was predicted to break out in five to ten years. Expansion of the multilateral embargo to include 1-B items would prevent the Soviet Union from stockpiling 'production equipment' for military purposes in the event of conflict with the West. Bevin dismissed the American proposal by asserting that any wholesale extension of the international embargo would involve CoCom 'getting dangerously close to the realm of economic warfare', a situation the Attlee government was anxious to avoid. Bevin argued that consolidation rather than expansion of the current East–West trade restrictions would be more effective in undermining Soviet military potential in the long run. Turning to mutual security, Bevin pointed out that Western European economic strength would be impaired if export controls were implemented to the extent required by the United States, and that an 'economic blockade' of Eastern Europe would have disastrous consequences for the OEEC economies.[8]

Edwin Martin of the State Department met privately with Bevin to discuss the 1-B list, but Bevin merely confirmed Britain's opposition to the American proposal. He suggested to Martin that a change in the direction of embargo policy was now imperative given the objection of Britain and France to a strategy of 'economic warfare' against the Soviet bloc.[9] The French delegation also expressed dissatisfaction with the Truman administration's export control policy. French officials believed that Western European acceptance of the 1-B list in full would be 'tantamount to large scale economic warfare and is out of step with developments in the field of military co-operation'.[10] The three powers left the talks divided; international cooperation on East–West trade now entered its bleakest phase thus far.

Worse was to follow. At a meeting of CoCom on 15–16 May the other European members of the group gave their full support to Britain and France. In unanimously rejecting the American proposal no CoCom member, with the exception of Britain, France and West Germany, was prepared to accept the inclusion of a single 1-B item on the International II list. Ambassador David Bruce, in a characteristically shrewd assessment of the mood in Paris, commented that there would be 'no possibility' of progress in CoCom unless Britain changed its position. Even then, Bruce argued, the United States would still be faced with trenchant opposition from the majority of CoCom members.[11] The acting secretary of state, James Webb, concluded that Britain and the United States had reached more agreement on policy at the tripartite meetings in early May.[12] It seemed to American policy makers that some European governments were even more opposed to the extension of export controls than both London and Paris.[13] In light of these highly unsatisfactory developments, the Truman administration moved to convene bilateral discussions with Britain with the express purpose of resolving the growing impasse over East–West trade.

On 31 May the Co-ordinating Group of CoCom met to discuss the crisis over East–West trade. While the group tried to find common ground between the American and British positions, the talks failed to produce a compromise on the 1-B list proposals. The principal point of contention between the United States and its CoCom partners was the control of items classed as semistrategic. These items, which constituted a large proportion of the 1-B list, consisted of industrial exports such as machine tools, diesel, ball bearings, iron and steel. The American delegation argued that all major industrial commodities could be construed as contributing to Soviet military production: the embargo should therefore be extended to all dual-purpose items. By contrast the British delegation stated that the embargo should be limited to materials of a strictly strategic nature: as industrial commodities would not contribute substantially to Soviet military production they should be traded freely with Eastern Europe.

Despite the fundamental difference between Washington and London over 1-B export controls, officials at the American embassy in Paris were anxious to reach agreement in CoCom. If the United States and its European partners remained divided over East–West trade policy, this might have severe ramifications for cooperation on other aspects of Western security. Ambassador Bruce, in a telegram to Webb, highlighted the geopolitical significance of the multilateral export control programme in the Cold War conflict with Moscow. He feared that the breakdown of cooperation between the United States and Western Europe over embargo policy might damage the Atlantic alliance. Such a scenario, the ambassador pointed out, would increase the likelihood of Soviet aggression in Europe.[14] However the efforts to convince the Attlee government to abandon its opposition to the 1-B proposals were to no avail. In informal talks at the American embassy in London, Sir Roger Makins of the Foreign Office continued to emphasise the value of industrial East–West trade to the British economy.[15]

By the end of the summer, cooperation on international export control policy had reached its lowest ebb. Disagreement about the strategic value of industrial exports had created a situation in which, in the words of Vibeke Sørensen, 'the common embargo was in complete disarray'.[16] On 24 August the NSC met to discuss the crisis. Dean Acheson outlined in detail the main points of disagreement between American and European export control policy. He told the council that CoCom would continue to block the 1-B proposal, given the importance of industrial East–West trade to the economies of Western Europe. Hinting at a possible compromise, he stated that it would be unwise for the United States to create a 'sore spot' over this issue as full support was needed from NATO for the rearmament effort. The NSC instructed Acheson to discuss the problem with Bevin and Schuman in September at the foreign ministers' meeting in New York.[17]

Towards compromise: the New York talks, September 1950

Dean Acheson was the statesman most responsible for the compromise negotiated between the United States, Britain and France in the latter months of 1950. The secretary of state had a good command of the intricacies of international embargo policy, unlike other senior officials in the Truman administration. Moreover he was well-respected in Western Europe, having played a substantial role in the political and economic reconstruction of the region after the Second World War. His close personal relationship with Ernest Bevin and Robert Schuman afforded him the opportunity to exert considerable influence over the British and French governments.[18] Thus if one wishes to understand the compromise on 1-B export controls that materialised in November 1950, the words and actions of Acheson must be studied carefully.

In a telegram of 5 August to David Bruce in Paris, Acheson set out his solution to the problem of the 1-B list. He believed that the United States should continue to press Britain and France to reconsider their opposition to restrictions on industrial exports to the Soviet bloc. But instead of presenting London and Paris with the entire contents of the 1-B list, the Truman administration should seek to get the two governments to agree to implement controls on a short list of items deemed to contribute to Soviet military production. Recognising the importance of non-strategic trade to the 'economic and political health of the West', Acheson suggested that the United States should attempt to persuade Britain and France through diplomacy as the use of coercion would only lead to more conflict. To Acheson's mind, the best way to secure CoCom's acceptance of further export controls would be to gain the support of Britain and France at the tripartite meetings in New York. Ending his telegram on an optimistic note, Acheson told Bruce that an agreement on the 1-B List 'is not … in our opinion yet out of the question'.[19]

Under Acheson's direction the State Department undertook a review of international embargo policy in August, prior to the New York conference. The review concluded that progress during the summer months had been most unsatisfactory from the American viewpoint. Of the 288 1-B exports proposed by Washington for control by the CoCom members, the European governments had rejected outright 253 items. This led State Department officials to conclude that only a small proportion of the items in the 1-B List were likely to be accepted for control by CoCom. Acheson and his colleagues decided to change tack. At the tripartite meetings in September the secretary of state would seek to obtain support from Bevin and Schuman for the embargo to be extended to industrial exports of high strategic value to the Soviet Union. In the spirit of mutual security, Acheson would stress to his British and French counterparts the importance of wider export controls, given the strategic threat to the global order posed by the

Korean War. If steps were not taken to delay the build-up of the Soviet military capability through an extensive embargo on East–West trade, Western Europe would be vulnerable to Soviet aggression.[20]

In the weeks preceding the New York conference Acheson was especially worried about Britain's disinclination to cooperate with the United States on the 1-B list. He expressed his deep concern about the Anglo-American conflict over East–West trade in a telegram to Ambassador Lewis Douglas in London. He appeared to be apprehensive about the wide divergence between the United States and Britain over industrial exports to the Soviet bloc. He was highly exasperated by London's refusal to restrict trade in industrial items of blatant strategic value to Moscow. To be sure, Acheson could not understand how Washington's closest ally could prioritise trade interests above mutual security concerns in view of the present strategic climate in Europe and Southeast Asia.[21]

During August, however, some British ministers began to rethink East–West trade policy. The minister of defence, Emmanuel Shinwell, in a paper submitted to the cabinet, questioned the existing policy by suggesting that the outbreak of war in Korea necessitated a more stringent embargo on trade with the Communist bloc (including China).[22] Winston Churchill also criticised the Attlee government's export control policy in a series of speeches in August and September. Churchill believed that the unrestricted shipment of machine tools to Eastern Europe was counterproductive to British strategic objectives in Europe and Southeast Asia. In a speech from the opposition benches on 12 September he called on the Labour government to ensure that:

> no more machine tools of a war-making character and no more machines or engines which could be used for war-making purposes should be sent from this country to Soviet Russia or the Soviet satellite nations while the present tension continues.[23]

Attlee's response was guarded. While he acknowledged that changing strategic circumstances required wider controls on East–West trade, he stated firmly that the current British trade agreements with Eastern European governments would be executed without alteration. Significantly, Whitehall's commitment to exports in industrial commodities to the Soviet bloc remained largely unchanged.[24] Yet domestic pressure from the Conservative Party, and the threat by the US Congress to withdraw economic and military aid, forced Attlee to move towards a limited compromise with the Truman administration on the 1-B list.

At the tripartite talks in New York, discussions on East–West trade were overshadowed by the pivotal issue of German rearmament. Once again the allies clashed over West Germany's future role in NATO. Acheson presented Bevin and Schuman with an ultimatum: the commitment of American troops to Europe would be dependent on British and French acceptance of the rearmament of West Germany. Bevin and Schuman were clearly surprised by this initiative. Schuman, in particular, thought that West Germany should be politically and economically integrated into Western Europe before actively participating in NATO. Unable to reconcile the American and French positions the talks ended in a stalemate.[25]

Disagreement about German rearmament did not, however, prevent the three powers from achieving some measure of progress on East–West trade matters. In a minute circulated to Bevin and Schuman, Acheson reiterated the importance of the 1-B list: 'it is essential to restrict exports to the Soviet bloc of selected items, such as those on the 1-B List, which are required in key industrial areas that contribute substantially to war potential'.[26]

Although the minute implied that the American delegation would continue to press Britain and France to accept wholesale 1-B export controls, in reality Acheson went to the meetings in New York seeking a compromise on East–West trade. Although the available evidence appears inconclusive, it could be argued that Acheson was concerned that further disagreement on embargo policy might affect cooperation on more pressing issues confronting Western security.[27] It seems that he wanted to resolve the dispute over the 1-B list in New York. To this end he proposed that the three powers withdraw 'from any extreme positions and make the best compromise possible'.[28]

In response to Acheson's proposal, Bevin gave his assurance that the Attlee government would institute an embargo on 1-B items of overriding strategic value to the Soviet Union. Some scholars have suggested that Britain and France capitulated to American demands on East–West trade during the tripartite meetings, but this did not appear to be the case. During August and September Britain had began to move towards acceptance of limited 1-B controls in light of the growing Cold War tensions with Moscow and the Korean War. At the talks in New York, Bevin was merely following current British policy when he agreed to restrictions on industrial items of a highly strategic nature. The reaction of senior policy makers in the Truman administration substantiates this claim. For example David Bruce commented that although Britain and France were now willing to support the extension of the embargo to 1-B items, the number of industrial exports they were pre-pared to control was limited.[29]

Yet the first step towards compromise had been taken. This was testi-mony not only to astute diplomacy on the part of Acheson, but also the mutual recognition by the three governments that cooperation had to be preserved within the Western alliance in the face of Soviet aggres-sion throughout the globe.[30] The strategic embargo was viewed as a secondary issue in the wider framework of Western security: German rearmament and the organisation of the military command of NATO required more urgent attention than East–West trade.[31] Thus the three powers at the New York conference chose to settle the question of export control policy swiftly in order to focus on more pressing con-cerns confronting the Western alliance.[32] Moreover Britain's commit-ment to assist the United States in the Korean War, demonstrated the Attlee government's willingness to maintain the close partnership that existed between Washington and London. With the Cold War at its height, British policy makers had no wish to jeopardise Anglo-American relations over East–West trade. National security con-siderations would prevail over trade interests as Britain began its preparations for war through a massive rearmament programme.[33]

Compromise: the London talks in October and November

In the winter of 1950 American diplomats sought to capitalise on the progress made at the meeting in New York by continuing to link econ-omic containment to the wider defence programme for Western Europe. In essence, policy planners at the State Department believed that denying industrial exports to Eastern Europe would further the objective of hindering Soviet military production. If effective, this would allow the Western alliance to maintain a distinct advantage over Moscow in terms of military and economic power. Hence the Truman administration attended the tripartite meetings in London during October and November with a view to securing a common agreement with Britain and France on a suitable list of 1-B items for control in CoCom.[34]

Acheson did not participate in the negotiations, but he remained actively involved in the making of export control policy. His brief to the American delegation embodied the Cold War tactics he had vehemently deployed with respect to the Kremlin since becoming secretary of state in January 1949.[35] He instructed the delegation to underline the impor-tance of building a strong Western defence programme against Soviet aggression in their talks with British and French officials. While Acheson did not expect Britain and France to agree to implement wholesale controls on 1-B items, he ordered the leader of the delegation, Charles Bohlen, to impress upon the allies the strategic value of industrial commodities to Moscow. Acheson was aware that some economic sacrifice would have to be made by Western Europe, but he believed that a loss of trade in the short term would serve the mutual security of the Western alliance in the long run. In any case he estimated that the shortfall in East–West trade produced by 1-B export controls 'would be small and manageable through ad hoc measures'. As a temporary solution he proposed that the United States could help Western European governments to find new markets for their 1-B exports.[36]

For its part the Foreign Office had two main concerns about the forthcoming tripartite talks in London. First, British officials were apprehensive about conducting talks on East–West trade with the United States outside the multilateral framework of CoCom. They feared that negotiations between the three countries without the participation of the other members of CoCom 'would engender the suspicions of the other Western European governments'. Meanwhile policy makers in the Mutual Aid Department of the Foreign Office were concerned that implementation of the 1-B proposals would cause 'a sharp reduction in trade with Eastern Europe'. They concluded that 1-B export controls would not 'greatly affect the United States', and that the restriction of industrial East–West trade would 'cause more harm to the United Kingdom and Western Europe than it would to the Soviet bloc'.[37]

Second, British officials were worried that the incorporation of 1-B items into an embargo aimed primarily at denying strategic exports to the Soviet Union would lead to an 'economic blockade' of Eastern Europe. Such a scenario, they thought, would have severe repercussions for the British economy. If Britain failed to deliver industrial shipments to the Soviet bloc as part of its trade agreements with the Eastern European governments, the British economy would lose valuable raw materials. From a list of imports most at risk, the Foreign Office concluded that imports of softwood and mining timber, coarse grain and bacon would be badly affected in the event of Soviet countermeasures against Britain. The Attlee government would then have no other option but to acquire these items from dollar markets. This would have serious implications for Britain's balance of payments position, further weakening the economy.[38]

Some progress was made at the tripartite meeting on 17 October in London, attended by American, British and French delegates. The three delegations reached agreement on the predominance of the strategic factor in governing future export control policy: 'the agreed objective of the three powers is that the strength of the West should be increased relative to that of the East. Economic sacrifices must undoubtedly be made in order that strategic considerations should be predominant.'[39] What is perhaps most striking about this statement was the acknowledgement by Britain and France of the centrality of strategic considerations in future multilateral embargo policy, a shift in emphasis from trade to security that had begun at the New York conference in September.

Several factors contributed to the decision to pursue wider controls on 1-B items. As noted above, the Attlee government was becoming increasingly alarmed by the attempt by congressional representatives in the United States to make East–West trade controls a condition of economic and military aid. Moreover diplomatic pressure from the State Department contributed to the British and French re-evaluation of trade policy towards the Soviet bloc. It could also be argued that criticism of the Labour government's East–West trade policy by Winston Churchill forced British ministers to adopt more stringent restrictions on industrial items.

Each of these factors arguably played some part in influencing the decision to view trade with the Soviet bloc in a more strategic light. Yet according to recently declassified British government documents, it appears that ministers had independently reached the conclusion that an extension of export controls was now a desirable security measure.[40] During September and October the Foreign Office and Ministry of Defence had begun to reassess British national security in light of the growing Soviet military threat to Western Europe. In a revealing memorandum on the tripartite talks the Economic Policy Committee (EPC) of the cabinet concluded that:

> it was necessary not only to limit the short-term striking power of the Soviet bloc but also to retard the development of its war potential in the longer term. For this purpose, it was essential, in addition to the embargo of direct military significance, to restrict exports to the Soviet bloc but also to retard the development of its war potential in the longer term. For this purpose, it was essential, in addition to the embargo of exports to the Soviet bloc [to control] selected items which are required in key industrial sectors that contribute substantially to war potential.[41]

But the acceptance by the Attlee government of controls on 1-B items did not signal a policy shift on non-strategic trade with Eastern Europe.

In fact ministers were careful to select for embargo dual-purpose items that would not damage trade agreements with the Soviet bloc governments. In a telegram to the British embassy in Washington the Ministry of Defence expressed its hope that the United States would not seek to transcend the agreement reached in New York by demanding an economic blockade of Eastern Europe.[42] This telegram was illustrative of Britain's approach to Anglo-American cooperation on East–West trade. At the London meetings the British delegation was prepared to agree to some export controls on industrial commodities, but it fought vigorously to preserve trade in items of significant economic value. If, as Sørensen and Mastanduno have argued, the Anglo-French acceptance of a wider East–West trade embargo was due to American pressure, why did not Washington extract wider concessions on the 1-B list? Neither Sørensen nor Mastanduno provide a satisfactory explanation. It would appear from an examination of the available evidence that the United States approached the London talks with a view to resolving the dispute with Britain and France over East–West trade. The American delegation was willing to compromise on the 1-B list to gain British and French support for an expansion of the strategic embargo in CoCom. With the spectre of a Soviet invasion hanging over Western Europe, Washington wanted to avoid disunity with its partners in the Western alliance.

On 20 November, after two months of intense negotiations, a compromise was reached on the 1-B list. Significantly Britain and France agreed to institute export controls on industrial items and the United States acknowledged the importance of non-strategic trade to Western Europe. This was a definite step forward. The essence of the compromise was explained in the report by the three delegations:

> The spirit of accommodation was sustained by the hope that, if an agreement satisfactory to all three governments emerged from the discussions, it might, subject to the necessary flexibility, be expected to prove in the present international situation to be of an enduring character.[43]

In other words the nature and scope of the East–West trade embargo had changed. Not only would the multilateral export control programme prohibit military commodities in trade with Eastern Europe, it would also restrict items of indirect strategic value. A recent study asserts that Britain and France were subjected to considerable pressure by the United States during the tripartite talks in New York and

London to accept an embargo on 1-B items.[44] This was clearly not the case. If one carefully examines the report by the three delegations and the list of agreed items a very different story emerges. By and large Britain and France succeeded in preventing the United States from including industrial exports of economic importance to the two governments. The new 1-B list contained only those exports that the three delegations deemed would contribute significantly to Soviet military production. It could be argued, of course, that Britain and France would have preferred to continue unrestricted trade in many of these items, but both governments realised that the current international situation required a much broader strategic embargo.

The American delegation was most satisfied with the tripartite talks, which they believed had exceeded the expectations of the Truman administration. In particular they welcomed the shift in British policy towards viewing East–West trade in a more strategic light.[45] Acheson greeted the outcome of the discussions by proclaiming that 'very substantial progress' had been achieved, and that a 'spirit of accommodation' had enabled the three allies to reach an agreement on the 1-B list. It was now possible, he argued, for the three governments to establish an effective multilateral export control programme to complement the security objectives of the Western alliance.[46] A communiqué from the American embassy in London to the Foreign Office also underscored the success of the tripartite meetings. It suggested in positive tones that the two governments had resolved their differences on East–West trade, and concluded that the London talks had been 'unusually successful, both as to the spirit in which they were conducted and the agreement reached'. Moreover 'opinion and policy' differences had been overcome by the three countries.[47]

Charles Bohlen, the chairman of the American delegation, authored the most insightful report on the tripartite talks. In his account of the negotiations he reiterated the theme of renewed cooperation between Washington and London on East–West trade policy. According to Bohlen:

> the principle result of the tripartite conversations was the reconciliation of the views of the United Kingdom and France, particularly those of the former, and those of the United States on specific international export controls concerning the Soviet bloc.

Rather than attributing the success of these negotiations to adroit American diplomacy, as same authors have claimed, he cited the willingness of the British and French delegations 'to accept the agreed controls because they considered strategic considerations over-riding'. Bohlen pointed out that while Britain and France were prepared to sacrifice some East–West trade, they had sought and received assurances from the United States that export controls would be limited to items of strategic value to the Soviet bloc.[48]

The agreement reached by the United States, Britain and France at the meetings in London paved the way for acceptance of wider export controls by the CoCom members. Between the 20 November 1950 and 16 January 1951 the governments of the East–West trade group agreed to institute an embargo on 244 of the 318 items originally proposed for control by the United States. In fact CoCom approved all but 47 of the items on the list drawn up by the three delegations in London.[49] In response to critics of the November compromise in Congress and the Commerce Department, the State Department warned that economically the revised East–West trade embargo would 'have a sufficiently marked effect on Western Europe to make it unwise to consider further substantial restrictions of exports until the effect of the adoption of new lists has been more fully observed'.[50] This was also the opinion of the British embassy in Lisbon. Citing additional dollar expenditure on supplies lost through increased restrictions on trade with the Soviet bloc, the embassy asserted that further export controls would be undesirable in the short term. Notwithstanding the loss to the British economy of valuable trade with Eastern Europe, the Attlee government had decided that some economic sacrifice was necessary in the interests of national security.[51]

By early 1951 the United States and its CoCom partners had appeared to embrace the 'spirit of accommodation' of the tripartite agreement of November 1950. Moreover Anglo-American cooperation on economic containment had resumed. Persistent opposition to the 1-B list from the European members of CoCom had forced the State Department to pay more attention to the economic needs of Washington's allies in the Western alliance. Acheson, in particular, had been keenly aware of the implications for mutual security of disunity over East–West trade. Yet in the latter months of 1950 Britain and France had abandoned their staunch opposition to a broadening of the embargo in light of the international strategic climate. Deeply concerned by the possibility of a Soviet invasion of Western Europe, they had begun to view the exportation of industrial goods in a more critical light. Without these policy shifts it seems likely that the three powers would have remained divided on East–West trade. The

November compromise also demonstrated the importance of Anglo-American cooperation to Washington and London.

Conclusion

The November 1950 compromise was a crucial event in the history of the East–West trade embargo. The United States and Western Europe disagreed about the efficacy of industrial export controls throughout most of 1950, but finally resolved their differences late that year. This was in part due to the perceptiveness of the State Department in recognising that East–West trade was an essential component of Western European economic recovery. Dean Acheson was not prepared to use coercive measures to secure the agreement of Washington's allies to the inclusion of 1-B export controls the multilateral embargo. He realised that any attempt to pressure the European governments to restrict goods of indirect strategic importance would be counterproductive. During the September and November tripartite meetings with Britain and France he sought to work closely with Bevin and Schuman to find common ground between the United States and the other CoCom governments. His approach yielded satisfactory results.

While the Attlee government remained adamantly opposed to any substantial broadening of the embargo during the first part of 1950, events in Korea and the threat of war with the Soviet Union forced Whitehall to execute a policy shift. Calls in August and September from the opposition benches to prohibit trade in certain industrial commodities also forced the Labour government to rethink East–West trade policy. Yet at the tripartite talks with the United States and France in New York and London, diplomats emphasised the continuing impotance of Eastern European trade to the British economy. Given the Attlee government's influence in CoCom, as well as Britain's importance as a Cold War ally, Whitehall was able to negotiate a compromise with the United States that preserved vital industrial trade with the Soviet bloc.

5
Trade or Aid? American Isolationists and East–West Trade, 1950–51

After protracted negotiations lasting two years the Truman administration finally managed to gain international support for a comprehensive economic containment strategy against the Soviet Union. During 1950–51, however, the administration encountered domestic opposition to its export control policy from Congress. Through the Mundt Amendment to the Foreign Assistance Act of 1948 and the Export Control Act of 1949, the legislature possessed significant powers in the field of East–West trade. Perturbed by the Truman administration's foreign policy, isolationist representatives began to protest about American international commitments and economic and military assistance programmes, and sought to make aid to leading powers in Western Europe contingent on their sharing with the United States the burden of containing communism throughout the globe.

Congress and the Korean War

Much has been written about the reaction of the US Congress to Harry S. Truman's decision to intervene in the civil war between North and South Korea in the summer of 1950. Concerned by the unilateral nature of American foreign policy, a powerful group of conservative Republican representatives in Congress took this opportunity to express their dissatisfaction with the Truman administration's handling of external affairs.[1] While the presidential administration had encountered some opposition to its foreign policy initiatives from a small but vocal clique of isolationists in the aftermath of the Second World War, the executive–legislative relationship was usually one of bipartisanship.[2] Nonetheless the rapid expansion of American commitments abroad in the late 1940s and early 1950s led many congressional representatives to question the objectives of Truman's national security policy.[3]

For the isolationist coalition the Korean War was a critical turning point. Under the leadership of Senator Robert Taft of Ohio and distinguished public figures outside Congress such as former president Herbert Hoover, the isolationists launched an assault on the administration's defensive perimeter strategy in East Asia. They accused the president and his secretary of state, Dean Acheson, of pursuing unwise policies that had contributed to the outbreak of the conflict in Korea. In the 'great debate' between the administration and its critics that followed the intervention of the United States in Southeast Asia, the president was criticised for failing to ask Congress for a declaration of war. Many conservative representatives believed that Truman had exceeded his powers as president by ignoring the legislature's constitutional prerogative to declare war. What is more they feared that an American victory in the war would result in a permanent commitment to the region by the Truman administration, much as had happened in Western Europe. This, they thought, would have an adverse effect on the domestic economy. In order to finance its international commitments the administration would be forced to place excessive controls on the economy, raise taxes to pay for military expenditure and incur undesirable budget deficits. Not only would the United States be stretched financially to meet its international obligations, the American standard of living would suffer from the burden of world leadership. In the long run democracy and civil liberties would be endangered by the development of a 'garrison state' in the United States.[4]

If the isolationists were perturbed by the actions of Truman and Acheson in East Asia, they were equally disturbed by the executive's foreign policy goals in Western Europe. They strongly opposed the stationing of American troops in Europe under the command of NATO. In fact Senator Kenneth Wherry of Nebraska – through the Wherry Resolution – demanded that any commitment of troops to the continent be contingent on congressional approval. It is important to note that although isolationists such as Taft and Wherry were averse to American intervention in Asia and Europe, they supported Truman's efforts to counteract the threat posed by the Soviet Union. However, they argued that national security interests could be served effectively by air–sea defence rather than the commitment of troops to foreign lands. A defence system based on air and sea power, they asserted, would not only protect the territory of the United States, but would also require much less in terms of military spending, thus alleviating the spectre of budget deficits.[5]

Yet perhaps the largest bone of contention for the isolationists was the reluctance of some NATO allies actively to support the United States in Korea. Many Republican conservatives were angered by the refusal of European governments to shoulder a proportionate burden of the military effort in Southeast Asia, even though they continued to receive considerable shipments of economic and military aid from the United States. To make matters worse, in the eyes of some isolationists the Western Europeans appeared to expect Washington to defend Europe from a potential Soviet invasion, as well as waging a successful military campaign in Korea. They pointed out that the United States was not only shouldering a disproportionate share of the military cost of the Korean War, at great expense to domestic prosperity, but was also contributing substantially to the security of Europe. Despite attempts by the Truman administration to justify its costly commitment to Western Europe and Korea, the isolationists continued to call for a reduction in economic and military assistance to Europe.[6] On discovering that certain countries were exporting strategic materials to the Soviet Union and China, Congress increased its pressure on Truman and the State Department to cut off shipments of aid to governments persistently trading with Soviet bloc countries. As we shall see, the Truman government faced an enormous challenge to its economic containment policy from an increasingly obdurate Congress throughout 1950–51.

The Wherry and Cannon Amendments

As observed in a previous chapter, executive–legislative relations were fraught with conflict over the issue of East–West trade. In 1948 Congress asserted its position on the export control process through the Mundt Amendment to the Foreign Assistance Act. This was followed by the enactment of the Export Control Act of 1949, which prohibited trade in strategic materials to nations deemed to pose a security threat to the United States. Since the beginning of the Cold War the Truman administration and conservative Republican representatives had been divided on the question of trade with the communist states. On the one hand the administration favoured a limited embargo on strategic exports to the Soviet bloc that would not interfere with Western European trade agreements with Eastern Europe. On the other, congressional isolationists in particular called for the total suppression of commercial ties with the Soviet Union and its satellite states.

By the summer of 1950 the debate between the administration and Congress began to focus on the contribution of the Western European governments to economic containment. Truman's intervention in Korea opened to question the contribution of Washington's most powerful allies to the cause of rolling back communism in Southeast Asia. Upon examining Western Europe's trading patterns with the Soviet bloc, a number of high-profile representatives accused some OEEC nations of supplying strategic equipment to the Soviet Union and China that was subsequently used to wage war against the United States. A sizeable contingent of isolationist politicians lobbied the administration and Congress for massive cuts in economic and military assistance to those nations that continued to maintain normal trading relations with Eastern Europe and China. Pressing relentlessly for the adoption by aid-receiving countries of more stringent East–West trade controls, the isolationists tabled a plethora of motions condemning the exportation of strategic goods by Western European nations to the Soviet bloc.[7] Unlike the Truman administration, which viewed economic and military assistance to Western Europe as essential to the maintenance of a viable balance of power in the region, these representatives saw aid as a gift from the American people that should be withdrawn in the event of non-compliance with American national security objectives. But the administration was largely successful in defeating these measures when they came before the House of Representatives' Rules Committee.

Nonetheless, in September 1950 Senator Kenneth Wherry of Nebraska proposed an amendment to the Supplemental Appropriations Bill of 1951 in an effort to deny aid to any nation that continued to export military items to the Soviet bloc. Sponsored by leading isolationists in the House and Senate, including James Kem, George Malone, Harry Byrd and John Rankin, the amendment threatened to 'cut off economic and financial assistance to all countries which export to the Soviet Union or its satellites any articles which might be used for the production of military materials'.[8] This development was greeted with much unease by the Truman government. At a cabinet meeting on 15 September the ECA administrator, Averell Harriman, expressed his concern that the Wherry Amendment could have dire consequences for assistance programmes to Western Europe. On the recommendation of the cabinet Truman wrote to the chairman of the House Appropriations Committee, Clarence Cannon, in an attempt to dissuade representatives from the Democrat Party from supporting the legislation.[9] In a thoughtful letter, Truman argued that the Wherry Amendment would strain relations between the United States and its allies in NATO. This would weaken the Western alliance, strengthen the hand of the Kremlin and ultimately jeopardise American national security. The president suggested, moreover, that adoption of the legislation in its present form would not only undermine Western European trade with Eastern Europe, it would also drive underdeveloped African and Asian countries into the Soviet sphere of influence.[10]

Leading diplomats in the State Department and Western Europe concurred with the president's assertion that the Wherry Amendment would cause disunity between Washington and its key allies. For example Ambassador David Bruce of the American embassy in Paris believed that the administration would have to encourage the CoCom governments to intensify the embargo on East–West trade or risk losing economic and military assistance from Congress. Bruce was of the opinion that if these nations were denied ERP funds, economic recovery would be delayed even longer.[11] Perhaps the most vocal critic of the legislation was Acheson's deputy in the State Department, James Webb, who urged the president to veto the measure in the interests of the Western alliance. He objected to the coercive nature of the Wherry Amendment, which he viewed as contrary to the State Department's diplomatic aims in its negotiations on embargo policy with Western Europe. Webb also underscored the impact that the legislation would have on European trading contacts with Eastern Europe. He commented that 'a rigid unworkable measure such as this might lead to a stoppage of all East–West trade'.[12]

It could be argued that the Wherry Amendment was part of a wider programme by the isolationists in Congress to challenge the foreign policy prerogatives of the president. The commitment by Truman of American armed forces to Korea, under the auspices of the United Nations, was seen by some congressional representatives as an abuse of the legislature's war-making powers, and the isolationist lobby viewed the Wherry Amendment as a necessary step to ensure the maintenance of effective checks and balances on East–West trade that posed a threat to national security. But Truman's threat to veto the Supplemental Appropriations Bill, to which the contentious measure was attached, placated conservative Democrats in the House and the Wherry Amendment was removed from the legislation after discussion in conference.[13]

Although the isolationists' efforts to force countries in receipt of American economic and military assistance to restrict trade with the Soviet bloc were initially thwarted, reports that the Soviet Union was acquiring military raw materials from Western Europe precipitated new legislation in Congress. The new measure, which was authored by

Clarence Cannon, was in effect a diluted version of the Wherry Amendment. Attached as a rider to the Supplemental Appropriation Act of 1951, the Cannon Amendment stated that:

> During any period in which the Armed Forces of the United States are actively engaged in hostilities while carrying out any decision of the Security Council of the United Nations, no economic, or financial assistance shall be provided ... to any country whose trade with the Union of Soviet Socialist Republics or any of its satellite countries ... is found by the National Security Council to be contrary to the security of the United States.[14]

The main difference between this measure and the Wherry Amendment was that discretion to withhold aid from nations violating the Export Control Act of 1949 was placed in the hands of the National Security Council. This would allow the president rather than Congress to decide whether or not assistance should be provided to offending governments. While disturbed by the measure, the Truman administration was certainly relieved that ultimate decision making in export control policy would be left at the door of the president.

The Kem Amendment

President Truman was far from satisfied with the Cannon Amendment, even though it ensured that the executive would have the power to grant waivers to nations that failed to comply with the objectives of the Export Control Act of 1949. The criticism levelled at the administration's foreign policy initiatives by the isolationists in Congress worried both Truman and Dean Acheson. In particular they were concerned about the influence wielded in the legislature by Senator James Kem of Missouri. Kem, an integral member of the isolationist camp, was leading the Republican campaign against the Truman administration's containment policy. Most notably, Kem had voted against the participation of the United States in NATO, opposed aid to Yugoslavia after Tito had withdrawn his country from the Soviet bloc and constantly demanded the resignation of Acheson as secretary of state. In March 1950 the senator had turned his attention to East–West trade.

Kem had become actively involved in American assistance programmes in the autumn of 1950 when he co-sponsored the Wherry Amendment. Like Wherry he believed that economic and military assistance should be linked formally to export control policy. In his opinion the Cannon Amendment, which replaced Wherry's measure, afforded too much discretion to the president in matters concerning the failure of nations to comply with the Export Control Act. Given the internationalist nature of Truman's foreign policy, Kem thought that the president would not deny assistance to key allies in Western Europe for continuing to export strategic materials to the Soviet Union. Thus throughout 1951 Kem attempted to overturn the Cannon Amendment by introducing new legislation that would place the power to distribute aid in the hands of Congress.

A letter from Kem to Truman on 9 March was to form the basis of an amendment to the military assistance legislation that Kem proposed to Congress in May 1951. In this letter Kem described a visit he had paid to wounded Korean War veterans recuperating at the Walter Reed Hospital in Washington. He accused several Western European countries of shipping strategic commodities to the Soviet Union and China that were subsequently used against American soldiers in the Korean War. Imploring Truman to withdraw assistance from these nations, Kem asserted that the Western Europeans had placed commercial gain before victory in the Korean War. Truman's response far from satisfied Kem.[15] On 9 May the senator introduced an amendment to the Third Supplemental Appropriation Bill of 1951 forbidding the executive to supply aid to allies that continued to export armaments and items used in military production to the Soviet bloc. The amendment was the most explicit attempt so far to link East–West trade to aid, as it espoused the unconditional withdrawal of military assistance from countries that violated the conditions of the Export Control Act. Most significantly the Kem Amendment removed the president's discretion to grant exceptions to allies that failed to comply with the legislation. Despite a concerted effort by the administration and the Democrat leadership in Congress to remove the amendment from the Third Supplemental Appropriation Bill, the legislation was signed into law by Truman on 2 June. The Kem Amendment did contain, however, a minor but significant modification: the NSC was granted the power to make exceptions in the interest of national security.[16]

The Kem Amendment, which had most serious ramifications for the future of multilateral cooperation in East–West trade between the United States and its allies, forced the Truman administration to reconsider its tactics with regard to negotiations in CoCom. With the visible presence of Congress in export control policy, the ability of American diplomats to shape policy in CoCom was considerably constrained. The State Department would now be required to ensure that the

Western European governments were restricting trade with the Soviet bloc to a level deemed acceptable by Congress. If nations refused to comply with the conditions set out in the Kem Amendment they were liable to forfeit economic and financial assistance from the United States. Predictably the measure was condemned by the CoCom members. The leading Western European powers, as the next chapter will demonstrate, were appalled by the attempt of a foreign legislature to dictate the terms of their trade policies. While sympathetic to the grievances of its allies, the Truman administration had to face the impossible task of conveying to Congress the commitment of some Western European nations to a strategic embargo without disclosing the existence of CoCom. In a reference to the secrecy of the Paris Group, Dean Acheson pointed out that 'no amount of general explanation and argument without facts to back them up, will convince Congress ... that Western Europe [is] in fact co-operating in this field'.[17]

On 25 May the State Department concluded that the Kem Amendment would seriously impede the negotiations with the Western European governments to forge an effective multilateral export control programme. From the administration's perspective the legislation would impinge upon the economic sovereignty of Washington's allies as it would force them to sever trade contacts with Eastern Europe as a prerequisite for American economic and military assistance. The Department of State observed that the Kem measure would give rise to resentment and indignation among the Western European nations about American interference in their international trade policies. According to the State Department, 'this resentment would impair the willingness of some of our European allies to co-operate in mutual defence arrangements'.[18]

In order to avert a clash between the United States and Western Europe over the Kem Amendment the NSC recommended that the Truman administration grant an interim exception to all states affected by the legislation. Not only would this prevent the development of a serious rift between Washington and its allies, it would also allow the NSC to investigate the export control practices of each aid-receiving government.[19] Implicitly, the granting of exceptions in the short term would allow the administration to regain control of embargo policy in the face of the congressional challenge to Truman's power to grant economic and military assistance to allies. Both the State Department and the NSC were keenly aware of the need to preserve aid allocations to Western Europe in light of the increasing Soviet threat to Western security. In stark contrast to the isolationist group in Congress, they

believed that the strength of the Western alliance was more important
to national security than an economic blockade of Eastern Europe:

> A Western Europe united in purpose and strong economically, polit-
> ically and militarily can serve, in association with us, as a strong
> deterrent to aggression not only in Europe but also in other areas of
> the world. The primary US objective in Western Europe is therefore
> the creation of military and economic strength required to deter
> aggression and to safeguard and develop the values of the civilisa-
> tion which we share.[20]

Thus while Congress viewed the issue as one of aid or trade, the
Truman administration wanted to reconcile a limited strategic embargo
on East–West trade with continued economic and military assistance
to Western Europe. Trapped in an invidious predicament, the administration commenced a series of urgent talks with its partners in CoCom.
The objective of these discussions was to tighten the multilateral
export control programme in order to protect Western European aid
from the onslaught of congressional legislation.

In response to the Kem Amendment, the State Department began
the task of convincing the OEEC nations to implement more stringent
controls on East–West trade based on the examples of the 1-A and 1-B
list.[21] To this end, if Western European export controls were somewhat
similar to those of the United States, President Truman's case for preserving economic and military assistance to Washington's allies would
be stronger. In a memorandum to Acheson the deputy assistant secretary for economic affairs, Harold Linder, stated that:

> In Western Europe our objective should be to obtain agreement by
> all the Western European governments to embargo shipments to the
> Soviet bloc of all items of primary strategic significance which are
> also embargoed by the US and to establish tighter quantitative con-
> trols for items of secondary significance.[22]

Meanwhile the NSC's recommendation on 14 June that Truman
should grant exceptions to all aid-receiving nations offered a welcome
break to the administration. The granting of this general amnesty to
all recipients of American assistance allowed the State Department
carefully to study the East–West trading patterns of each of its allies.
The initial reports showed, however, that a great many nations were
still engaging in strategic trade with the Soviet bloc. What most con-

cerned some senior officials was the fact that the Kem Amendment would have devastating implications for economic recovery in Western Europe. As the undersecretary for commerce, Thomas Blaisdell, pointed out, 'we can stop trading with the Communists with little loss – [the] Western Europeans lose much by stopping [trade] which we probably would not replace or could not replace fast enough'.[23] From the Truman administration's perspective, the Kem Amendment threatened to undermine not only the progress made by CoCom in 1950, but also economic recovery. With this in mind, Truman called on Congress to repeal the measure and produce 'more workable legislation' that would return decision making on this most important national security issue to the White House.[24]

The Battle Act

It was the president's dissatisfaction with the Kem Amendment that led to a congressional inquiry into East–West trade practices under the leadership of Representative Laurie Battle of Alabama. Battle's report, which was produced by a subcommittee of the House of Representatives' Foreign Affairs Committee, proposed new legislation to replace the Kem Amendment. The report criticised the Truman administration for failing to ensure that all Western European nations placed adequate export controls on strategic trade with the Soviet bloc. But it concurred with the president and the State Department that a comprehensive embargo on East–West trade would strain relations with NATO allies. In the words of Acheson, the report recognised 'the validity of our basic premise that while certain goods should be completely embargoed there are economic and military advantages to be derived from continued trade in other goods of lower strategic significance'.[25] The report showed a surprisingly subtle appreciation of East–West trade in that it identified two distinct categories of exports: strategic and non-strategic. Like the Truman administration it favoured a total embargo on items in the former category and quantitative controls on items in the latter. Yet while senior executive officials viewed the Battle report in a positive light, Roy Bullock of the House Foreign Affairs committee was more sceptical. Bullock was certain that Congress would be unwilling 'to give the president or any other individual as wide discretion of granting exceptions as [the] proposed clause appeared to'.[26] Nonetheless the legislation introduced by Battle to the House of Representatives on 2 August allowed the executive clear powers of discretion to deny assistance to nations violating the Export Control Act of 1949.

There were some key differences between the Battle bill and the Kem Amendment. First, the new bill authorised the president and not the NSC to grant exceptions in the interests of national security. Unlike the Kem Amendment, which did not define what constituted a strategic good, the Battle bill divided exports to be embargoed in East–West trade into two separate categories. The first contained war materials such as 'arms, ammunition, and implements of war, atomic energy material, petroleum, transportation materials of strategic value, and those items of primary strategic significance used in the production of arms, ammunition and implements of war'. The second was composed of exports not specified in the first category but threatened the national security of the United States.[27] The legislation also provided for a mutual defence assistance officer to oversee the operation of the export control process: the officer, chosen by the president, would report to Congress biannually on the effectiveness of the embargo.[28]

The Battle bill (the Mutual Defence Assistance Control Bill) was passed by the House of Representatives on 2 August and the Senate on 28 August. Truman did not, though, sign it into law until 26 October as he wished to allow the new mutual security director, Averell Harriman, time to publish the new list of items to be controlled in East–West trade under the legislation. The new act repealed the Export Control Act of 1949, Section 117 (d) of the Foreign Assistance Act of 1948 and the Kem Amendment.[29] Vibeke Sørensen, in an insightful study of executive–legislative relations and East–West trade, describes the Battle Act as 'a victory for President Truman's administration over an increasingly hostile Congress'.[30] While this is an accurate appraisal of the legislation, it should be noted that both the Kem Amendment and the Battle Act created problems for the State Department in its negotiations with CoCom. In fact Truman and Acheson spent their remaining year in office trying to comply with the conditions of the Battle Act to appease Congress, while simultaneously attempting to grant exceptions to allies whose trade was being profoundly affected by the legislation. It is to the Truman administration's negotiations with Western Europe that we now turn.

A troubled partnership

The Western European governments were most disturbed by Congress's involvement in East–West trade.[31] They feared that economic and military assistance from the United States would be discontinued if Congress investigated their trading patterns with Eastern

Europe. In London the Foreign Office was so concerned about the implications of the Kem Amendment on military aid that it ordered the British embassy in Washington to consult with the ECA and the State Department. The embassy reported with confidence that assistance to Britain was 'not in jeopardy'.[32] Nonetheless by January 1952 Britain and its continental partners in CoCom were struggling to preserve the multilateralism of the Paris group against the unilateral nature of the Battle Act. Although the Truman government was generally successful in obtaining exemptions for its allies from the legislation, relations between Washington and its allies over East–West matters were decidedly prickly.

Of all the Western European participants in CoCom the Attlee government was the most vocal critic of Congress's intervention in international export control policy. Despite reassurance from the State Department that the Kem Amendment would not be applied to Britain, the British ambassador to Washington, Sir Oliver Franks, complained about the legislation to Harold Linder. In a conversation with Franks, Linder asserted that if the gulf between International List I and the 1-A list was narrowed significantly, then Congress could be assuaged. Franks reacted sharply to this suggestion. He argued that Britain was principally a trading nation and was averse to any restrictions on trade that posed no threat to its national security. Declaring his opposition to a wholesale embargo on trade with Eastern Europe, Franks commented that a hot war with the Soviet Union was unlikely in the short run. Accordingly the British government's policy was to continue its commercial relationship with Moscow as a means of preventing conflict. To Franks' mind, if the CoCom members were forced to comply with the provisions set out in the Kem Amendment and sever their trading links with the Soviet bloc, this action would be construed by the Soviets as an act of economic warfare. Tension between the two blocs would be exacerbated, making the prospect of war more likely.[33]

Franks disclosed the full extent of his feelings on the matter in a top secret telegram to the Foreign Office on 11 May. In his opinion the Kem Amendment was designed to bring 'European and particularly United Kingdom trade to a standstill'.[34] He suggested that the legislation was not the result of a 'sudden burst of anger', but an attempt by Congress 'to impose [its] own views over patterns of trade between Western and Eastern Europe'.[35] In a report to the Foreign Office analysing the implications of the Kem Amendment for East–West trade, Franks concluded that if the Western European governments complied with the measures they would be deprived of basic raw materials and strategic items necessary for the common defence effort. The report also noted that should the Western European nations refuse to adhere to the guidelines of the legislation, they would be liable to forfeit economic and military assistance from the United States.[36]

During the summer of 1951 the British and French governments were very concerned about the influence of Congress on American export control policy. The Foreign Office in particular was disturbed about the political, economic and financial ramifications of the Kem Amendment for British trade policy.[37] A multitude of reports and memoranda highlighting the Attlee government's contribution to the international embargo on East–West trade were produced by the Mutual Aid Department. A telegram sent to the Commerce Department in Washington summarised the position of the Foreign Office with respect to the Kem Amendment. The Foreign Office argued that Britain had intensified its strategic export control programme over the previous six months and therefore could not understand the 'bitterness of American public opinion' towards Western Europe. Moreover it dismissed as preposterous the charge by Congress that Britain was 'trading with the enemy'.[38]

These developments created a dilemma for the Truman administration. Faced with the dual problem of appeasing Congress and preserving the multilateralism of CoCom, the State Department began to assess the effect of the Kem Amendment on the broader issue of the United States' relationship with its allies in Western Europe. The well-respected diplomat and ambassador to Paris, David Bruce, gave a characteristically astute analysis of the situation. He judged that the future of relations between Washington and its CoCom allies would be based on either the multilateral 'give and take' approach or the unilateral 'take or leave it' option. Clearly Congress wanted Truman to pursue the latter course. But as far as Bruce was concerned, much progress had been made in CoCom through the multilateral nature of the Paris group so the 'give and take' option was more desirable in the context of the Cold War. At a time when Western Europe appeared vulnerable to attack from the Soviet Union, Bruce urged Acheson to place the interests of mutual security ahead of congressional disgruntlement with East–West trade.[39]

Acheson agreed with Bruce. The State Department strove to avert a breakdown in cooperation by proposing to discuss the congressional legislation at both the trilateral level with Britain and France, and then at the multilateral level with the other members of CoCom.[40] Acheson's objective with regard to these informal talks was to gain assurance from the CoCom members that controls on exports to the Soviet bloc would be applied rigorously in line with other security measures for the defence of the 'free world'. Likewise he suggested a review of the 'strategic character' of the three international export control lists: items of strategic value on List II to be transferred to List I and items no longer of military importance on List I to be downgraded to List II.[41]

A tripartite working group composed of experts from the United States, Britain and France met in early July in London. Defending the East–West trade interests of Western Europe, British officials stressed the importance of maintaining some trade in exports of strategic value to enable OEEC governments to procure essential raw materials from Eastern Europe. From the viewpoint of Britain's precarious balance of payments situation, the British delegation argued that it was necessary to permit significant trade in items on International List II 'to make sterling acceptable to the [Soviet] bloc'. Wishing to reach agreement with Britain and France before discussions at the multilateral level in CoCom, American officials were prepared to accept the argument that it was crucial 'not to sacrifice UK imports' from Eastern Europe.[42] In Washington Acheson endorsed the position taken by the American delegation. He believed that any satisfactory outcome in CoCom depended on the support of Britain and France. Yet he realised that the Truman administration would be open to criticism from Congress if it acceded to the demands of Whitehall in order to obtain 'a large measure of UK support'.[43]

What is more, the deal that Acheson managed to secure on International List I was far from satisfactory. Walter Gifford of the American embassy in London predicted that the Attlee government would only accept 60 per cent of the proposed American additions to the list. Although unhappy with this predicted outcome, Gifford commented that the United States 'will have to accept [it] or destroy [the] multilateral approach'.[44] Meanwhile British ministers had struggled to reach common ground on the American proposal. The Board of Trade and Ministry of Supply clashed with the Foreign Office and Ministry of Defence over the number of items to be added to International List I. A compromise between the two groups was finally reached and the cabinet recommended that Britain agree to two thirds of the American recommendations. While Gifford declared this offer to be the 'best obtainable co-operation without the breakdown of multilateralism' between the United States and its allies, the spectre of Congress loomed ever closer. Nonetheless his reading of the climate of opinion at the Foreign Office led him to deduce that London would 'simply refuse to budge if we push too hard'.[45] Ever hopeful, Acheson was still convinced that the United States might be able to extract more concessions from the Attlee government before the multilateral talks in CoCom.[46]

Outlining the position of the State Department prior to the CoCom meetings of 19–20 July, Acheson reiterated that the United States would 'continue to attach great importance to [the] continuation and strengthening of a genuinely multilateral approach to the problem of export control'.[47] To this end the Truman administration would pursue three objectives in embargo policy. First, Washington would continue to advocate restrictions on strategic exports to the Soviet bloc and it would seek to ensure that its allies in CoCom continued to embargo items of military value to Moscow as part of the mutual defence effort of the Western alliance. Second, the Truman administration wanted to ensure that the loss of imports from Eastern Europe resulting from economic containment would not affect the economic strength of Western Europe. Finally, the administration wished to avoid further confrontation with Congress over East–West trade. By encouraging its allies to bring the international export control lists into line with the American lists, the Truman government hoped that the multilateral embargo would be stringent enough to placate public opinion in the United States.[48]

The American delegation underscored these objectives in their opening speech to CoCom on 19 July, and stressed the need for the 'fullest possible agreement among the governments' on the International List I.[49] Eric Berthoud of the British delegation offered support for the American proposal by declaring that his government was prepared to accept 33 of the additional items on the list. Britain would, however, reserve its verdict on the remaining 20 items proposed for control by the United States until it was aware of the intentions of the other members. According to the Foreign Office these remaining items were reserved by the British delegation because of the 'great importance we attached to maintaining an adequate volume of East–West trade'.[50] With the decision of Whitehall to follow Washington's lead, Bruce, in an account sent to Acheson of the proceedings in Paris, described the negotiations as a 'successful session'.[51]

After four days of discussion between the United States and its partners in CoCom, Sidney Jacques of the American delegation reported that the Western European governments were now prepared to embargo 90 per cent of the 1-A list.[52] This was welcome news for Acheson.

While satisfied with the progress made, he urged the American delegation to bridge the very slight gap between the 1-A list and International List I. If this could be achieved the Truman administration, he imagined, would have little difficulty gaining exceptions from the Kem Amendment for all the members of CoCom. But the Attlee government was not prepared to sacrifice essential trade with Eastern Europe by expanding International List I. In a 'hold the line' policy the Western European members, led by Britain, remained steadfastly opposed to the incorporation of any further 1-A items into the international list. The United States decided against forcing the issue. Having secured some concessions from the Western Europeans, the State Department did not want to undermine cooperation in CoCom.[53] Instead Ambassador Gifford broached the matter at a meeting in London with the newly appointed foreign secretary, Herbert Morrison. He had no success. Morrison insisted that the Attlee government could not afford to place any more restrictions on East–West trade as commercial contact with Eastern Europe was crucial to Britain's economic survival.[54]

On 1 August, at a meeting of the Consultative Group of CoCom, the United States once again urged its European allies to increase the number of strategic items under embargo. The British delegation retained the position it had held during the general meeting of CoCom in July. Rejecting export controls on coal-mining, earth-moving, construction and transportation equipment, the delegation argued that these commodities were necessary for 'the normal peace-time and industrial activity of the modern state'. They pointed out that to place such items 'on the list for complete embargo would in our view involve a definite change in policy'.[55] In short the Attlee government believed that if International List I were extended to include items of secondary strategic value, this would lead to an economic blockade of Eastern Europe – a scenario they wanted to avoid. The Consultative Group agreed to expand International List I by 34 items: 19 short of the number originally proposed by the United States. By this action the Western European members of the Paris Group provided a ringing endorsement of the position advanced by Britain.[56]

Although CoCom had accepted only 60 per cent of the items proposed by the United States embargo, the State Department adjudged the preceding two months of trilateral and multilateral negotiations to be a success. Confident that further progress would be made at future CoCom meetings, the Truman administration was optimistic that exceptions would be granted to Western European governments under the Kem Amendment.[57] Now that the international embargo list more or less mirrored the 1-A list, Truman and Acheson would be able to inform Congress that Western Europe was pursuing a trade policy with the Soviet bloc that was consistent with the national security interests of the United States.

Conclusion

During 1950–51 isolationist politicians in Congress began to express their dissatisfaction with the Truman administration's economic containment strategy through a series of important legislative initiatives. The isolationists were particularly concerned by reports that Western European governments were continuing to ship strategic exports to the Soviet Union despite the Korean War and the escalating Cold War. By tying economic and military assistance programmes to compliance with the Export Control Act of 1949, they hoped to force these nations to sever their trading links with the Soviet bloc. The Kem Amendment and the Battle Act were the most significant attempts to compel Western Europe to implement wholesale restrictions on East–West trade.

As a result of the new role forged by Congress in American export control policy, the Truman administration was forced to reexamine its position *vis-à-vis* its European partners in CoCom. While trenchantly opposed to congressional interference in international embargo policy, Truman and the State Department feared that the essential economic and military assistance programme would be jeopardised by the Kem Amendment and the Battle Act. The administration thus acted swiftly to protect aid allotments to its Western European allies, while urging CoCom to expand and tighten the multilateral embargo in order to appease zealous isolationists in Congress. For the most part the Truman administration was successful. It managed to secure discretionary powers through the Battle Act – a compromise measure that allowed the president to grant waivers from the legislation to key allies. Moreover the administration, was able to mobilise support in CoCom for an extension of International List I: as a result the international embargo list closely paralleled the domestic 1-A list.

6
Troubled Partners: Anglo-American Relations and the Battle Act in 1952

The Battle Act, enacted on 26 October 1951, was the cause of much tension and resentment in Anglo-American relations. This controversial legislative measure, which was the result of a compromise between Congress and the Truman administration, threatened the *raison d'être* of multilateral cooperation between the United States and its Western European allies in East–West trade policy. Forcing nations receiving economic and military assistance from Washington to curtail their commercial contacts with Soviet bloc countries was viewed by the Churchill government as violating the sovereignty of international trade. Thus Britain, in conjunction with the largest CoCom members – France, Italy and West Germany – sought to make the Truman administration accountable to the multilateral principles of the international export control regime. The subsequent confrontation between the United States and its partners produced a major review of the direction and scope of policy in CoCom. Yet when faced with the decision of whether or not to terminate military assistance to allies that violated the Battle Act provisions, the American government chose to preserve the unity of the Western alliance instead of placating a hostile Congress and public opinion.

Anglo-American relations, 1952

On returning to office in October 1951, Prime Minister Winston Churchill sought to revive the 'special relationship' that had existed between Britain and the United States during the Second World War.[1] Although Harry Truman and Clement Attlee had forged a close alliance during the early years of the Cold War, the period 1945–51 had not been one of intimacy between London and Washington. Britain was very much the junior partner in the Anglo-American partnership, and like other Western European nations it was dependent on the United States for economic and military aid, given its severe financial difficulties and burgeoning overseas commitments. Yet the Attlee government had been a valuable ally of the Truman administration in respect of containing communism in Europe and Southeast Asia and playing a leading role in the Western alliance. Despite the relative decline of Britain as a global power, London had still been influential enough to moderate the perceived excesses of American policy, especially in the Middle East and Southeast Asia.[2]

But Churchill had a different vision from Attlee. He wanted a more formalised alliance with the United States that would allow for closer cooperation on policy making between the two powers. Churchill attempted to fulfil this objective during a visit to Washington in January 1952, but he had little success. President Truman, in his final year in office, was averse to establishing an exclusive relationship with Britain that might alienate the other Western European powers. Embroiled in the Korean conflict and preoccupied with the integration of West Germany into a European Defence Community (EDC), Truman was not disposed towards a formal alliance with London.[3]

After a series of informal discussions on a wide range of international issues, it became apparent that the two powers were divided on policy towards certain regions. As a firm advocate of European integration the Truman administration wanted Britain to participate actively in the Schuman and Pleven Plans. Churchill stuck rigidly to Attlee's policy of non-committal to supranational institutions in Western Europe. Although Churchill and his foreign secretary, Anthony Eden, favoured a European army, they did not wish Britain to become entangled in the affairs of the continent at the expense of its global and imperial obligations. Divisions also remained over policy towards the People's Republic China (PRC). Churchill gave Truman his assurance that Whitehall would support the United States in the Korean War, but the prime minister was not prepared to retract Britain's formal recognition of Communist China. Likewise Churchill was reluctant to restrict exports to China for fear that Britain's considerable financial interests in Hong Kong might be jeopardised. The two leaders also disagreed over the Middle East. Truman's interest in the region extended to bolstering the area against Soviet expansionism and protecting access to vital raw materials necessary for Western European economic recovery. By contrast Churchill wanted to assert British primacy in the region and lobbied the president and his secretary of state, Dean Acheson, for a battalion of American troops to help Britain defend the Suez Canal from Egyptian nationalists. On the subject of nuclear weapons, Churchill failed to persuade Truman to cooperate extensively with Britain on the atomic bomb. Constrained by the McMahon Act of 1946, the president could offer its ally only limited access to technical information on atomic matters.[4]

Despite Churchill's valiant efforts to rekindle a close association with the United States, the Truman administration was unmoved by his elegant pronouncements on the importance of an intimate Anglo-American partnership. Truman and Acheson, while valuing Churchill's support in the struggle against global communism, refused to cast diplomatic relations with Britain in a special light, and now looked to France to lead European economic and military integration.[5] An economically viable Western Europe with the industrial strength of Germany at its core, they thought, would be able to withstand a potential Soviet invasion. Nonetheless American policy makers believed that Britain had a crucial role to play in Western Europe and the rest of the world. Even if Britain did not join the European integration project, the United States still expected the Churchill government to be actively involved in the creation of the EDC. As the strongest military power with the largest economy, Britain, in the eyes of Truman and Acheson, was Washington's single most important ally in respect of the Cold War.[6]

Not all British officials had Churchill's faith in the 'special relationship'. Anthony Eden, for one, was of the opinion that Britain should begin to assert its independence in the international system. Instead of viewing Britain as a trusty servant of American hegemony, Eden believed that Britain was making a most significant contribution to the Western alliance of its own accord. As the historian John Charmley has written, Eden was apt to remind audiences in the United States that Britain would 'not tow America's line'. Far from merely acting as a junior partner to the United States, Britain, in Eden's mind, not only had the largest armed forces in Western Europe, it also had commitments in Korea, the Middle East and Malaya.[7]

Whatever the differences between Churchill and Eden over Britain's international role, a close alliance with the United States was vital. During 1951–52 the British economy was in a state of turmoil, brought on by the expensive rearmament programme and a down turn in export trade. Marshall Aid to Britain had ended in 1950, but the Attlee and Churchill governments once again found themselves dependent on financial assistance from the United States. In fact Britain was to receive $300 million worth of military aid in the fiscal year 1952–53. In the endeavour to become self-sufficient, with freedom to manoeuvre in the international arena, London had to forge strong ties with Washington in the early 1950s. But dependence was not one-sided. The Truman administration required Britain's support throughout the globe in waging the Cold War against the Soviet Union.[8] This chapter explores the nature of Anglo-American relations in the area of embargo policy in 1951–52. First, it is necessary to examine Britain's reaction to the Battle Act.

Britain and the Battle Act

In early August 1951 the Foreign Office sent a most poignant telegram to the State Department concerning the role of Congress in East–West trade. Briefly, the telegram was an expression of dissatisfaction with the Kem Amendment and the Battle bill. From the perspective of the Attlee government, this legislation interfered in the making and execution of international trade policy. While viewing the Battle bill as 'less restrictive' than the Kem Amendment, the Foreign Office stated that both 'seek to ensure that foreign governments should make their common East–West trade policies conform to a pattern established by the United States by stipulating that failure to do so would involve a cessation of US aid.'

The telegram also provided a striking overview of the main objections of London to the attempt by Congress to make economic and military assistance conditional on compliance with American export control legislation. Disturbed by what it perceived as blatant unilateralism by Congress in international trade policy, the Foreign Office was critical of the legislation in two respects. First, it argued that the United States had no right to judge where the balance of advantage lay in East–West trade for Britain. Congress, as far as the Foreign Office was aware, did not appear to realise the importance of Eastern European raw materials to the British economic recovery programme. Second, by making military and economic aid conditional on the Attlee government pursuing a policy that was detrimental to British interests, Congress was not only alienating America's allies but also jeopardising the Western alliance.[9] From the perspective of the Cold War, the Kem Amendment and the Battle bill contradicted the Truman administration's strategy of building a strong unified alliance to contain Soviet expansionism. Clearly American diplomats were worried by Britain's reaction to the legislation. In particular they were anxious to dispel London's fear that the participation of Congress in export control policy would hinder 'free negotiation' in CoCom.[10]

The irrepressible British ambassador to Washington, Sir Oliver Franks, led the charge against the Kem and Battle measures. He urged Attlee and his newly appointed foreign secretary, Herbert Morrison, to 'stand up' to the United States in East–West trade matters; for failure to do so would mean that Britain's influence over American policy be less effective in the future. Franks believed that Britain and the other members of the multilateral export control programme could constrain and perhaps modify the excesses of the congressional legislation if they acted with a united voice in CoCom.[11]

In fact Britain's continental partners in CoCom had reached the same conclusion as Franks with regard to the Kem and Battle legislation. Significantly, Italy and West Germany both called for a strengthening of the Paris Group through multilateralism in order to withstand the pressure that was being applied to European East–West trade policy by Congress. Notwithstanding the bilateral approach of negotiations on the Kem Amendment, the OEEC delegations in Paris most affected by the legislation resolved to 'stand together in defence of their interests'.[12] There is no doubt that the decision of leading Western European governments to speak as a collective voice against the Kem and Battle measures had a profound impact on the Truman administration. Whereas Truman and Acheson had preferred to deal with the Kem Amendment on a bilateral basis in negotiations with each government affected by the legislation, they were now forced to confront the issue at the multilateral level in Paris. Either way, from the viewpoint of the administration the outcome would be unsatisfactory.

Throughout the latter months of 1951 British officials sought to impress upon the Truman administration the extent of Western European discord with the Kem and Battle legislation. For example, in a speech delivered in Truro, Cornwall, intended for the American public, Sir Hartley Shawcross called on Congress to recognise the vastly different perceptions towards East–West trade held by Western Europe and the United States. The president of the Board of Trade told his audience that unlike the United States, Western Europe benefited greatly from the advantages of importing key raw materials from the region.[13] Similarly, in a brief prepared for Herbert Morrison for his trip to Washington in September, Foreign Office officials underscored the importance to Britain of trade with Eastern Europe. They pointed out that a reasonable volume of trade between Britain and the Soviet bloc was necessary, given that 'there is no alternative source of supply particularly for timber and coarse grains'. With reference to the wider strategic value to Britain of East–West trade, they asserted that Britain required a strong economic base if it was to be an effective military power. If London were denied either military assistance or East–West trade under the Kem and Battle measures, Britain's role in the Western alliance against communism would be diminished, at great cost to the 'free world generally'.[14]

Morrison and the chancellor of the exchequer, Hugh Gaitskell, discussed the issue of East–West trade with Acheson and Linder at a foreign ministers' meeting in Washington on 11 September. Both ministers expressed the concern of Whitehall about the Kem and Battle legislation. Outlining the problems for the British economy of excessive restrictions on trade with Eastern Europe, Gaitskell informed Acheson that Britain was at the 'beginning of a very serious dollar crisis'. The chancellor estimated that unless Britain was allowed unrestricted access to timber and grain from the Soviet bloc, it would be unable to constrain a dollar deficit of $500 million in 1951–52. Moreover he argued that, with respect to rubber, the present export control regime was far too restrictive. As far as he was concerned the embargo on East–West trade threatened to deprive Britain of favourable trading contracts and thus valuable raw materials, at enormous cost to the British economy in the long run. Morrison, in concurrence with his cabinet colleague, suggested to Acheson that the Labour government's plight would worsen if Britain was forced to comply with the Kem and Battle legislation. When pressed by Acheson and Linder to reconsider 20 items held in dispute with the American delegation in CoCom as a means of circumventing the Kem measure, Morrison refused to budge. He replied that Britain had 'gone a devil of a long way' towards accommodating the Truman administration in respect of bringing the international lists into line with the American domestic lists.[15] The two parties left the meeting in a cloud of uncertainty. It seemed clear that Acheson would work slavishly to protect his allies from the provisions of the Kem and Battle legislation, but first he wanted CoCom to tighten the multilateral embargo.

While the enactment of the Battle Act on 26 October repealed the Kem Amendment, the Truman administration continued to encounter resentment and disgruntlement in Western Europe. In comparison with the Kem Amendment, Truman and Acheson viewed the Battle Act as the lesser of two evils. Although the new legislation continued to demand that the United States' allies prohibit strategic trade to the Soviet bloc in exchange for military assistance, the power of discretion clearly lay in the hands of the president.[16] Given the importance of Western European defence to American national security, Truman, during the remaining months of his tenure as president, would not apply the provisions of the Battle Act to any key ally. Nonetheless the Battle Act was to prove a serious bone of contention in relations between the United States and Western Europe.

By 1952 relations between the Truman administration and Congress had deteriorated. As a lame-duck president during an election year, Truman was faced with extreme opposition to his foreign policy initiatives in Korea and Western Europe.[17] On the contentious subject of East–West trade a significant group of conservative isolationists, led by Senator James Kem, implored the president to take a tougher stand on allies that persisted to trade with communist nations. It was the secrecy of the CoCom organisation that made confrontation between Truman and Congress inevitable. Unable to disclose to the legislature the substantial progress that had been achieved in international export control policy, the administration's bargaining position with Congress on military aid had been severely undermined. This was the intractable dilemma in which the Truman administration found itself. The majority of the Western European governments did not want to reveal the existence of CoCom for fear of domestic opposition by interest groups, the business community and communist political parties.[18] Under these circumstances Truman had to haggle with Congress to ensure that military assistance programmes to Western Europe would continue. In an effort to placate the worries of its allies, the United States moved to convene a meeting of CoCom in early January 1952 to reassure the Western European governments that the items contained on the Battle lists were analogous to those on the international lists.[19] At this stage, senior State Department officials were confident that the Battle legislation was 'reasonable' and would be 'workable' once a selective approach to export controls was attained.[20]

The initial reaction of the two leading European members of CoCom – Britain and France – to the Battle Act was representative of the general Western European mood towards the direction of economic containment strategy. France demanded that the operating date of the act be postponed for almost a month while officials at the Quai d'Orsay considered the implications of the legislation for French foreign trade. The French government responded angrily to the Battle Act. It believed that the Act threatened to undermine the Western alliance in four respects. First, it found the Act contrary to the spirit of international cooperation that had inspired the Marshall Plan and NATO. Second, it objected to the unilateral nature of the Act, accusing the United States of attempting to control the trade of foreign powers.

Third, from the perspective of East–West trade, the measure forced France to procure raw materials from dollar sources. If it continued to trade with Eastern Europe its allocation of military aid would be reduced or even terminated indefinitely. Lastly, the Battle Act advocated an economic blockade of Eastern Europe; an act deemed by France to be unacceptable in peacetime.[21]

Although not as explicit as the French critique, the Foreign Office also expressed its reservations about the Battle Act. But London's criticisms, which were more constructive in nature, were aimed specifically at the Truman administration. The American government, Foreign Officials reasoned, should consult its partners at the multilateral level of CoCom before proposing further extensions to the international lists. While consensual agreement between Washington and the other CoCom partners was unlikely, at least the spirit of multilateralism that had characterised the formation of the group would be preserved.[22] Moreover the Western Europeans would have an opportunity in CoCom to vent their fury at the direction being taken by international export control policy under the shadow of Congress.[23]

In an important position paper outlining suggested British tactics in CoCom, the Joint War Production Committee (JWPC), composed of representatives from the Foreign Office and the Ministry of Defence, recommended the following approach. First, the newly elected Churchill government should continue its policy of supporting a limited multilateral East–West trade embargo, and should encourage its continental partners to do likewise. Second, the British delegation to CoCom should assert that the Battle Act was 'inconsistent with the NATO partnership concept'. However the British delegation should work closely with its American counterpart 'to secure the agreement of the US government to administering the Act in a manner consistent with the Paris Group's principles and procedures'.[24]

Senior Foreign Office officials adopted these tactics in talks with diplomats from the American embassy in London. In conversation with embassy representatives, Eric Berthoud stated that the Churchill government would endeavour to 'stand by' the international lists agreed in CoCom and refuse 'to yield to the US in this matter'.[25] He informed the Americans that London viewed the Battle Act as a violation of Britain's right to trade with other nations.[26] As Ronald Slater of the Mutual Aid Department wrote in a paper explaining Britain's unease with the Battle Act: 'We deprecate the use by the United States of aid legislation to enforce Cold War trade policy. We protested formally against the intention to do this before the Battle Act was passed.'

Slater then recommended that the Churchill government 'reach a modus operandi with the Americans rather than make further efforts to change legislation which is anchored in public opinion'. Like the JWPC, he suggested that London should work with other Western European governments to force the Truman administration to abide by the multilateral spirit of CoCom, rather than 'adhere blindly to the American proposals'.[27] London remained defiant. It would, according to a report by the secretariat of the JWPC, 'continue to trade with the East where we are satisfied that the balance of advantage is with the free world'.[28]

The Battle Act and CoCom

Although the impact of the Battle Act on Western European East–West trade has been frequently mentioned in the historiography of the early Cold War years, it has not been examined in great detail. Nonetheless it is possible to discern two conflicting lines of thought in the literature. Gunnar Adler-Karlsson and Vibeke Sørensen argue that the Truman administration drew on the provisions of the Battle Act to force its CoCom partners to bring the international export control lists into line with the American domestic lists.[29] By contrast Alan Dobson and Helen Leigh-Phippard have demonstrated, with the help of British government documents, that despite pressure from Congress the American government was sympathetic to the Western Europeans. They point out that Truman managed to obtain waivers from the legislation in order to preserve military assistance to Washington's allies. What is more, the president ensured that non-strategic trade with the Soviet bloc was not affected by the Battle Act.[30] Relations between the United States and its allies were certainly strained by the Act, as the following account will illustrate, but in the interest of allied unity the Truman administration sought to accommodate the economic and military needs of the Western European governments.

In early January 1952 Britain and France continued to lobby Truman and the State Department to hold discussions on the Mutual Defence Control Act at the multilateral level. In conversation with State Department officials the French ambassador, Henri Bonnet, declared that his government hoped that the legislation might be implemented multilaterally rather than bilaterally.[31] Officials at the Foreign Office echoed this sentiment. They believed that the Western Europeans would be better placed to air their grievances with the United States as a unified group than on a government-to-government basis. The problem for Britain and its continental partners was how to reconcile the moderate multilateral export control programme implemented under the auspices of CoCom with the much broader embargo implicit in the provisions of the Battle Act.[32] The perceptive British ambassador to the United States, Sir Oliver Franks, was convinced that the Europeans could exert enough pressure on the United States through the Paris Group to modify the unilateral approach to American policy. To this end the mutual security administrator, Averell Harriman, would be forced to consult with CoCom on the Battle lists or face the danger of destroying the 'co-operation he seeks to achieve'.[33]

Yet the State Department was sympathetic to the grievances of Britain and France concerning the Battle Act. Acheson was well aware of the dangers of disharmony between Washington and its allies over East–West trade. It was important that policy divergences on economic containment policy should not compromise the wider objectives of the Western alliance in the face of Soviet expansionism in Europe and Southeast Asia. Acheson anticipated that an arrangement could be worked out between the United States and Britain whereby the 'principles and procedures in Paris and Washington can exist together'.[34] But herein lay a potential obstacle that threatened to plague Anglo-American relations in East–West trade policy. It had become apparent to the Foreign Office that the decision-making powers of CoCom would be rendered ineffectual by the presence of the Battle Act in American policy. Unless the Truman administration could prevent Congress from encroaching on international embargo policy, the United States and its allies would remain divided in CoCom.

Prior to the meeting of CoCom scheduled for mid January, British and American representatives met to discuss the emerging crisis. The talks made little progress. Once again the British delegation argued strongly that decisions about the future direction of the East–West trade embargo was the preserve of the Paris Group and not Congress. While divided over policy, the two delegations vowed to work towards an 'acceptable modus operandi' in Paris.[35] Despite this commitment to solidarity, the different views of the two delegations were evident at the CoCom meetings of 15–16 January. In their opening remarks to the assembled members on 15 January, the British delegation, referring to the unilateral nature of the Battle legislation, stated that London 'wished to avoid action prejudicial to the workings of CoCom'. What concerned British diplomats was not the Battle lists, which they viewed as quite similar to the international lists, but the way in which the American government would administer the act. They implored the

Truman administration to ensure that the provisions of the Mutual Defence Control Act were executed 'in a manner consistent with the principles and procedures' of CoCom.

Acknowledging that President Truman would probably seek to grant exceptions to the Western European nations under the legislation, the British delegation asserted that the decision not to control certain items in East–West trade should reside with each individual country. It was not, they commented, for the American government to judge where the balance of trade lay for any nation. If the United States resorted to coercion to impel any Western European government to place further restrictions on exports under the Battle Act, this action would be inconsistent with the multilateral spirit of 'give and take' in CoCom. This approach, the British delegation concluded, would have enormous repercussions for the *raison d'être* of the multilateral export control regime.[36] Not only would economic containment cease to be an effective Cold War strategy against the Soviet Union, the strength and unity of the Western alliance would be undermined. This in turn would increase the potential of Soviet risk-taking in areas of strategic significance such as Europe, Southeast Asia and the Middle East. The British delegation stated categorically that should the United States decide not to apply the provisions of the legislation at the multilateral level, London would intervene 'to prevent the US from using Battle Act sanctions to override agreements' reached in CoCom.[37]

The French delegation concurred with Britain. Protesting against the Battle Act for advocating the suppression of East–West trade, the French representatives underscored the dollar gap crisis between the United States and Western Europe. If French manufacturers were prohibited by the Battle Act from obtaining raw materials from non-dollar sources such as Eastern Europe, France's balance of payments situation would become increasingly untenable.[38] Many of the concerns voiced by the British and French delegations were reiterated by other Western European governments during the two-day session. The contingents from Western Europe supported Britain's proposal that the multilateral application of East–West trade controls be maintained despite the Battle Act legislation.[39] From this viewpoint, then, the CoCom meeting of 15–16 January can be seen in a positive light. In effect Washington was sent a resounding message by its allies: the Truman administration would be faced with the prospect of disunity and conflict if it attempted to apply the Battle Act unilaterally.[40]

Observing a session of CoCom on 21 January, a large American delegation appeared suitably impressed by the demonstration of unity and defiance against the Battle Act by the Western Europeans. Whether the delegation's report had any impact on policy making in the State Department is uncertain from an examination of the available documents. But officials in Washington and some American embassies in Europe were unquestionably worried about developments in CoCom. Discussions between policy planners in Washington and Europe revealed the Truman administration's commitment to NSC 91/1 to deny aid to any nation exporting strategic goods to the Soviet bloc. They would work, however, to obtain waivers from the Battle Act for crucial American allies. The United States nonetheless refused to discuss the Battle Act with its partners at the multilateral level.[41] For this reason Sir Edmund Hall-Patch of the British delegation to the OEEC fretted that American actions would have grave consequences for Western Europe should Washington choose to override the multilateral basis of the embargo negotiated two years previously.[42] Hall-Patch was not as certain as some of his colleagues in the British delegation that the talks of 15–16 January had been successful.[43]

Anglo-American discord over prior commitments in East–West trade

In May the Truman administration and Western Europe was confronted with another possible threat to the international export control programme. Disgruntled with the Battle Act on the ground that it granted too much discretion to the executive, Senator James Kem sought to revive his infamous amendment in a different form. Kem's bill once again strove to make Congress the sole gatekeeper for American economic and military assistance. The measure was introduced to the Senate by Kem on 28 May and provoked much debated between the isolationist group and supporters of Truman. Kem's efforts were to no avail, however, much to the relief of the president and Acheson, who both lobbied intensely to defeat the measure.[44]

The bill's defeat was due in large part to the intervention of the powerful chairman of the Senate Foreign Affairs Committee, Tom Connolly of Texas. In a letter to Connolly in the aftermath of the drama, Acheson offered a well-measured defence of the Truman administration's economic containment policy. He stated that the Western European governments were 'wholeheartedly committed to a policy of economic defence and applying strict controls on items of strategic significance'. These nations, Acheson explained to Connolly, would not institute the embargo on trade with the Soviet bloc demanded by recent congressional legislation because of political and economic reasons. As the secretary of state made clear, 'They will not adopt such a policy and … in the circumstances, they cannot do so without seeming to their own people to have surrendered an essential element of their national independence and sovereignty'.[45]

Ironically, Kem's bill acted as a stimulus for Acheson to begin a series of talks with key ambassadors in Washington to persuade Western European governments to bring the international export control lists into line with the American domestic lists. In June Acheson conducted separate talks with the British, French and Italian ambassadors on the state of the East–West trade embargo. He informed each ambassador that Kem's campaign to repeal the Battle Act had been halted. But he warned the three ambassadors against adopting a complacent attitude towards the Battle Act and future congressional export control measures. It was imperative, Acheson stressed, that the Western Europeans continued to exercise restraint in trade with the Soviet bloc, or else military assistance could be threatened.[46] On behalf of the Churchill government, Sir Oliver Franks inquired whether the United States would be willing to support the expansion of 'peaceful' trade with Eastern Europe in 1953. Harold Linder of the State Department replied that it was unlikely that any future administration would sanction increased trade contact with the communist nations given the strength of the isolationist lobby in Congress.[47]

The hardening of the Truman administration's attitude towards East–West trade in the summer of 1952 disturbed the Foreign Office. Some officials were worried that the mutual security administrator, Averell Harriman, would take a dim view of British trade with the Soviet bloc and refuse to grant exceptions to the Battle Act.[48] They feared that American proposals to grant uniform exceptions on items for control in East–West trade would discriminate against British exports to Eastern Europe. The Foreign Office was anxious to ensure that each member of CoCom would have the freedom to select exports in certain commodities to be exempted from the legislation. However the State Department proposed to draw up several lists of items to be exempted from embargo. These lists, which would be carefully monitored by CoCom, would contain items deemed by the mutual security administrator not to contribute to Soviet war-making potential. British officials were incensed by this proposal, which appeared to reserve for the United States the right to determine the content of Western European trade with Eastern Europe.[49] Despite disagreement about the application of exceptions to the Battle Act, Britain and the United

States began to reach common ground on the importance of multilateral cooperation in CoCom.[50]

On 12 June Acheson met Franks in Washington to discuss the trade commitments Britain had had with Eastern Europe before the Battle Act had taken effect in January 1952. Acheson wanted the Western European governments to suspend their contracts with the countries of Eastern Europe with respect to items on the Battle lists. His hard-line position was undoubtedly the result of intense pressure from Congress to ensure that the executive carried out the provisions of the Mutual Control Assistance Act. The State Department was particularly alarmed by reports that the Western Europeans were shipping $7 million worth of strategic exports to the Soviet bloc during the course of 1952. By June commodities to the value of $4 million had been exported to Eastern Europe, and during the following 12–15 months the Western Europeans planned to ship $21 million worth of items on the Battle lists to the Soviet bloc. Significantly the British shipments amounted to $5 million. Although Acheson acknowledged that these trade commitments had been agreed between the parties prior to the implementation of the Battle Act on 26 January 1952, he informed Franks that Britain's actions would undermine Anglo-American cooperation in East–West trade.[51]

Later in the month British officials met an American delegation at the Foreign Office to discuss the thorny issue of prior commitments. At a meeting on 20 June Harold Linder, representing Acheson, expressed the State Department's concern about the shipment of strategic exports to the Soviet bloc by Britain. Linder implored British policy makers to review their prior trade commitments to the Soviet bloc in the interests of mutual security. He warned that military assistance to Britain and Western Europe would be jeopardised if the OEEC nations continued to engage in strategic trade with the Soviet Union. In response Eric Berthoud pointed to a factual error in the American estimates of Britain's prior commitments for items on the Battle lists: the value of these was not $5 million but $1.5 million. Furthermore Britain was reluctant to break government and private trade contracts with Eastern Europe in a policy reversal that would have 'grave implications', and no decision would be made about prior commitments until ministers had discussed the issue at cabinet level.[52]

The subject of prior commitments in East–West trade was raised by the American delegation at a meeting of the Consultative Group in Paris on 24 June. In their opening statement the delegation stressed that the Truman administration did not wish to 'prejudice [the] multilateral control arrangements', but Washington feared that prearranged strategic trade to the value of $23 million would 'make a significant contribution to the military potential of the [Soviet] bloc'. The American delegation thus urged the members countries to make a 'special effort' to avoid shipping strategic commodities in order to safeguard the strategic balance of power in Europe.[53]

Harold Linder called on the larger members of CoCom, notably Britain, France, West Germany and Italy, to lead by example and renege on $6 million worth of their commitments to Eastern Europe, comprising steel processing equipment, metal working machinery, ball bearings and industrial diamonds. Linder commented that if a substantial proportion of these commodities were shipped to the Soviet bloc 'the whole mutual aid programme might be jeopardised'. Given the wider security ramifications of the American delegation's statement, Eric Berthoud of the British delegation seemed inclined to support Linder's call for a review of prior commitments in CoCom. Yet he contended that as a matter of principle nations should be allowed to honour the trade contracts they had established with Eastern European governments.[54]

However Linder and Berthoud remained locked in dispute over the matter, and efforts by the State Department to impress upon the Foreign Office the military value of these agreements to the Soviet Union were to no avail. American diplomats continued to argue that substantial fulfilment of the prior commitments would defeat the purpose of the multilateral embargo. Unmoved by this line of reasoning, British officials were determined to carry out their commitments, which they believed did not conflict with the principles and policy of CoCom. Despite Linder's warning that military aid would be forfeited if Congress was made aware of the value of British strategic exports to the Soviet bloc, the Churchill government refused to revoke the trade agreements it had negotiated prior to the Battle Act.

With the development of an impasse between London and Washington a meeting was convened at the foreign minister level in late June. Eden, Acheson and Robert Schuman of France attended the talks. Acheson sought to persuade Eden and Schuman that if the $23 million worth of military items discussed at the Consultative Group conference on 23–24 June were shipped to the Soviet bloc, the implications for Western security would be grave.[55] While Acheson did not propose to undermine the embargo agreements in CoCom, he suggested that the members should remain flexible in order to fulfil the objective of economic containment. In other words the Western

European governments should put security priorities before trade interests in cases where the military potential of the Soviet Union would benefit considerably. If these governments chose to ignore the warnings of the State Department, Acheson asserted, not only would American military assistance be jeopardised but also the East–West trade embargo would be rendered ineffectual. In defence of British trade interests, Eden replied that Britain would continue its policy of controlling exports in materials of military value to the Soviet Union and Eastern Europe, but that it intended to honour its non-strategic trade agreements. Eden also dismissed the American estimates of the value of Britain's strategic East–West trade. Like Berthoud, he suggested that the State Department had grossly overestimated the value of this trade, according to the calculations of the Foreign Office.

In July Churchill ordered Eden and the president of the Board of Trade, Peter Thorneycroft, to conduct a review of Britain's East–West trade. First, Eden and Thorneycroft were to consider the American request that shipments agreed with the Eastern European governments prior to the Battle Act be restricted. Second, they were to consult tool manufacturers on the status of orders contracted with the Soviet bloc before the enforcement of the legislation by the United States. Given the volume of Britain's prior commitments, Eden and Thorneycroft not surprisingly concluded that London should honour the existing agreements with the exception of items of 'overriding' strategic significance.[56]

At a meeting of the Coordinating Group in mid July, British representatives outlined the Churchill government's position on prior commitments. The American delegation, however, asserted that the wholesale fulfilment of Western European trade agreements with the Soviet bloc would pose serious problems for CoCom's system of export controls, particularly with respect to items on International List II. Yet with potential discord between the United States and Western Europe over East–West trade looming, the American diplomats did not reject the British proposal in entirety. Most notably, the other European members of the group embraced London's initiative.[57] By the end of the summer it appeared that the British government's prior commitments proposal was the most acceptable resolution to the impending crisis in CoCom and was supported by the majority of members.[58] Following the lead of Britain, eight members submitted a list of items negotiated before the implementation date of the Battle Act to be honoured in trade with Eastern Europe by November 1952.[59] Inevitably, it was an Anglo-American compromise that averted further discord over East–West trade.

Coping with Congress: the visit to Europe by Laurie C. Battle

In autumn 1952 Congressman Laurie Battle, the instigator of the Mutual Defence Control Act, travelled to Europe to monitor strategic shipments to the Soviet bloc. He met representatives of every major government engaged in East–West trade. At a meeting with Battle in Paris, Ivor Pink of the British delegation to the OEEC gained the impression that the US Congress and American public still believed that the Western European nations were supplying strategic materials to the Soviet Union. He suggested in a telegram to the Foreign Office that it was necessary 'to clear up misunderstandings on this issue' lest Battle inform Congress that Britain was not complying with the provisions of the legislation.[60] In a letter to Eric Berthoud, Harry Gresswell of the Ministry of Defence called on the Foreign Office to adopt a firm line towards Battle. He remarked that:

> We are not, and have never been, dragging our feet in the field of true security. If we have shown any reluctance, it is merely because we see no good reason to roam somewhat aimlessly down the devious by-paths suggested by public opinion in the United States.[61]

Notwithstanding their determination to set the record straight on British export control practices, Foreign Office officials decided to act with caution and tact in their discussions with Battle. They would emphasise the importance to the British economy of Eastern European markets for non-dollar raw materials. But they would also assert that the differences between London and Washington over embargo policy were 'marginal' and that the British export control lists mirrored those of the United States.[62]

In preparation for the talks with Battle, the Foreign Office consulted members of the British delegation in Paris and the British embassy in Washington to gain an insight into the character and views of the congressman. Sir F. R. Hoyer-Millar bluntly described Battle 'as a slow thinking democrat from the Deep South and although well meaning rather alarmingly obtuse'. Moreover Hoyer-Millar was most disturbed by Battle's lack of knowledge and command of Western European embargo policy.[63] Alan McCall-Judson of the British embassy in Washington also painted a less than flattering portrait of Battle in a telegram to Berthoud. According to McCall-Judson, Battle was prone to press on European officials the necessity of controlling trade with communist nations as a prerequisite for receiving military assistance from the United States. Recounting an error of fact made by Battle in an interview with a journalist on Western European East–West trade, McCall-Judson expressed the view commonly held by British officials of Battle's apparent 'simple mindedness'.[64]

With these impressions in mind, on 19 September representatives from the Foreign Office and the Ministry of Defence sought to enlighten Battle on British economic containment policy towards the Soviet bloc and described Britain's role in the multilateral export control programme for East–West trade. They outlined the dollar shortage problem that had plagued Britain since the Second World War and the importance to Britain's economic recovery programme of Eastern European markets for raw materials. However they asserted that the Churchill government accepted in principle the objectives of an embargo on East–West trade. Battle replied by acknowledging that the gap between the American and international export control lists was slight, but he encouraged officials to work to overcome the disparity for the benefit of mutual security.[65]

When Battle met Roger Makins for talks three days later at the Foreign Office he took a much tougher stand on British trade policy towards the Soviet bloc. Battle reiterated his warning to Makins that if Britain did not bring its export control lists into line with those of the United States, as required under the Mutual Defence Control Act, the American government would be forced to withdraw its assistance to Britain. Rather than interfering in the trading practices of nations, Battle insisted that the legislation was a defence measure instituted by Congress in the interest of Western security. In a remarkably calm response to Battle's tirade, Makins replied that there was no real difference in policy between London and Washington on the subject of East–West trade. But he stated that the Western European countries should be 'entitled to some freedom of action in certain cases' where trade commitments had been negotiated before the Battle Act came into force.

Battle's efforts proved futile. He failed to persuade the Churchill government to move towards more uniform Anglo-American export control lists. Furthermore his uncompromising stance on East–West trade and his limited knowledge of Western European embargo practices only succeeded in antagonising British officials.[66] He returned to Washington far from satisfied with the findings of his eight-nation tour of Western Europe. He reported in a letter to Averell Harriman that the European members of CoCom were exporting 28 items of strategic value to the Soviet bloc, even though the United States had embargoed these commodities. He was most critical of the Western

European response to the Mutual Defence Control Act. As far as he could discern from Western European export control practices, decisive action was not being taken to help 'win the war in Korea or to gain the advantage over Russia in the Cold War' by adequately restricting strategic exports to the Soviet bloc. His sharpest criticism was reserved for Britain. Alluding to British exports to Eastern Europe since the beginning of 1952 without recourse to the Battle Act, he wrote: 'I do not understand how this can occur without an exception being made as provided in the Act'.[67]

What was most significant about Battle's visit was that it revealed the chasm between the perceptions of Congress and the Western European members of CoCom towards East–West trade. Unlike the State Department, Battle seemed oblivious to the importance that Britain and its continental partners attached to commerce with Eastern Europe. The divergent viewpoints of Congress and London were further confirmed by the manner in which Foreign Office officials greeted the *First Battle Act Report to Congress*. Their attitude was that the Churchill government 'does not take official cognisance of the Battle Act and hence cannot in any way "approve" any announcement connected with the legislation'.[68]

By contrast the American government was sympathetic to the arguments of its European allies. When faced with the decision of terminating military assistance to Britain, France and Italy as punishment for shipping over $2 million worth of strategic materials to Eastern Europe in December 1952, President Truman refused. In consultation with Harriman, he recommended to Congress that aid to the three countries should continue. In a letter addressed to six congressional committees, Truman gave two reasons for his decision. First, he argued that the shipments in question had been negotiated prior to the date on which the Battle Act had come into force (January 1952). Thus the three countries had been obliged under trade agreements with Eastern European governments to honour the transactions. Second, Truman declared that he could not terminate the aid provided to any of the three nations as they contributed four-fifths of the European NATO defence commitment. Any attempt to alienate these nations over East–West trade would have grave implications for the future of Western security. Guided by what he saw as 'the strength of the Act', Truman wrote that 'to terminate aid to the United Kingdom, France and Italy would seriously impair that security because it would jeopardise the effectiveness of the free nations' first line of defence in Europe'.[69]

Despite the uneasy nature of relations between the United States and its allies in CoCom, the president's action in this case indicated the administration's commitment to mutual security in the context of East–West Cold War rivalry. Inherent in Truman's decision to grant waivers to Britain, France and Italy under the Battle legislation was the primacy of allied security considerations over commercial interests. Representatives of the British delegation in Paris nonetheless complained to the Foreign Office that the Truman administration had been responsible for the 'deterioration of relations in CoCom'. They remarked that the American CoCom delegation were

> for the most part merely puppets manipulated by many hands with as many motives: the fear of Congress and the risk of more extreme legislation than the Battle Act, the fear of public criticism of 'arms' being sent to the Soviet bloc, mingled with a genuine conviction that (because the USA need not do so) it is wicked to trade with Russia.[70]

In general the feeling in Whitehall was that the United States had replaced the voluntary and multilateral spirit developed in CoCom in 1950 with a hard-line approach promoted by Congress that advocated 'less and less trade with the Soviet bloc', strategic or otherwise.[71] Senior export control officials at the Foreign Office and the Ministry of Defence predicted that Western Europe, and Britain in particular, 'could expect continued and continual efforts to tighten up security controls' by the United States.[72] However, aware of the concern of the British and other Western European governments about the effect of the Battle Act on policy in CoCom, the Truman administration worked frantically to protect its allies from the legislation throughout 1952. In fact on no occasion did the president terminate military or economic assistance to any CoCom member accused by Congress of violating the Mutual Defence Control Act. While it could be argued that relations between the Western allies were severely strained over the hardening of the American attitude towards East–West trade in CoCom, the position of the administration was more moderate than that of Congress.

Conclusion

In 1951–52 the increasing power and influence of Congress in American export control policy alarmed the Churchill government. In particular, British policy makers resented the Battle Act. From the perspective of Whitehall, the legislation impinged on the sovereignty of British trade policy. It made economic and military assistance from the United States conditional on the restriction of East–West trade, as delineated by Congress. Moreover the existence of two separate lists of strategic items under the Battle Act ran contrary to the multilateral and voluntary spirit of CoCom. Anglo-American relations over embargo policy towards the Soviet bloc were fraught with conflict over the Battle measure. Constrained by the legislation, the Truman administration requested its allies to extend International List I to incorporate items on the Battle lists. While the administration clashed with the Western European governments over the future direction of policy in CoCom during the summer of 1952, the multilateral character of the Paris Group remained intact. This was largely due to the refusal by President Truman to suspend aid to allies that continued to export strategic commodities to Eastern Europe in violation of the provisions of the Battle Act.

7
Relaxing the Embargo: Eisenhower, Churchill and East–West Trade, 1953–54

The years 1953–54 marked a watershed in the history of the Western embargo on trade with the Soviet bloc. The relaxation of tensions between East and West during the early months of 1953 led the newly elected Eisenhower administration and the Churchill government to conduct independent reviews on trade policy with Eastern Europe. There has been much debate in the literature on the August 1954 revision of the international export control lists. Robert Mark Spaulding has argued that the impetus for the relaxation of the embargo came from President Dwight Eisenhower,[1] but British archival research by John Young demonstrates that Winston Churchill initiated the revision of the international export control lists.[2]

This chapter reviews this debate by examining the Eisenhower administration's perception of East–West trade in 1953–54. It concludes that the policy document on economic defence policy, NSC 152/2, was a compromise between the president's radical position and the more conservative standpoint of the majority in the National Security Council (NSC). The chapter also considers the enquiry into export control practices by British ministers in the autumn of 1953. It demonstrates that London favoured a more substantial revision of the embargo than Washington.

The 'new look' Cold War

On winning office in November 1952 Dwight D. Eisenhower brought to the presidency a lifetime of international experience and expertise. In a distinguished military career he had led the allied forces in Europe during the Second World War and became the first supreme commander of the allied powers of NATO in 1951.[3] As president he sought to draw on this vast experience when waging the Cold War against the Soviet Union. While he supported the Truman administration's containment policies in Europe and Southeast Asia, Eisenhower was concerned about the fiscal implications of NSC-68. He believed that the creation of a costly national security state in peacetime would bankrupt the federal government, force citizens to pay intolerably high taxes and impinge on individual freedoms. Nonetheless the new president realised that the Republicans, having won the presidency for the first time since 1928, could not afford to return to a policy of isolationism given the international strategic situation. Rather the United States had to continue to exercise leadership in the non-communist world, bolster Western Europe and Southeast Asia and ensure that the Western alliance remained unified against the forces of Sino-Soviet communism.

In his first years in office, then, Eisenhower strove to establish a national security strategy that would allow the federal government to cut budget deficits, maintain a strong dollar and encourage free enterprise.[4] In order to execute this policy of 'solvency and security' the president and his newly appointed secretary of state, John Foster Dulles, argued that the United States should develop its nuclear arsenal at the expense of more costly conventional weapons. Such an approach, which was to be codified in NSC 162/2, would allow for a 'flexible response' in the event of open conflict with the Soviet Union.[5]

Like Truman, Eisenhower pursued a 'Europe-first' strategy. He thought it vital to preserve the close alliance that had existed between Washington and its Western European allies in the formative years of the Cold War. In fact Eisenhower and Dulles were of the opinion that a strong, cohesive alliance with the major powers of Western Europe was just as important as the military element of American national security policies.[6] Without the full support of the Europeans in the Cold War, they thought, the United States would not be able to contain and deter the Soviet military threat. Eisenhower and Dulles were also worried that Moscow might attempt to capitalise on any rifts over policy making that developed between the United States and its allies. If Washington did not safeguard the democratic freedom of nations in the so-called 'free world', the Kremlin might exploit political instability and economic disorder by seeking to co-opt these countries into the Soviet orbit. Likewise both Eisenhower and Dulles were convinced that a strong, unified Western alliance based on multilateralism and mutual security could attract Soviet satellite states in Eastern Europe to break away from the Soviet Empire.[7]

Thus the Eisenhower administration's first priority was to attempt to overcome the differences between the United States and its European allies over policy towards German rearmament, the Korean War and East–West trade. Although committed to the defence of the continent, Eisenhower and Dulles expected the Western European governments to play an active role in NATO and develop a supranational European community.[8] A unified Europe, American policy makers had argued since 1947, would build bridges between the peoples of Western Europe, bring economic prosperity to the region and establish an effective bulwark against Soviet aggression. The formation of a European Defence Community (EDC) would also allow West Germany to rearm within a supranational framework, allaying France's fear of a German military resurgence. As firm supporters of the EDC, Eisenhower and Dulles maintained that an integrated European army could achieve the dual objectives of preventing future German military aggression in Europe and developing closer political ties between the continental neighbours in a European community.[9] In the long run the political and military integration of Europe would allow the Eisenhower administration gradually to reduce military assistance to the region.[10] This would enable Eisenhower to stave off criticism by the opponents of foreign assistance within the government and Congress.[11]

Despite the initial goodwill of Eisenhower and Dulles towards Western Europe, Britain remained sceptical about and suspicious of the motives of the new Republican administration. Winston Churchill, the British prime minister, welcomed Eisenhower's election to the presidency, but was concerned by the appointment of Dulles as secretary of state. Churchill was even more perturbed by the president's refusal to establish an exclusive 'special relationship' with Britain. Eisenhower, much like Truman, believed that Churchill exaggerated the influence of Britain and the importance of its world role. Moreover he was not disposed to develop an exclusive relationship with Britain at the cost of alienating the other European powers.[12]

What strained relations between the United States and Britain, especially in Foster Dulles' mind, was the reluctance of Britain to play a meaningful part in the political and military integration of Europe. Furthermore Churchill's desire tò hold a summit between Britain, the United States and the Soviet Union to discuss the possibility of relaxing the tension between East and West was not shared by Eisenhower or the State Department. While Churchill wanted to seize the olive branch of 'peaceful coexistence' offered by the new Soviet leaders – Malenkov and Beria – Eisenhower and Dulles remained suspicious of the Kremlin.[13]

Their cautious response was also conditioned by the extremely anticommunist political climate in the United States that arose from the controversial investigations by Senator Joseph McCarthy. The two powers also clashed over colonisation. Eisenhower's opposition to the imperial aspirations of Britain and France in the Third World led to differences between the allies over global containment policy. Conflicting with Britain over the Suez Canal and France over Indochina, the Eisenhower administration encouraged nationalism and neutralism in the underdeveloped world. In the Far East, however, Britain and France supported Eisenhower's decision to end the Korean War and provide economic aid to Japan in order to build up regional strength against communist infiltration.[14] During the Eisenhower administration the contentious issue of East–West trade, as this chapter will argue, once again led to confrontation between the United States and Britain.

Eisenhower and East–West trade

Renewed study of the Eisenhower presidency was stimulated by the declassification of thousands of documents during the 1980s and 1990s, providing historical evidence that contradicted the traditional interpretation of Eisenhower as a passive and ineffectual president.[15] Yet in attempting to set the record straight many scholars have created a distorted image of Eisenhower's leadership in foreign affairs. They argue that the president not only made the key executive decisions in national security policy, but also took full command of the policy-making process. An examination of records of the export control process in the United States during the 1950s demonstrates that Eisenhower was an active participant in the making of embargo policy towards the Sino-Soviet bloc, but that opponents of his views within the administration and in Western Europe frustrated his attempts to provide international leadership in CoCom.[16]

The issue of East–West trade was discussed frequently by the NSC during the Eisenhower presidency. According to the minutes of NSC meetings, Eisenhower was a vocal participant in discussions on matters relating to international embargoes. Indeed it appears that he closely studied the question of trade with the Soviet bloc and prepared well in advance of meetings.[17] While the president was keen to express his own views on East–West trade, he encouraged debate amongst the other members of the NSC. The minutes of meetings on embargoes and economic defence policy further reveal that Eisenhower was largely unsuccessful in persuading the NSC to share his somewhat radical views on East–West trade. Unlike his secretaries of commerce and defence, the president believed that controls on trade with the Soviet bloc should be relaxed. The NSC minutes depict an astute president passionately and vigorously arguing the case for increased trade with Eastern Europe.[18]

The pre-inaugural cabinet meeting on 12 January 1953 in Washington was the first occasion on which Eisenhower expressed the view that increased trade between East and West could be used to improve diplomatic relations between the United States and the Soviet Union. At the NSC meeting of 30 March he suggested that trade could be a valuable weapon 'in the hands of the diplomat'. In a radical departure from the Truman administration's policy blueprint, NSC-104/2, Eisenhower believed that by opening commercial contact with Eastern Europe the United States could entice the satellite states to break their economic dependency on Moscow and enjoy the fruits of the international economy. If successful, this would 'split the Soviet world' and weaken the Soviet Union 'in a broad and subtle way'.[19] Whereas Truman had attempted to limit the military potential of the Soviet Union by denying shipments of strategic and industrial commodities to Eastern Europe, Eisenhower was convinced that the Soviet bloc could be weakened if the satellite countries were exposed to favourable trading terms with the West.

Eisenhower wanted to heal the rift between the United States and its partners in CoCom over policy direction and the scope of the embargo. In contrast to his predecessor he was sympathetic to Western Europe's complaint that the embargo was too broad. During the early years of CoCom, strategic considerations had governed the Truman government's approach to East–West trade policy. The economic welfare of the United States' allies, although viewed as important by the State Department, had been of secondary importance to the policy planners responsible for export control policy. Eisenhower disagreed profoundly with this attitude. To his mind NSC 104/2 was flawed in that it had forced the Western European governments to sever vital trade links that were necessary for economic recovery and military strength. At an NSC discussion on East–West trade he commented that 'it would be impossible to win any war with such severe restrictions placed on our allies especially a cold war'. In much the same vein as Truman's secretaries of state, Marshall and Acheson, Eisenhower was of the opinion that a stringent embargo on exports to the Soviet bloc would prove to be counterproductive to the objectives of the Western alliance. He warned the NSC that if constant friction between the United States and its allies prevailed over the making of East–West trade policy, Washington could not expect 'to keep these nations on our side in a struggle with the Soviet Union'. Once again pointing to the economic plight of the Western European nations, he asserted that it was both 'foolish' and 'impossible' to continue to demand that these governments place wide-ranging restrictions on trade when their 'standard of living was too damned low'.[20]

Eisenhower further asserted that if the United States wanted to preserve the unity of the 'free world' and win the Cold War it should not 'stifle the trade' of Western Europe. He urged the NSC to take a long-term view of the problem. If the Western Europeans were forced to maintain severe restrictions on the sale of industrial items to the Soviet bloc, this would weaken both their economies and mutual security. Not only would economic vulnerability increase the likelihood of Soviet infiltration into Europe, conflict between Washington and CoCom might lead to a rift in the Western alliance. Eisenhower feared that a breakdown in multilateral cooperation over East–West trade would mean that 'these nations in the coalition will go to pot one by one'.[21] It could be argued that Eisenhower expressed these sentiments in a dramatic fashion in order to gain the support of the NSC for his views. But as an experienced military leader with many years of command during the Second World War and as a former supreme commander of NATO, he was keenly aware of the dangers that Western European economic weakness posed to American national security.

For Eisenhower a close working relationship with the Churchill government in economic defence policy was imperative. In recognition of Britain's influence in CoCom, he thought that the United States should bend 'as far as possible' to London's demand to reduce the number of industrial items under embargo. Departing from the Truman administration's position that the Western European governments should bring the international lists into line with the American lists, Eisenhower declared that Washington must begin 'to place itself in the minds of the British'. Viewed from the perspective of Britain and other Western European nations, the demand for East–West trade 'after years of struggle and privation' during the post-war years could be better understood by American policy makers. Eisenhower once again illuminated the implications for Anglo-American relations if the United States continued to force Britain to maintain a stringent embargo on trade with the Sino-Soviet bloc. To make his point he declared that the Churchill government might decide unilaterally 'to go it alone in their trade with the USSR'.[22] While he did not seriously believe that such a scenario would occur, given the importance of the 'special relationship' with Britain, he was anxious to build strong ties of cooperation with London in a Cold War alliance against Moscow. It should be noted, however, that although Eisenhower wanted to narrow the scope of the embargo, he was prepared vigorously to oppose efforts by the Churchill government to delete from the international lists industrial items he considered to be of military value to the Soviet Union.[23]

To what extent did Eisenhower seek to relax the controls on trade with the Soviet bloc? From the available evidence it is difficult to discern which items the president wanted to remove from the embargo. The NSC minutes imply that Eisenhower's main goal in East–West trade policy was substantially to reduce the number of exports under control. Despite opposition from the Commerce and Defense Departments, he favoured a comprehensive overhaul of the three international lists established by CoCom in 1950. Eisenhower recommended that these lists be shortened to 'the maximum possible extent'. Furthermore he insisted that the United States and its partners in CoCom should strive to 'pare' International List I 'down to its fundamentals'.[24] It is not clear from the NSC minutes which items Eisenhower had in mind for removal from the three lists, but he did indicate to senior officials that items that were readily available to the Soviet Union from non-Western sources should be deleted from the domestic and international lists immediately. Nonetheless he stated at the NSC meeting of 20 March 1954 that the embargo should reflect a 'net advantage to the free world'.[25] To Eisenhower's mind, the international export control programme should be restricted to items of strict military value to the Soviet Union and should not hinder the access of Western European nations to Eastern European markets. When directed by Congress, under the terms of the Battle Act, to suspend military assistance to Britain, Norway and West Germany, the president refused. In a letter to Senator Styles Bridges he wrote that terminating aid to these countries would jeopardise 'the unity and strength of the Western nations'. He informed Bridges that the objective of American export control policy was to prevent the Soviet Union from acquiring strategic materials for military production, and that this would 'serve the unity and security of the free nations'.[26]

Despite Eisenhower's many pronouncements in favour of revising the East–West trade embargo during 1953–54, the NSC was reluctant to support his viewpoint. There are several possible reasons why Eisenhower failed to take command of domestic and subsequently international export control policy. First, while he often spoke at length about expanding trade with Eastern Europe, he did not believe that economic defence policy was a top priority national security issue. At the NSC meeting of 18 March 1953 he revealed his true feelings about the issue. As far as he was concerned the United States had devoted too much attention to economic containment. He remarked to his colleagues in the NSC that it 'was little less than crazy to waste as much talent on this problem as was represented by the individuals in this room'.[27] It was for this reason that he did not use his considerable power of persuasion to gain the support of his key cabinet secretaries for a wholesale revision of trade with the Sino-Soviet bloc.

Second, the NSC minutes, while fragmentary, show that Eisenhower was ill at ease with the mechanics of embargo policy. He did not appear to grasp the fundamental issues that had led to discord between the United States and its allies in CoCom during the Truman years. Although he was aware that the Western Europeans were disgruntled by the export controls, he could not articulate to the NSC in a convincing manner why these nations were opposed to American demands for a broad embargo on East–West trade. His exasperation was evident at an NSC discussion on 1 July 1954, when he exclaimed 'that he might just as well sit back and listen to what the members of the Council had to say on the problems of East–West trade because as the members of the Council well knew, he thought they were wrong on the subject'.[28] This contradicts the assertion by some scholars, notably Robert Mark Spaulding and Philip Funigiello, that Eisenhower was the driving force behind the revision of the international lists by CoCom in August 1954.[29] In order to understand the shaping of international embargo policy, the perspectives of the other NSC members and the Churchill government must also be examined.

A house divided: Eisenhower and his critics

The Commerce and Defense Departments did not share Eisenhower's commitment to East–West trade liberalision. Even John Foster Dulles, the president's closest advisor on foreign policy, was sceptical about the changes proposed by Eisenhower in the field of economic containment policy. Secretary of Commerce Sinclair Weeks and Secretary of Defense Charles Wilson frequently clashed with Eisenhower over East–West trade at NSC meetings during 1953–54. Both Weeks and Wilson argued forcefully that the multilateral export control system created by CoCom should be maintained and even enlarged. Senior members of the military establishment such as the chairman of the Joint Chiefs of Staff, Admiral Arthur Radford, also held this view. In fact Eisenhower often found himself in the minority during NSC discussions on economic defence policy.

Wilson was consistently critical of Eisenhower's position. At the pre-inaugural cabinet meeting, when Eisenhower spoke of his plan to increase trade with the Soviet bloc and China, Wilson suggested that this would be analogous to 'selling firearms to the Indians'. The president-elect gently reproached his outspoken critic, but Wilson remained opposed to relaxation of the East–West trade embargo. In fact he held the view that economic containment was a valuable strategy for maintaining the superiority of Western military power over the Soviet Union.[30] During the NSC meeting of 11 March 1954 he claimed that export controls had placed 'heavy pressure' on the economies of the Soviet bloc countries.[31] He stressed that the United States should continue to ensure that the Western alliance applied a broad strategic embargo on military and industrial goods. This, he argued, would help to create a clear military advantage on the part of the non-communist world over the Soviet bloc. He asserted that increased diplomatic pressure should be brought to bear on the Western European governments to narrow the gap between the international and the American export control lists. Otherwise the Eisenhower administration might be perceived as 'a special enemy' of Moscow by virtue of the fact that American restrictions on East–West trade were more extensive than those of the Western European governments.[32]

Admiral Arthur Radford supported Wilson's contention that the administration should not pursue 'a radical revision' of the embargo. Radford considered that extensive relaxation of the export controls would not yield the high level of trade between the CoCom members and Eastern Europe predicted by the Churchill government. On the contrary, a reduction in restrictions on the exportation of industrial items with potential strategic value would allow Moscow to acquire raw materials and equipment for military production. Radford was convinced that Moscow would ignore civilian commodities and target strategic and dual-purpose goods from the West.[33]

Sinclair Weeks also opposed any reversal of the Truman administration's export control policy and appeared to embrace the conservative attitude towards East–West trade held by his predecessor, Charles Sawyer. In fact Weeks emerged as Eisenhower's most trenchant critic on trade with the communist nations. Under Weeks the Commerce Department remained antipathetic to any form of commercial contact with the Soviet bloc. Moreover it continued to criticise the Western European governments for preserving their trade in industrial exports to Eastern Europe. In many respects the trenchant opposition of the Commerce Department to East–West trade was due to the virulently anticommunist leanings of Sawyer and Weeks. Much like his predecessor, Weeks chided the Western European nations for imposing less restrictive controls than the United States. Not only was he perturbed that American manufacturers were losing business in Eastern Europe to their Western European counterparts, he also believed that the trading practices of the CoCom members were assisting the build-up of the Soviet and Chinese war potential. In criticism directed at Eisenhower he remarked that it was indefensible for the United States to tolerate the sale of strategic materials to the Soviet bloc in light of the Cold War. Paradoxically, he also stated that he was 'one hundred percent in favour of expanding international trade'.[34] Weeks' intractability on the question of export control policy contrasted sharply with the Eisenhower administration's commitment to a liberal world economy based on the principles of free trade.[35]

The Churchill government bore the brunt of Weeks' diatribe against trade contacts with the Soviet bloc. In a letter to John Foster Dulles, Weeks commented that the main motive for Britain's call for relaxation of the East–West trade embargo was enlightened self-interest. He charged London with seeking to dismantle the international export control system in an effort to obtain 'profitable orders for machines and equipment' from the Soviets. He warned the president against supporting the British initiative to reduce substantially the number of items under control by pointing out that this would be going 'too far too fast'. Furthermore the relaxation of the embargo demanded by London would have grave ramifications for national security.[36] Vice President Richard Nixon also urged caution. For Nixon the biggest problem would be the reaction of Congress to the British proposal. He recommended that Eisenhower remain resolute in the face of pressure from the Western Europeans. Failure to follow the provisions of the Battle Act, Nixon stated, would have 'most serious repercussions in Congress'.[37] The irrepressible Charles Wilson entered the debate on the side of Weeks and Nixon with the assertion that while he was a 'free trader too, to give in to the British right now would simply be another communist victory'.[38]

Surprisingly Dulles remained relatively silent on the issue of economic defence policy and tended to occupy the middle ground in NSC discussions on East–West trade. He did not appear to support Eisenhower's view that the embargo be radically revised. On the other hand he was generally receptive to Eisenhower's theory that trade could be employed as a strategy to loosen the Eastern European satellites from the grasp of Moscow. According to Dulles the president should veto the Churchill government's proposal to liberalise trade with the Soviet bloc because the United States would not be able to monitor shipments to the region and thus prevent military build-up in the Soviet Union.[39] Yet if limited trade was allowed between East and West, he argued, Washington could attempt to lure the satellite governments away from the Soviet bloc by impressing upon them 'the fact that they can get commodities from us that they cannot obtain from Russia'. It was Dulles' belief that trade could be used as a psychological weapon not only to detach the Eastern European satellites from the Soviet Union, but also to accelerate the growing split in the Sino-Soviet alliance.[40]

NSC 152/2

The Eisenhower administration's economic containment strategy was outlined in NSC policy document number NSC 152/2. This new statement of American export control policy was the product of NSC discussions on East–West trade in 1953. It represented a compromise between Eisenhower's commitment to the liberalisation of trade with the Soviet bloc and the more conservative stance adopted by Radford, Weeks and Wilson. But NSC 152/2 was also conditioned by three external developments.

First, the death of the Soviet leader, Joseph Stalin, in March 1953 offered hope for a period of peaceful coexistence between the Soviet Union and the West. As the new Soviet leadership was showing signs that it might pursue a policy of détente towards the United States, the NSC was willing partially to open trading links with Moscow. Second, Eisenhower successfully negotiated the armistice that ended the Korean War in July. With relative peace in Southeast Asia and abatement of the Cold War tensions, Washington signalled its intention to rethink export control policy towards the Sino-Soviet alliance. The decision to review the East–West trade embargo was part of a general reconsideration of American national security policy.[41] Given that the imminent threat of war that had characterised the early years of the Cold War had subsided, policy planners decided to reorganise national security strategy for the 'long haul'.[42] Finally, the Eisenhower government was particularly worried by the poor state of relations between the United States and the Western European governments in CoCom.

The new administration acknowledged that it would have to listen more carefully to the grievances of its allies on the subject of East–West trade if it wished to avoid the breakdown in cooperation that had plagued effective policy making during the Truman era.[43]

NSC 152/2 attempted to address each of these issues. While the new policy document concluded that the fundamental concepts underpinning the previous administration's export control strategy needed to be revised in light of the relaxation of Cold War tensions, it was generally cautious in tone. It recommended that the United States institute a 'gradual and moderate relaxation' of the international embargo. Although it recognised that the death of Stalin and the armistice in Korea had significantly altered the global strategic climate, it warned against changing the structure of the multilateral export control system. The reason for this reticence was explained in paragraph two of the document: 'we are faced with a long period of tension short of war and ... regardless of gestures made by the Soviet bloc, the motives of the Communist countries are properly to be viewed with suspicion and scepticism'. As far as NSC 152/2 was concerned, a major revision of the restrictions on exports to the Soviet bloc was not a viable option despite peaceful overtures by the Kremlin. Rather the Eisenhower administration should remain wary of the intentions of the Soviet Union. In effect NSC 152/2 ordered that only items deemed not to pose a threat to national security if shipped to the Soviet bloc should be released from the embargo. Although the document favoured a multilateral review of the three international lists, it concluded that each list should remain in its present form. Clearly, the document was at odds with Eisenhower's view that the East–West trade embargo should be 'pared down to its fundamentals'.

Another important issue that NSC 152/2 addressed at length was the state of US–Western European relations in CoCom. In a telling statement the document acknowledged that:

> our economic defence programme must be framed and administered with full recognition of the fact that the economic defence system of the free world is part of the larger system of military and political alliances and, like them, depends upon the co-operative efforts of the free nations.

Following the president's thinking, NSC 152/2 was anxious to avoid the conflict and confrontation that had threatened to undermine decision making in CoCom in 1950–52. Nor did the Eisenhower administration want to neglect the economic recovery concerns of the Western European governments. Instead of insisting that these countries increase their restrictions on sales to the Soviet bloc, NSC 152/2 pressed American diplomats to take account of the 'views and intention' of the other CoCom members in multilateral negotiations.

At the same time the Eisenhower administration's 'new look' economic defence strategy aimed to reduce the dependence of the OEEC countries on East–West trade. NSC 152/2 concluded that if the Western Europeans could find alternative sources of raw materials and foodstuffs, the Soviet Union would not be able to obtain strategic goods through trade agreements with the West. Even though the Cold War tensions had relaxed, American policy makers were worried that the Soviet Union would continue to stockpile military hardware for a future conflict with the Western alliance. It was therefore essential for the United States actively to encourage its allies to develop new trading links with non-communist countries. NSC 152/2 did not elaborate on how the Eisenhower administration might be able to coax the Western European governments away from the Eastern European markets without avoiding full-scale conflict between the allies.[44] All in all NSC 152/2 was an extremely vague policy statement. While it stressed the necessity of improving relations in CoCom, its policy recommendations did not offer any concrete solutions to the problem of establishing effective cooperation in East–West trade. Nor did it reflect the views of the senior members of the NSC. It certainly did not heed Eisenhower's call for a radical overhaul of the embargo, nor did it provide a ringing endorsement of Weeks' and Wilson's view that export controls should continue to be used as a weapon against the Soviet Union in the Cold War.

The British perspective

In March 1953 Anthony Eden raised the question of East–West trade during a meeting with Dulles in Washington. He assured Dulles that Britain was committed to restricting exports of strategic goods to the Soviet Union and China. He also emphasised that the Churchill government was anxious to leave 'the way clear for trade in all other materials'. Moreover he informed Dulles that while London would work closely with Washington to improve the present multilateral export control system, Britain would refuse to consider placing any more items under embargo.[45] It was evident from this meeting that Britain and the United States had divergent perceptions of trade policy towards the Soviet bloc. Clearly the former envisaged a much narrower strategic export control programme than the latter. As we shall see, the conclusions reached in a British ministerial review of East–West trade in autumn 1953 contrasted starkly with the recommendations of NSC 152/2.

At the official level, diplomats in the Foreign Office were worried about the direction of American export control policy. Ronald Arculus was most disgruntled about the American attitude towards CoCom. He described the *Third Battle Act Report to Congress* as 'a rather childish document which tries to make sport out of hunting strategic consignments'. In a scathing critique of the document's analysis of East–West trade, he remarked that 'in the present political circumstances it is not opportune to dress the controls (which are defence measures) in a hostile guise as if they were a punitive weapon'.[46] This view was held not only by officials at the Foreign Office and the British delegation to CoCom, but also by senior ministers as they began to review international trade policy in August.[47]

Prime Minister Churchill's interest in East–West trade ensured that the matter would be given serious attention at the cabinet level. Having devoted the latter years of his illustrious career as an international statesman to achieving détente with the Soviet Union, Churchill believed that increased trade between the West and the Soviet bloc would bring about a thaw in the Cold War. Ironically, the ageing prime minister had been a conspicuous critic of the Attlee government's decision to ship machine tools to the Soviet Union at the height of the Korean War. In his many years of public service, this was not the first time he had changed his stance. As already noted, Churchill had been anxious to improve relations between the Western alliance and Moscow since becoming prime minister for the second time in October 1951. His personal involvement in economic relations between Britain and the Soviet Union had elevated the public profile of East–West trade internationally,[48] but his determination to remove the barriers to trade with Eastern Europe culminated in a clash between London and Washington over the revision of the international lists in the spring and summer of 1954.

Stalin's death and the general relaxation of tensions between the West and the Soviet bloc paved the way a review of East–West trade practices by British ministers in the autumn of 1953. The Economic Steering Committee (ESC), a cabinet subcommittee, was charged with conducting an inquiry into domestic and international export control procedures. Attended by senior ministers with responsibility for economic matters, the ESC concluded that the embargo, in its present form, was largely ineffectual. The committee found that the Soviet Union had successfully circumvented the embargo by acquiring certain strategic materials from alternative sources. As some items under control since 1950 were now being readily procured from non-CoCom countries, the committee recommended that these commodities be decontrolled, given that the 'economic, political and strategic considerations' had changed. In marked contrast to the proposals in NSC 152/2, the ESC suggested that since any modern conflict would be fought with nuclear weapons rather than by conventional warfare, many of the items restricted by CoCom would not contribute to Soviet military build-up. What was required, the ESC argued, was an international, 'item by item' review of international export controls to prepare for a future nuclear conflict with Moscow. While the ESC did not advocate 'sweeping changes' to the 'system of security export controls on trade with the Soviet bloc at this juncture', it called for a full cabinet discussion on the scope of relaxing the present controls.[49]

Having secured cabinet approval to undertake a comprehensive review of export control policy, the ESC met on 2 September for further discussion on steps that could be taken to revise the East–West trade embargo. The ESC's most significant finding was that International List I was too long in light of the current economic and strategic situation. Arguing that the list contained many items that were no longer of strategic value to the Soviet Union, it concluded that 'it may be quicker to eliminate doubtful items' from the embargo than to 'construct a new list from scratch'. The ESC highlighted two main advantages of shortening the export control list. First, items of no beneficial strategic value to the Soviet Union could be released from the embargo for the purposes of normal trade. Second, CoCom could more effectively manage and enforce a shortened list composed of key military goods. This 'would not produce a perfect list but may produce a more sensible one' that Britain could divulge to the United States 'at an appropriate time'.[50] The president of the Board of Trade, Peter Thorneycroft, emerged as a keen exponent of this proposal and believed that it would benefit Britain's international trading position. A consistent critic of export controls, Thorneycroft declared that the 'exigencies of the Cold War have prevented the UK from taking ... trading opportunities'.[51] In his eyes there were two options available to the Churchill government: it could limit export controls to commodities of military potential; or it could continue to support the costly long-term strategy of economic warfare against the Soviet Union. As far as the Board of Trade was concerned, the former option best suited Britain's economic and strategic interests.[52]

Conclusion

By the winter of 1953 both the United States and Britain had reached the conclusion that the East–West trade embargo needed to be reformed. In Washington the Eisenhower administration was divided over security export control policy. On the one hand the president was in favour of a major revision of the domestic and international export control lists. Anxious to improve multilateral cooperation over trade policy in CoCom, Eisenhower insisted that opening trade contacts with Eastern Europe would strengthen the Western alliance *vis-à-vis* the Soviet Union. On the other hand Charles Wilson and Sinclair Weeks advocated caution. From their perspective, any expansion of trade with the Soviet bloc would allow the Kremlin access to key strategic materials at great expense to Western security. Wilson and Weeks recommended that the NSC continue the Truman administration's policy of maintaining comprehensive restrictions on strategic and industrial exports to the Soviet bloc. The Eisenhower administration's policy blueprint on economic defence policy, NSC 152/2, incorporated both of these contrasting viewpoints. It recognised the necessity of a 'gradual and moderate relaxation' of the embargo, but recommended that the United States retain its present export control system. Despite peaceful overtures by the new Soviet leadership, the NSC remained suspicious of the Kremlin's foreign policy motives and tactics.

Across the Atlantic the Churchill government had also initiated a review of export control policy. The British inquiry, which had been undertaken independently of the United States, yielded rather different findings. Much like its American counterpart, the British review concluded that the export control system developed by CoCom in 1950–52 required urgent reform, but it went much further and recommended a complete overhaul of the East–West trade embargo, given the reduction in Cold War tensions since the death of Stalin. Churchill was the driving force behind the British review. He sensed that trade could be used to improve relations between the Western alliance and the Soviet bloc. A report by the ESC in September 1953 stated that Britain would benefit from an expansion of trade with Eastern Europe if a substantial number of items under multilateral control were relaxed. It therefore proposed that the three international lists be reduced to one short list, composed of military goods of strategic value to the Soviet Union. As London and Washington prepared for a series of bilateral discussions on East–West trade in December 1953, a clash between the two powers over export controls was inevitable. While the United States wished to preserve the embargo in its present form, Britain wanted a wholesale renovation of the multilateral export control system.

8
Economic Containment for the 'Long Haul', 1953–61

By 1953, both American and British policy makers realised that the export control programme instituted against the Soviet bloc in January 1950 had become obsolete, but they differed over the shape and content of the embargo to be applied to East–West trade during the period of the 'long haul'. Both governments thought it unlikely that war would break out between the Western alliance and the Soviet Union in the near future, yet they had divergent approaches to economic defence policy in the 1950s.

The United States argued that the revised export control programme should continue to include a wide range of industrial and dual-purpose exports. The Eisenhower administration was therefore of the opinion that the embargo should merely be updated: in effect, items that had been restricted in 1950 but were now readily available to the Soviet Union should be decontrolled. Britain, however, wanted a substantial relaxation of controlled exports on the three international lists; it also wanted to abolish the 'China differential', which allowed for more restrictive trade with the People's Republic of China (PRC). British ministers argued that the Soviet economy was extremely sophisticated in technological terms, thus little would be gained by preserving an embargo on industrial and dual-purpose commodities. The Conservative governments of the 1950s were also under domestic pressure to relax the restrictions on trade with Eastern Europe and the PRC for commercial reasons.

This chapter examines the continuing Anglo-American conflict over East–West trade, focusing on the August 1954 international list revisions, the Geneva Conference of 1955, the controversy over the abolition of the 'China differential' in 1956–57 and the continued effort by the Macmillan government to obtain a further liberalisation of the embargo in 1956–60.

Anglo-American negotiations, October 1953 to January 1954

Following the NSC review of economic defence policy, on 6 October 1953 the American State Department sent an *aide mémoire* to the British government outlining its proposals for a relaxation of the East–West trade embargo. The *aide mémoire* stated that some of the controlled exports 'should, perhaps be relaxed if new information indicates particular items to be of less importance than previously thought'. In a radical departure from previous export control policy, the Eisenhower administration acknowledged that excessive restrictions on trade with the Soviet bloc had contributed to local unemployment and economic difficulties in Western Europe. These two issues were to form the basis of the discussions between the United States and Britain on revising the embargo for the 'long haul'. The *aide mémoire* recognised that the immediate threat of conflict with the Soviet Union had subsided and that a revision of the multilateral export control programme was urgently required.[1] On 11 September the State Department had revealed the change in policy to all American embassies and consulates through a secret policy directive. The directive, which mirrored the *aide mémoire* sent to Britain, advocated 'increased emphasis on the multilateral approach to security trade control problems, with more account to be taken of economic and political impacts and conditions in participating countries'.[2]

The British reaction to the *aide mémoire* was for the most part positive. Ambassador Roger Makins in Washington informed the Foreign Office that the American government now seemed to view East–West trade 'in a much broader and more sympathetic manner than previously'.[3] Yet while applauding the willingness of the Eisenhower administration to contemplate a revision of the embargo, British diplomats believed that the American proposals were not substantial enough. At a meeting between representatives of the British embassy in Washington and the State Department, diverging attitudes towards the relaxation of export controls began to surface. The American delegation held that any revision of East–West trade controls was subject to strategic considerations, while the British delegation was disappointed by the extent of the relaxation proposed by the United States.[4] In the opinion of one official at the Foreign Office, the Eisenhower administration's proposal had 'not much to offer'. At best, he concluded, the United States was 'looking to trim the Battle Act' without significantly altering the international export control system. Nevertheless the general consensus amongst policy makers in London was that the Churchill government should attempt to 'exploit' this 'noteworthy and welcome development'.[5]

In preparation for the bilateral talks in London with the United States, scheduled for November, Whitehall officials carefully analysed the implications of the American proposal. Although the *aide mémoire* suggested that the United States would be prepared to support a partial relaxation of trade controls, it was unclear to British policy makers what this revision would entail. The Churchill government hoped that Washington would sanction a substantial relaxation of items on each of the three international lists, but there was little optimism amongst officials at the Foreign Office, the Board of Trade and the Ministry of Defence that the United States would agree to a substantial shortening of these lists. Nevertheless they regarded the American initiative as an important step forward.[6]

British and American officials duly met in London in November for the planned talks. The purpose of the meetings was to establish a common position on export control policy prior to the consultative group discussions in January 1954. While both governments agreed that the embargo should be revised in accordance with the new strategic situation, they differed on the scope and pace of the relaxation of controls on trade with the Soviet bloc. During the prebilateral talks of 3–6 November it became apparent that the United States and Britain would have difficulty reaching an agreement on the extent of the new embargo.[7]

Closely observing the recommendations of NSC 152/2, the American delegation warned that any radical attempt to overhaul the present export control system would be unwise, given the 'serious risk of war' with the Soviet Union. From the perspective of the Eisenhower administration, restrictions on strategic commodities to Eastern Europe should be 'designed to create a clear advantage to the West'. The American delegation also cautioned against removing the embargo as it was an 'integral part of the total mutual security effort of the free world'. Rather than attempting to open trading links with Eastern Europe, the Churchill government would be better advised to break Britain's economic dependency on the Soviet bloc. If Britain and Western Europe relied too heavily on the Soviet bloc for imports and exports, the Soviet Union might seek, through psychological warfare, 'to influence the political policies or disrupt the economies of the free world'. In their concluding statement the delegates revealed the Eisenhower administration's official position on the revision of the embargo. The United States did not 'envisage ... a wholesale downgrading' of the international export control programme at the present time, but Washington gave its assurance that it would not press the Western European governments to 'bring the international listings to the level of the current US lists'.

Reluctant to give positive and immediate support to the American proposal, the British delegates chose not to respond directly to this statement. Instead they summarised the position of the Churchill government on East–West trade: in effect they spoke of the desirability of relaxing a large number of controlled items. They argued that the present export control system had been devised at the height of the Cold War when military confrontation with the Soviet Union was likely. Now that the Soviet 'threat' had subsided with the death of Stalin a much narrower and compact embargo was required for economic containment over the long haul. They stated bluntly that the current export control programme was 'too cumbersome for the period which both the United States and Britain consider will be "tension short of war" for an indefinite time'. A 'substantially curtailed list' of key military items strictly enforced by the CoCom members, they pointed out, would be more effective for a period of tension that fell short of war. Moreover the new list would allow for a 'real expansion of trade' between East and West that would benefit not only the European economies but also mutual security in the long run. According to Britain, Moscow was not solely interested in acquiring strategic materials through East–West trade, rather the Soviet leadership believed that increased trade with the capitalist nations in the West could strengthen the internal and political system of the Soviet Union.[8]

The prebilateral talks demonstrated the wide gap that existed between Britain and the United States on the future direction of international embargo policy. While the situation was not ominous, it would take many months to produce a compromise satisfactory to both governments. The two delegations had reached some agreement, however, on the need to tighten the existing control framework and encourage other participating governments to cooperate 'more actively' in the process.[9] Yet the Churchill cabinet was concerned by the reticence shown by the American representatives towards the liberalisation of trade with Eastern Europe. It had become apparent that the Eisenhower administration would proceed in a very cautious and tactful manner towards the relaxation of certain items under embargo. Even when the United States gave its consent to an international revision of export controls on East–West trade, Whitehall believed that there would still be a wide gap between the positions of the two governments: Washington would propose incremental changes to the international lists based on strategic considerations, while London would favour a much narrow embargo based on a single list of key military items.[10] Amidst this initial discord the two delegations met for further discussions on 21–22 November. The British delegation presented a detailed statement reflecting ministerial thinking on the relaxation of East–West trade controls. First, a more narrowly focused embargo would be more effective in the long term, and would also allow the Western European nations to benefit from increased trade with the Soviet bloc in exports of 'near military value'. Second, there had been instances where the Soviet Union had been able to acquire strategic items contained on the international export controls lists from alternative sources, so it was futile to continue to prohibit trade in items readily available from non-CoCom countries. Finally, the delegation unveiled the Churchill government's 'short list' proposal. Without revealing the contents of the list, the delegation described the merits of a single embargo list containing only items that would contribute significantly to Soviet military production. The list would comprise atomic and other war equipment, tankers, merchant ships, selected electronic items and assorted metals. According to the British statement, this list would be binding on all CoCom members, providing an effective means of economic containment over a long period.[11]

The American representatives were disturbed by the British delegation's statement and were most critical of the 'short list' proposal. Voicing their disapproval at the extent to which the Churchill government wanted to revise the embargo, they stressed the importance of mutual security considerations. In particular they thought that the 'eradication' of International List II and 'the greater part of List I' would provide the Soviet Union with unhindered access to strategic materials from the West. Nor did they believe that an extensive revision of the embargo would yield the volume of trade envisaged by Britain. Estimates prepared by the NSC predicted that an expansion of East–West trade would not benefit the Western European nations to a sizeable degree since the Soviet Union would confine its imports to military materials and goods of strategic potential. Recapitulating the recommendations in NSC 152/2, the American delegation concluded that the economic 'needs of the free world should not be met at the expense of free world security'. In an effort to avert a breakdown in the negotiations, they urged the Churchill government to shelve its plans to dismantle the multilateral export control system and agree to the 'moderate approach' proffered by the United States.[12]

In response to the grim outcome of the November meetings, Ambassador Winthrop Aldrich of the American embassy in London wrote to the Foreign Office to express the Eisenhower government's anxiety about the short list proposal. Aldrich commented that Washington was 'greatly concerned at the possible course of action suggested by the United Kingdom and feels that so drastic a revision of the scope of the control system is not justified under present circumstances'. He stated that American policy dictated that 'certain capital goods and raw materials, whether or not currently used for the production of war materials, constitute a reservoir of productive capacity which could be readily mobilised for war production'. He did not suggest a possible compromise position between the American and British approaches. In fact he may well have made matters worse by imploring Whitehall 'to modify its earlier views' so that agreement could be reached before the multilateral discussions took place in CoCom. This highlighted once again the Anglo-American difficulty of mutually defining dual-purpose items and exports of indirect military value. The British definition of strategic trade was clear-cut: items of military value such as atomic weapons, armaments, merchant ships and certain chemicals that could contribute *directly* to the Soviet war-making capacity. By contrast the American definition of strategic trade was much broader: almost any item used in military production was construed by the United States as strategically valuable to the Soviet Union.[13]

In Washington, however, senior officials did not dismiss the short list proposal as incompatible with American economic defence objectives. Harold Stassen, the mutual security director, recommended that the United States consider the complete relaxation of all commodities on the international lists with the exception of 'direct military and highly strategic mandatory items of the Battle Act'.[14] The secretary of state, John Foster Dulles, also thought that the British proposal merited careful attention. In a letter to Stassen, Dulles wrote that:

> the fact that the British recently proposed a drastic curtailment of East–West trade controls and that we might be met with similar proposals in the future, do argue for the utility of our quietly exploring the economic and security impacts of implementing this sort of policy reversal.[15]

Despite the musings of Stassen and Dulles, however, negotiations between the United States and Britain on the future direction of embargo policy remained deadlocked at the end of 1953. It would take the personal intervention of Winston Churchill in early 1954 to provide the impetus necessary for a common agreement.

Churchill takes command: January–March 1954

The cabinet approved the short list proposal on 17 November 1953, prior to the second round of bilateral talks between Britain and the United States in London.[16] But no agreement was reached on the contents of the new embargo: the Foreign Office and the Ministry of Defence preferred modest revisions within the framework of the present multilateral export system, while the prime minister and the Board of Trade wanted to prune the international lists down to items of direct military significance. Anthony Eden, in particular, was worried about the reaction of the Eisenhower administration to the British proposal. His protestations against submitting the short list to the United States fell on deaf ears. Churchill, supported by Peter Thorneycroft, argued that the short list proposal would act as a yardstick in the negotiations with the Americans. He did not believe that Eisenhower and Dulles would accept a drastically reduced embargo on East–West trade, but that the short list would at least enable Britain to secure some concessions.[17]

After the failure of the November bilateral talks to achieve any meaningful progress, at a cabinet meeting on 18 January 1954 Churchill ordered ministers to construct a single list containing the strategic and military items of most value to the Soviet Union. An interministerial group of senior officials was established for the purpose of compiling the list. Churchill personally formed an ad hoc cabinet committee to monitor the progress of the interministerial group; the prime minister's committee would review items in dispute.[18] The ad hoc committee met on 25 January to report on the work of the interministerial group and discuss the contents of the new short list, which would comprise fewer than 100 items selected from the three international export control lists. The new list clearly reflected the views of Churchill and Thorneycroft rather than those of Eden and the Ministry of Defence. Objections to the list were raised by Lords Reading and Alexander, representing the Foreign Office and the Ministry of Defence respectively, who both felt that the United States would reject the short list outright. They pointed out that the proposal would create a rift between London and Washington in respect of East–West trade. Churchill, however, was unmoved by their arguments. He stressed that if Britain wished to obtain substantial revisions to the international lists it had to press for a wide-ranging reform of the scope and content of the embargo.[19] Approximately 29 items were reappended to the list to assuage the concerns of the Foreign Office and Ministry of Defence after a subsequent meeting of the ad hoc committee in early February. But when the full cabinet convened on 17 February it approved the short list, which was composed of 135 items, signalling a victory for Churchill.[20] In future talks British diplomats would present the short list as a bargaining lever to force the Eisenhower administration to support a substantial relaxation of East–West trade controls.

On 26 February in a widely publicised speech to the House of Commons, Churchill divulged the cabinet's commitment to the liberalisation of trade with the Soviet bloc. Presenting East–West trade within the context of his grand scheme for an 'easement' of tensions with the Kremlin, he declared that 'The more trade that is through the iron curtain – and between Great Britain and Russia and its satellites – the better will be the chance of our living together in increasing comfort.'[21] Not only did Churchill believe that increased trade with the Soviet bloc would be beneficial to the British economy, he also thought that commercial contact might enable the West to 'infiltrate' the iron curtain and loosen Moscow's grip on the Eastern European satellites. As Robert Spaulding has written, Churchill's speech marked a turning point in the history of the East–West trade embargo for three reasons. First, it made world public opinion aware of the prime minister's determination to liberalise trade with the Soviet bloc and improve relations between the Western alliance and the Kremlin. Second, the speech, which was directed at American political leaders as well as the British public, confirmed the Churchill government's intention to press the CoCom membership to relax the East–West trade controls. Finally, 'Churchill signalled other countries that a major policy change was in the offing'.[22] In short the speech would profoundly influence the direction of international embargo policy in CoCom for nearly four decades.

In the short term the speech forced the hand of the Eisenhower administration both domestically and internationally. The administration would have to deal with pressure not only from the European members of CoCom to initiate a change in policy direction, but also from a staunchly anticommunist Congress. Some diplomats stationed in Western Europe began to call for affirmative action from the State Department with respect to the British short list proposal. Winthrop Brown of the American embassy in London implored Dulles to consider the implications of the short list on relations between the United States and its allies in CoCom. He recommended that 'the US should be ready to take concrete steps towards narrowing the present lists in order to provide the basis for subsequent negotiation with the British prior to international consideration of the problem'. If an agreement with the Churchill government could not be reached on the terms and procedure for revising the embargo, Brown noted dryly, the United States would be 'wholly isolated in any CoCom discussions of proposals for a reduced programme of controls'.[23] Ambassador Aldrich confirmed the pessimistic mood that pervaded the embassy. In a telegram to Dulles he remarked that the United States would find itself in an 'awkward position' in CoCom as the other members of CoCom were sure to support the British initiative.[24]

Several days after Churchill's landmark speech the British government sent a memorandum to the American embassy in London detailing the short list proposal. The memorandum reviewed the international strategic situation since the death of Stalin, and contended that new developments had rendered obsolete the export control system established in 1950–51. Given the changed circumstances and the absence of an imminent military threat from the Soviet Union, the Churchill government proposed a new embargo for a long period of tension with Moscow short of war. The new embargo list would consist only of the most potent military and strategic items. All other items currently under control would be released for normal trade with Eastern Europe if the proposal were adopted. By way of explanation for this policy reversal, the memorandum alluded to the potential danger of maintaining the current embargo over the 'long haul'. It suggested that if the present international lists remained intact, Western Europe would continue to suffer economic hardship due to lack of access to imports from traditional sources and markets for capital goods. Furthermore the British government could not see the logic of persisting with an embargo on items that were readily available to the Soviet Union from other sources. Thus the memorandum called on the Eisenhower administration to reconsider the policy of restricting exports of secondary and indirect strategic significance.[25]

American diplomats were against the 'short list' proposal for two reasons. First, the British list fundamentally altered the complexion of International List I. It was approximately half the length of the embargo list and was largely restricted to items of direct military importance such as materials related to atomic energy and military production, omitting dual-purpose exports and items of indirect strategic value to Soviet war production.[26] Second, it threatened to alienate the United States in CoCom. The French and Italian governments had responded swiftly to

Churchill's historic speech by calling for a multilateral meeting in CoCom to discuss the British proposal. In a diplomatic move designed to gain the support of the French government for the liberalisation of East–West trade, the Foreign Office instructed that the contents of the short list be relayed to the Quai d'Orsay. With French support the Foreign Office hoped to improve Britain's bargaining position *vis-à-vis* Washington.[27]

Alarmed by these developments the State Department sought a bilateral meeting with British officials to discuss the short list proposal. According to Walter Bedell Smith, the United States had to move rapidly if it was 'to change in any marked degree the British views on this subject'. As far as Smith was concerned, Churchill's personal intervention in British export control policy created problems for the United States. It would be difficult to force Britain to shelve the short list with the spectre of the prime minister looming over proceedings. Disturbed by Britain's insistence that International List II, which was composed of items under quantitative control, be abolished entirely, Smith appealed for bilateral discussions with Britain before the CoCom meeting on 9 March.[28]

The available evidence suggests that no such bilateral talks took place, and even if they did they failed to produce a compromise between the two governments. On 9 March the Anglo-American differences over the future of the East–West trade embargo were revealed to the CoCom members. The meeting consisted of an exchange of statements by Britain and the United States on their proposed changes to the export control system in light of the recent changes in the international strategic climate. Without divulging the contents of the short list, the British delegation spoke of Whitehall's commitment to substantial changes to the international export control lists. They remarked that the abatement of the Soviet military threat necessitated a new form of economic containment. In short, what was required was a much narrower embargo that could be enforced effectively over the 'long haul'. The American delegation concurred with the British analysis of the strategic situation, but suggested that a comprehensive export control system composed of exports of strategic and dual-purpose value should be maintained, given that the threat of war with the Soviet Union had not disappeared. Not surprisingly, all the other Western European members sided with Britain, confirming the worst fears of the State Department. The members resolved to explore the implications of both the American and the British statements at a future meeting of CoCom.[29] Left with no alternative but to bargain with London, the White House would have to try to moderate the British stance on export controls.

Eisenhower's response: March–April 1954

Western European demands for the liberalisation of trade with the Soviet bloc produced a crisis in American government circles. Efforts by the State Department and the British and French ambassadors to modify the Churchill government's short list proposal had proved ineffectual. Conscious that the international export control system was on the verge of being disassembled by Britain, the NSC Planning Board prepared a memorandum listing possible policy actions that could be taken by the president and his senior advisors.

In essence, the main recommendation of the Planning Board was that the Eisenhower administration should 'seek such substantial modification of the British proposal as would permit its acceptance within the terms of US economic defence policy'. If the British proposals to reduce International List I and abolish List II were adopted by CoCom, many items that could contribute to the Soviet war potential would be left uncontrolled. In conclusion, the memorandum proposed that a modification of the short list proposal would 'avoid a major and open clash with our leading ally in the Consultative Group'. To avert a breakdown in Anglo-American cooperation on East–West trade, a written communication from the president to Prime Minister Churchill might help to get Britain and France to the negotiating table to hammer out a compromise. According to the NSC the communiqué should be couched in terms upholding the virtues of close cooperation between the two countries and appeal to Churchill for flexibility towards the security priorities of the Western alliance. It should also argue the merits of quantitative controls on dual-purpose exports that in the opinion of the NSC would contribute considerably to Soviet military production.[30]

Any assessment of the East–West trade embargo revision must begin with the Eisenhower–Churchill correspondence of March 1954. The exchange of letters between the two leaders was notable for three reasons. First, since the inception of economic containment in 1948 it was the only occasion when a president and a prime minister intervened directly in CoCom negotiations. During the brief history of the embargo, export control policy had always been the preserve of ministers and civil servants. Second, the correspondence highlighted the degree of difference between the two governments on the liberalisation of trade with the Soviet bloc. Although both Eisenhower and Churchill wanted to revise the three international lists for the 'long haul', the prime minister envisaged a much more substantial relaxation of trade controls than did the president. Unlike Churchill, Eisenhower believed that industrial exports should be kept under embargo, as such items were potentially valuable to the Soviet military machine. Finally, the direct intervention of the two leaders in the proceedings provided the necessary impetus to drive forward the negotiations on revision of the international export control lists. In the early months of 1954 little progress had been achieved between American and British policy makers at the official or ministerial levels. The personal interest taken by Eisenhower and Churchill in East–West trade pressed home the need for an Anglo-American agreement on export control policy.

On the advice of the NSC, Eisenhower wrote to Churchill on 19 March to discuss the growing impasse on East–West trade. In a short letter the president delineated the policy of the American government on security export controls. He stated that the United States was pre-pared to 'go a significant distance' towards the 'contraction and simplification' of the embargo on exports to the Soviet bloc. The presi-dent warned, however, that Washington would not support the British short list proposal in CoCom. He reasoned that 'to do so would be ... to go beyond what is immediately safe or in the common interest of the Free World'. He continued by underscoring the domestic pressure his administration faced from Congress through the Battle Act legislation. If the United States were to support the British proposal, the Eisenhower administration would be subject to harsh criticism from a virulently anticommunist Congress. Yet he hoped that 'pressures in either of our countries' would not adversely affect Anglo-American relations, 'politi-cal, economic, and military – as well as the strength of the NATO coali-tion'. Eisenhower pointed to what he perceived as the two issues that threatened to undermine cooperation between Washington and London in respect of embargo policy: the desire by the United States to retain the controls on certain industrial exports and the preservation of International Lists II and III. The president added optimistically that he was adamant that the Anglo-American differences could be overcome during trilateral talks with France, so that 'we can continue jointly to provide constructive leadership' in CoCom.[31]

Churchill's reply reflected the views he had expressed on East–West trade during his provocative House of Commons speech on 26 February. He reiterated his belief that trade should be increased with the Soviet bloc and explained the logic behind his commitment to the relaxation of export controls. The former Cold Warrior placed East–West trade in the context of his preoccupation with promoting 'an easement of relations with Soviet Russia'. For Churchill, expansion of commercial contact with Moscow would offer the Western alliance a means of 'achieving friendly infiltration which ... would be to our advantage from every point of view including military'. From his perspective, liberalising trade with Eastern Europe would not lead to the wholesale exportation of weapons and military equipment to the region. Given the prevailing international economic circumstances, restrictions on dual-purpose exports – items of indirect strategic value – should be removed to enable Western European countries to benefit from the untapped markets of the Soviet bloc. Churchill appealed to Eisenhower to appreciate the importance of East–West trade to the British economy. Now that Germany and Japan had become major commercial competitors, Britain was obliged to expand trade 'in every possible direction' if Britain was to feed a population of 50 million and serve as a key ally of the United States in the Western alliance.[32]

Despite their pronounced differences over the direction and scope of the international export control revisions, Eisenhower and Churchill realised that a compromise on East–West trade was necessary for close cooperation between their two nations in CoCom. Disharmony over embargo policy would not only hinder effective leadership in CoCom, but might also strain Anglo-American relations in a wide range of other international issues. Thus both leaders declared their support for a series of trilateral ministerial meetings between Britain, the United States and France, to be held at the end of March. The object of the discussions was to reach a common ground in advance of the multilateral talks in CoCom.

The August 1954 international export control revisions

The trilateral meetings duly took place during 29–30 March. In attendance were Thorneycroft, the American mutual security director, Harold Stassen, and Maurice Schuman of the French Foreign Ministry. Thorneycroft, who shared Churchill's views on East–West trade, presented a brief overview of British thinking on international export control policy. The new strategic circumstances since the death of Stalin in 1953, Thorneycroft argued, allowed a more limited trade embargo composed exclusively of items of direct military importance to Moscow. He stated that the embargo would consist mainly of items on International List I, and he was confident that a single export control list would be 'effective' and 'enforceable' over the 'long haul'. Thorneycroft pointed out that the release of exports from the present embargo would be beneficial to the trading interests of Britain and Western Europe, but that Whitehall's decision to recommend that CoCom release certain items from the international lists was based on strategic considerations and not the 'commercial advantages' that Britain might gain from the liberalisation of East–West trade.

Stassen did not respond directly to Thorneycroft's statement. Presumably he had been instructed by Eisenhower and the NSC to obtain a compromise with Britain, and he suggested that the three governments recommend to the other CoCom members a 'category by category' review of the multilateral export control programme. Once a general consensus had been reached that certain items were no longer of military value to the Soviet bloc, these goods would be immediately released from the embargo. This proposal was greeted warmly by both Thorneycroft and Schuman. Thorneycroft replied that the Churchill government would support such an approach on the understanding that the review process would allow a 'substantial relaxation' of items on the international lists. He then sought Stassen's assurances that if the review did not result in what London viewed as satisfactory deletions from the embargo, Britain would have the right to table the short list in CoCom.[33]

Despite this tentative progress the issue of quantitative controls remained unresolved. Whereas Thorneycroft pushed for the elimination of quantitative controls from the embargo, Stassen pressed for the retention of quotas on industrial exports to Eastern Europe.[34] When the final communiqué was released by the participants no mention was made of Anglo-American differences over quantitative controls. It reported that a large measure of progress had been made on the future direction of policy on East–West trade and all three governments supported a general, category by category review of the three international lists, to be conducted by CoCom. There were no specific details on the extent to which the embargo was to be revised, shrouding key points of departure between the American and British standpoints.[35]

Without exception the members of CoCom agreed that a category by category review of the international export control list should be undertaken.[36] The review process commenced in early April and took almost three months to complete. The items under review were divided into three categories – exports of nuclear and military significance, technologically advanced exports and exports of materials in critically short supply in the Soviet bloc – and were analysed in working groups comprising representatives of each nation. The three largest CoCom governments – Britain, France and the United States – also conducted a preliminary review in trilateral working groups to establish a common position. It was hoped that they could overcome any major differences over contentious items prior to the convocation of the CoCom working groups on each category.[37]

During the eight-week review Britain and the United States constantly clashed over quantitative controls on dual-purpose items. Most notably, on the question of power equipment the British representatives contested the American insistence that these items, which were in critically short supply in the Soviet bloc region, should remain under embargo.[38] There was also controversy over the refusal by the American representatives immediately to release items from the export control lists upon the completion of each category review; British officials claimed that Stassen had agreed to a so-called 'peel off' procedure during the trilateral ministerial talks in March. Given the worsening crisis in Indochina, both the United States and France wanted to wait until the full review process had been completed before approving deletions from the three international lists *en masse*.[39] The Churchill government was enraged by this development. The Foreign Office protested to the American embassy in London that the Labour Party and the British public expected the Conservative government to deliver rapid and sweeping changes to the East–West embargo, but it appeared to British diplomats that the United States might seek to prolong the revision of the international lists until well after the CoCom review had been completed.[40]

By the time the review had finished in June, Britain had managed to secure the acquiescence of the Eisenhower administration for the outright removal of 217 items from the embargo, but more than 80 items remained in dispute. Stassen and Thorneycroft met in London in an effort to hammer out a final agreement.[41] During the talks, which lasted from 3–7 July, the two politicians debated the strategic significance of the controversial items. Eager to deliver a substantial relaxation of East–West trade controls before the parliamentary recess in August, Thorneycroft retracted his opposition to 40 items and agreed to their remaining on the lists. In the spirit of compromise, Stassen gave his support for the deletion of all but six of the remaining items under consideration.[42] One obstacle to a unanimous agreement remained: a suitable date for the changes to be enforced. According to Stassen, the Eisenhower administration was reluctant to allow the revisions to take effect with war raging in Indochina. Similarly the French government declared that it would not sanction any alterations to the multilateral embargo until a peaceful resolution of the conflict in the Far East was forthcoming.[43]

On 19–21 July the Consultative Group met in Paris to approve the results of the CoCom review. It was not until a ceasefire had been negotiated in Indochina on 21 July that the United States and France gave their full consent to the removal from the international lists of items deemed by CoCom to be no longer of strategic value to the Soviet Union. The revised lists came into force on 16 August and were amended as follows: International List I was reduced from 250 to 170 items; International List II from 90 to 20 items; and List III was to contain only 34 items.[44] An analysis of the embargo revisions suggests that the Churchill government had succeeded in its attempt radically to reduce the number of exports under control in East–West trade. In fact several American diplomats expressed their disappointment with the results of the review.[45] Clearly the shortened multilateral export control programme did not dovetail with the recommendation of NSC 152/2 that any relaxation of the East–West trade embargo should be 'gradual' and 'moderate'.

Conflict revisited: the Geneva Conference and East–West trade controls, 1955

In early 1955 a paper prepared by the American Council for Foreign Economic Policy (CFEP) assessed the August 1954 international export control revisions. It concluded that the relaxation of the trade embargo on the Soviet bloc could be attributed to the strongly held view of the other CoCom governments that export controls should be substantially reduced for the 'long haul'. From the perspective of the Eisenhower administration, the results of the review were not 'wholly consistent with the recommendations of NSC 153/3, which advocated a 'gradual and moderate relaxation' of East–West trade controls. Indeed the CFEP thought that the new export control programme was 'not completely adequate to meet the US objective of controlling all those commodities which would contribute significantly to the war potential of the European Soviet bloc'. Thus while the revised embargo restrictions were considerably more tightly enforced than their predecessors, the CFEP was concerned about the strategic implications of the new multilateral export control programme.

The CFEP also analysed the effect that the international embargo had had on the growth of the Soviet war machine. It deduced that the strategic trade controls had caused 'some retardation' of the Kremlin's military production programme during the early years of economic containment. Although less potent in the early 1950s, the trade restrictions had continued to prevent Moscow from acquiring valuable strategic materials. However the August 1954 revision of the international lists meant that the Soviet Union was now able 'to gain access to a wide-range of important industrial equipment and materials formerly denied them'.

Another problem requiring immediate intention, according to the CFEP, was the attitude of the United States' allies to the relaxation of East–West trade controls. The CFEP underscored the divergent approaches of Washington and the other CoCom governments towards economic defence policy. While the United States saw the strategic embargo as an integral component of mutual security, the Western European nations attached much less importance to the trade control programme'. According to the CFEP there were essentially three reasons for the Western European position. First, the Eisenhower administration and its allies had a 'different evaluation of estimates as to the threat and means of avoiding war' with the Soviet Union. Most notably, Britain argued in respect of thermonuclear war that restricting industrial exports to the Soviet bloc would not hinder Moscow's ability to sustain a conflict with the West. Second, domestic commercial considerations had compelled the Western European members of CoCom to press for an expansion of trade with Eastern Europe. Unlike the United States, these nations required access both to new markets for exports and to traditional sources of essential supplies. Finally, internal political and commercial pressures had forced the European governments to push for the relaxation of controls on East–West trade. Given that these nations had been strongly influenced by Churchill's speech of 26 February 1954, calling for increased trade with the Soviet bloc, the CFEP stressed that any attempt by the United States to propose further additions to the international lists would be met with multilateral opposition. In conclusion, the CFEP suggested that while Washington was sympathetic to the economic predicament of its allies, it was reluctant to support the wholesale liberalisation of trade with the Soviet bloc.[46]

Despite the substantial relaxation of the international lists, British ministers continued to demand further concessions from the Eisenhower administration. They saw little point in maintaining restrictions on industrial items as any future conflict between East and West would be nuclear rather than conventional in nature. Thus any attempt to prevent military build-up by targeting the Soviet military–industrial complex would be a futile endeavour, given that a thermonuclear war would be of short duration. It was therefore sufficient to restrict the embargo to items of strategic and nuclear importance. Furthermore the expansion of trade in industrial items between the West and the Soviet bloc might help reduce international tension and avert a nuclear or conventional conflict. Given these strategic considerations, the Churchill government could not understand why Washington was refusing to decontrol items such as merchant ships, copper wire, rolling mills and electric generators.[47]

Alarmed by this British proposal further to reduce International List I, Foster Dulles wrote to Anthony Eden urging restraint. Dulles expressed his 'deep concern' about the problems that continued to plague Anglo-American cooperation in economic defence policy. Turning to the question of exports controls on merchant ships, copper wire, rolling mills and electric generators, Dulles requested Eden carefully to study the strategic implications of removing these items from the embargo. It was Dulles' contention that 'these particular goods should not move to the Soviets in such quantities as to constitute a real contribution to the potential military strength of the Soviet bloc'. He hoped that the United States and Britain would be able swiftly to overcome their differences on these commodities to enable the 'continued existence and effectiveness of the multilateral organisation in Paris'. Most importantly, he emphasised the necessity of close cooperation between the two governments in East–West trade matters, as failure to resolve disagreements in CoCom would inevitably lead to 'dangerous frictions in Anglo-American relations'.[48]

Yet Dulles' warnings were for the most part ignored. Despite several telegrams between Dulles and Eden, as well as between Harold Stassen and Peter Thorneycroft, neither government was prepared to cede ground on the disputed items. British ministers were adamant that the export controls on ships and copper wire should be removed immediately,[49] but the American State and Defense Departments refused to allow concessions to the Churchill government on either of these items as they deemed them to be of great value to the Soviet Union for the purposes of military production.[50]

The dispute between the United States and Britain over these items dragged on for many months. Efforts by the State Department to resolve the issue through a bilateral, item-by-item review of the commodities in question were unsuccessful as the Foreign Office pressed for a full settlement of items held over from the August 1954 revisions.[51] In fact the mood in London suggested that the Churchill government was 'very dissatisfied' with the extent of the August international list reductions. The American embassy in London informed the State Department that British ministers would not entertain any additions to the embargo and were determined to secure further deletions.[52] Sinclair Weeks of the Commerce Department was most concerned about Britain's demands. He suggested that the failure of the CoCom governments to apply strict quotas on machine tools and merchant ships, together with London's proposal to remove copper exports from the embargo, had 'rendered international controls more of a myth than a reality'.[53] While some shipping controls were relaxed by CoCom in September, the United States and Britain were unable to reach a compromise on copper and rolling mills before the four-power foreign ministers' meeting in Geneva in October.[54]

During 18–23 July, the United States, the Soviet Union and Britain, held their first collective meeting since the Yalta Conference in 1945. The period of relative détente that had characterised international relations between the Soviet Union and the Western alliance since Stalin's death in March 1953 had culminated in this major conference in Geneva. Although still highly suspicious of each other's motives, both Moscow and Washington were keen to establish a lasting peace settlement in Europe. The conference did not produce any concrete results on the key issues – arms control and the reunification of Germany – but the fact that the four powers were meeting for the first time since the outbreak of the Cold War offered the hope of future cooperation between East and West.[55]

The NSC placed much emphasis on trade as a 'trump card' at the Geneva conference. Foster Dulles was a keen proponent of the view that East–West trade could be used to extract concessions from the Kremlin on important issues.[56] He received the enthusiastic support of President Eisenhower, who felt that trade in non-strategic goods could be offered to the Soviet Union 'whenever the United States believed that its interests would be advanced thereby'. He advised, however, that the United States should coordinate with Britain and France on trade policy, lest Washington find itself 'on one side of the argument while our allies and the Soviets were on the other'. The Defense Department was more reticent about drawing on trade as a bargaining lever in Geneva. Charles Wilson asserted that the United States should only contemplate a relaxation of export controls it was sure of Moscow's willingness to ameliorate the fundamental sources of tension between East and West. Admiral Arthur Radford was even more sceptical than Wilson, commenting that trade concessions in non-strategic goods would not appease the Soviet Union as the Kremlin was only interested in exports of military value. Nevertheless the majority in the NSC supported the Eisenhower and Dulles proposal to liberalise East–West trade if the Soviet leadership appeared willing to offer concessions on arms control and the security of Europe.[57]

Trade did not feature as a major point of discussion at the Geneva conference,[58] although each of the four heads of state alluded to the benefits for peace of removing barriers to commerce and cultural exchange. In a statement to the delegates at the conference, Eisenhower said that trade, free travel and communication that served to increase commerce between the West and the Soviet bloc would not only help to dispel mistrust, but could also foster understanding between the two blocs:

> If we could create conditions in which unnecessary restrictions on trade would be progressively eliminated and under which there would be free and friendly exchange of ideas and of people, we should have done much to chart the paths towards the objectives we commonly seek.[59]

There is no evidence that the Anglo-American differences over East–West trade were visible at the conference. The two governments, in conjunction with France, agreed that the liberalisation of export controls would not be tabled at the summit unless Moscow was willing to offer major concessions on arms control and security issues. But Eden's statement on trade and cultural exchanges revealed a subtle departure from Eisenhower's stance on the development of economic ties with the Soviet bloc.[60] Significantly, Eden proclaimed that 'we, for our part, would welcome an expansion of the existing channels of trade between East and West.[61]

The subject of East–West trade was discussed at greater length during meetings between the foreign ministers of the four powers in Geneva during October and November. Encouraged by the 'spirit of Geneva', Dulles was anxious to use trade as a bargaining lever to extract a positive settlement with Moscow on the reunification of Germany and other pressing security issues.[62] He suggested to officials during a meeting at the State Department that the Soviets should 'pay the price for the new posture'. If the Soviet Union were offered concessions on trade by the United States, the Kremlin would be put under pressure to respond positively to a political settlement of the Cold War.[63] However Dulles' gambit received a negative response from the Soviet delegation. American officials blamed the Soviet Union for the lack of meaningful progress at the foreign ministers' meetings. Yet while the Western Europeans continued to argue that Washington was 'flexible and reasonable' in its treatment of the strategic export control issues, they were inclined to believe otherwise.[64]

Abolition of the China trade differential, 1955–57

So far this book has been concerned exclusively with the Anglo-American embargo on trade with the Soviet bloc (the Soviet Union and its Eastern European satellite states). During 1955–57, however, the United States and Britain clashed fiercely over economic defence policy towards the People's Republic of China (PRC). Since the outbreak of the Korean War in June 1950, trade with the PRC and North Korea had been controlled by the CoCom members. When the PRC had joined the war effort on behalf of North Korea in December the Truman administration had completely prohibited trade with the communist government, led by Mao Zedong. Export controls, (imposed on the same items as those prohibited to the Soviet bloc), had been increased following a UN resolution on 18 May 1951. By the autumn of 1952, under the direction of the United States, the CoCom governments had not only embargoed the items on the three international lists but also drawn up a supplementary list of restricted exports. A China Committee – known informally as ChinCom – had been established to monitor strategic shipments bound for the PRC.[65] The 'special list' of embargoed commodities, which comprised approximately 207 items in 1955, became a great bone of contention between the United States and Britain. This was ostensibly because of the greater scope of the ChinCom controls in comparison with the embargo applied by CoCom to the Soviet bloc. Moreover, when the three international lists were revised in August 1954 the restrictions on trade with the PRC were not included in the decontrol process, creating an even wider divergence in content between the Soviet and Chinese embargoes. Thus throughout 1954 and 1955 the Churchill government, with the support of France, lobbied the Eisenhower administration for the removal of this differential.[66]

It took many months to begin discussions on the Chinese trade controls. The United States remained staunchly opposed to the removal of the differential on the ground that it considered the PRC to be an aggressor nation. The Geneva Summit and the foreign ministers' meeting also forestalled any progress towards a resolution of the conflict. In fact Eisenhower insisted that export controls on trade with the PRC should be excluded from the agenda at the four-power talks in Geneva. It was France that took unilateral steps to convene a Consultative Group meeting to air Western European dissatisfaction with the China differential in September 1955.[67]

Trilateral talks between the United States, Britain and France eventually took place on 5 October in Paris.[68] The French delegation asserted that there was nothing to justify discrimination between the PRC and the Soviet Union as the hostilities in Indochina and in Korea, which had been the only justification for such discrimination, were over. The British delegates argued along similar lines – the greatest threat to Western security was not the PRC but the Soviet Union, and it was politically indefensible for the British government to institute a more restrictive embargo on trade with the PRC than the Soviet Union. Now that the Korean War had ended, the commerce that had been restricted between British territories in Southeast Asia and Beijing should return to normal as this was vital to the economic survival of Hong Kong, the Federation of Malaya and Singapore. The American delegation remained impervious to these grievances. They pointed out that despite the cessation of hostilities in Korea, the PRC still posed a threat to the security and stability of the region. Furthermore the fact that the embargo on trade with the PRC had been approved by the UN was tangible evidence that a large group of countries continued to regard Communist China as a pariah in the family of nations. American diplomats also cited congressional and public pressure as a reason for the Eisenhower administration's commitment to the retention of the China differential; the effects of the Korean War had led the public to adopt a more uncompromising attitude towards the PRC than the Soviet Union.[69]

Foster Dulles was particularly worried by Anglo-American friction over the ChinCom trade controls. On 8 December he wrote to Eisenhower to inform him of the Anglo-French proposal to align the PRC export control list with the three international lists currently embargoed by the CoCom members. Dulles noted gravely that if the United States did not accept a 'graduated reduction in the China controls', Britain would act unilaterally to end the differential without observing the multilateral procedures of the Consultative Group.[70] In a personal communication to the British foreign secretary, Harold Macmillan, Dulles urged his counterpart to refrain from unilateral action on the PRC trade control list. He asserted that disunity between the two governments in ChinCom would result in 'not only a collapse of the entire co-operative structure but also a high degree of ill feeling ... between our nations'.[71] Gordon Gray of the Defense Department shared these sentiments, and argued that unilateral British action on trade controls would be detrimental to American national security. On balance, Gray concluded, if a choice had to be made between the loss of security and possible injury to Anglo-American relations, he was inclined to favour the latter option.[72]

At a CFEP meeting in early January 1956 the council took heed of the growing disgruntlement in Washington about the Eden government's proposal to eliminate the China differential. The CFEP recommended that the Eisenhower administration should stiffen its resolve against British, French and Japanese criticism by seeking to 'strengthen rather than soften' the multilateral controls on exports to the PRC.[73]

During Eden's visit to Washington in late January a series of high-level talks were held in an effort to avert a crisis between the two governments. The first of these meetings took place on 31 January at the State Department, involving Dulles and the newly appointed British foreign secretary, Selwyn Lloyd. While acknowledging the importance of the multilateral export control system, Lloyd remarked that Britain and its Far Eastern territories had a long history of trade with China. It was difficult, he suggested, for the Eden government to justify a more stringent embargo on trade with the PRC than on the Soviet Union when faced with intense pressure from parliament and the British public to relax the restrictions on exports to communist nations.[74] At a meeting between the two heads of government later in the day at the White House, Eden reiterated Lloyd's contention that the Soviet Union posed a greater threat to British interests than the PRC, and that the application of more restrictive controls on trade with Beijing was indefensible in parliament. Eden also attempted to impress upon Eisenhower the necessity of trade for the economic survival of the British territories, particularly Hong Kong. Eisenhower listened with a sympathetic ear, but whilst he did not wish to deprive Japan and the British territories of the benefits of trade with the PRC, the defence establishment and Congress were adamant that a comprehensive embargo was essential to American security interests in the Far East.[75]

Although Eisenhower gave no assurance to Eden that the United States would relax the PRC trade controls to the extent of the CoCom international lists, he promised to convene a meeting of the Consultative Group to discuss Britain's proposals. Yet no such meeting was convened, and despite incessant pressure from the British embassy in Washington and the Foreign Office for a multilateral meeting to be held the State Department stalled.[76] The United States' slow response was due to two factors: the insistence by Congress that a comprehensive embargo on trade be maintained against both the Soviet Union and the PRC, in return for economic and military assistance through the mutual security programmes; and divergent views in the NSC on what action should to be taken in response to the Anglo-French proposal to abolish the China differential. On the one hand Eisenhower and Dulles were worried that persistent disharmony with London on export controls would lead to a deterioration in relations with Britain and other major Western European governments. They were therefore receptive to the idea of liberalising the controls on trade with the PRC. It should be noted, however, that neither Eisenhower nor Dulles were prepared to support the complete abolition of the China differential. On the other hand defence officials, led by Radford and Wilson, were opposed to any alteration of the PRC restrictions. As far as Radford was concerned, each and every item denied to the communist countries was of strategic value, while all items of non-strategic value already flowed freely between Japan and the PRC.[77]

Persistent enquiries by the Eden government about the Anglo-French proposal to abolish the China differential finally elicited a response from Eisenhower and Dulles in mid April 1956.[78] With NSC approval of negotiations with London, Dulles forwarded a proposal to Lloyd in an attempt to settle the dispute. The United States would not agree to the major relaxation of trade controls desired by Eden and Lloyd, but it would accept the deletion of rubber and 'thirty or forty' miscellaneous items from the ChinCom list on condition that Britain gave its tacit support for copper wire to be put back on the international lists.[79] In a personal message, Eisenhower implored Eden to agree to the reinstatement of copper wire on the CoCom embargo. He informed Eden that military, defence and intelligence experts had advised him of the strategic necessity of instituting an international restriction on copper exports. He ended his communication by saying that Washington would be prepared to tolerate the use by London of exceptions on certain goods in trade with the PRC.[80]

British ministers immediately rejected Dulles' proposal. When informing Dulles of the response of the British government, Ambassador Roger Makins said that the American suggestion was 'helpful', but that Britain would not agree to any further additions to the international export control lists. He told Dulles that the Eden government had recently conducted trade talks with Nikolai Bulganin and Nikita Khrushchev of the Soviet Union and for political reasons could not sanction any new restrictions on East–West trade.[81] Replying to Eisenhower's letter, Eden was more forthright. He declared that the American proposal 'presents serious difficulties for us. I do not see how we could agree to this now'.[82]

A further attempt was made by Dulles at the North Atlantic Council meeting in May, but Foreign Secretary Lloyd merely reaffirmed London's aversion to any extension of the international embargo.[83]

Charles Wilson, in a letter to Dulles, registered his protest at what he perceived as British obduracy. He fretted that the actions of the Eden government – the use of exceptions procedures, public announcements and collusion with other participating countries – was 'undercutting the United States in the field of trade controls and is seriously weakening the United States' position in the Far East'. Wilson went so far as to accuse London of trying 'to pull away from a close alliance with us in these important and far-reaching matters'.[84] Dulles' response was thoughtful and quite surprising. While he did not condone the actions of the British government in ChinCom, he pointed out that 'each nation remains the final judge of its national interest and retains the freedom to act accordingly'. He argued that in the past the United States had often acted unilaterally and therefore should not apply double standards in its relations with allies. Dulles also dismissed Wilson's concern about Anglo-American disunity, commenting that 'from time to time there will undoubtedly be differences on particular issues between the British and ourselves'.[85] In hindsight this statement appears most prescient given that the foundations of the Anglo-American 'special relationship' were rocked by the Suez crisis within a matter of months. As 1956 came to a close, British and American diplomats concerned themselves with Middle Eastern issues, leaving unresolved the less important though significant dispute over PRC trade controls.[86]

When Harold Macmillan became prime minister in January 1957 after the sudden resignation of Eden because of illness he sought to rebuild the Anglo-American relationship in the aftermath of the Suez debacle.[87] But ever since his tenure at the Ministry of Defence and the Foreign Office Macmillan had been a leading proponent of the relaxation of controls on trade with the Soviet Union and the PRC. Thus continuing disagreement between London and Washington over the embargo marred the early months of his premiership. The Eisenhower administration refused to alter the multilateral export control framework to accommodate its leading European ally, while the Macmillan government held that the additional restrictions on the PRC were 'illogical and ought to be abolished'.[88]

At the Bermuda Conference in late March Dulles and Lloyd briefly discussed the trade problem. Lloyd told Dulles that the British government was under constant pressure from parliament to eliminate the differential between the Soviet and PRC lists . He warned Dulles that the main British political parties were united against any extension of the international export controls. Failure to resolve the Anglo-American differences, Lloyd stated, would lead to the alienation of the United States in CoCom and 'anti-American feeling in Britain'.[89] The following day Lloyd sent Dulles a message summarising the views of the Macmillan government on economic defence policy towards the PRC: he informed Dulles that London would only tolerate the China differential 'for a very short period'.[90]

Lloyd's impatience forced Dulles' hand. Having been conferred by the NSC with the authority to negotiate with Britain on PRC trade controls in a note to the foreign secretary, Dulles made yet another offer to settle the dispute. In essence the new proposal, if accepted by Macmillan and Lloyd, would lead to the amalgamation of the ChinCom and CoCom lists, adding to the new embargo items deemed to be of strategic significance by Washington and creating a single list of exports to be monitored in trade with the PRC.[91] On the surface Dulles' proposal appeared promising, but in reality it was far from acceptable to the Macmillan government, whose refusal to bargain on American terms can be attributed to two factors: the refusal of British ministers to contemplate any further additions to the international control lists and a motion tabled by over one hundred members of the House of Commons calling for the elimination of the China differential.[92] Britain's response dismayed Dulles, who remarked to Lloyd that the Eisenhower administration had 'torn [its] heart out' to make concessions to London.[93]

The two governments were still divided when a crucial meeting of ChinCom was held on 7 May. During the talks the American delegation tabled a proposal to revise the embargo on trade with the PRC, but refused to sanction the abolition of the differential. In turn the French delegation submitted a proposal to amalgamate the ChinCom and CoCom lists. This was more acceptable to the majority of the delegations, but nonetheless the talks ended in deadlock, without unanimous approval for either the American or the French proposal. Significantly, the failure of the Dulles proposal to gain the support of the members signalled the transfer of leadership of ChinCom from the United States to Britain.[94] At the Bermuda Conference in March, Lloyd had remarked to Dulles that British ministers would only consider a coordinated list that would 'command general respect' in ChinCom. Merely transferring items from one list to another, he had argued, would not, in the opinion of the Britain, obtain general acceptance.[95]

At a ChinCom meeting on 17 May the American delegation presented a revised version of the proposal submitted ten days previously. As Eisenhower had informed Macmillan in a personal note prior to the meeting, the United States remained reluctant to abolish the China differential due to security considerations, together with congressional pressure.[96] The revised package modified the original additions to the CoCom lists demanded by Washington. Yet Dulles still wanted to place controls on approximately 80 new items, to be added to International Lists II and III. Not surprisingly the majority of members rejected the American submission and rallied around the French proposal. The delegates left the meeting with an uncertain future looming over ChinCom and the multilateral export control programme.[97]

Macmillan confirmed Britain's decision to reject Dulles' proposal in an apologetic letter to Eisenhower: 'I am very sorry to tell you that I shall have to stick to the line shared by a large number of countries, including the great majority in Europe, who want to bring the Russia and China lists together'.[98] Despite the last-ditch effort by Dulles to hammer out an agreement with Lloyd, the two governments could not overcome their fundamental differences over the PRC trade controls.[99] Under increasing strain from parliament and the public to relax the controls on exports to the PRC, Macmillan instructed the British delegation to announce London's unilateral decision to abolish the differential at a meeting of ChinCom on 27 May.[100] In a letter to Eisenhower explaining his decision, Macmillan stated that his government had no alternative but to abandon the China differential. He concluded by saying that Britain and the United States 'must try to play down this difference of view between us' on strategic export controls. In reference to the importance of the Anglo-American partnership to Western security, Macmillan hoped that their disagreement over trade with the PRC would not hinder cooperation on economic defence policy or 'on the great issues that lie beneath all this'.[101]

Economic containment for the 'long haul': the CoCom review of 1958

Having secured a major victory on the relaxation of trade controls in respect of the PRC, the Macmillan government turned its attention to the CoCom international lists. During the final years of Eisenhower's presidency, Britain and the United States would once again clash on the size and scope of the strategic embargo on East–West trade. Anxious to exploit the support of the other Western European governments in CoCom for a further revision of the international lists, London pressed Washington for a multilateral review of the export control system in the latter months of 1957. An agreement was reached by CoCom to initiate a review of the embargo during the spring and summer of 1958.

In preparation for the review, British and American representatives met in January 1958 to explore the possibility of reaching a common position prior to the CoCom multilateral meetings in March. Yet the two sides appeared to be poles apart on the complexion of a revised embargo for the 'long haul'. Essentially the discussions between the two delegations centred on a suitable definition of what constituted a strategic export in a period of tension between the Western alliance and the Soviet Union short of war. The American delegation expounded the view that any export that could contribute to the Soviet Union's capacity to produce military equipment for use in a future war should be retained under embargo. By contrast the British delegates, referring to estimates provided by the Ministry of Defence, argued that controls should be limited to exports of clear strategic value to Moscow. As any future war with the Soviet Union was likely to be of a thermonuclear nature, the Macmillan government thought that the restriction of industrial exports would do little to curtail the Soviet Union's ability to wage war. They also argued that should a nuclear war break out, it would be of short duration. A programme of economic warfare targeted at the enemy's military–industrial complex would thus be of little consequence.[102]

With these strategic considerations in mind the Foreign Office contacted the State Department in January to outline Britain's proposals for revising the multilateral embargo. The Macmillan government favoured the relaxation of approximately 43 per cent of International List I and the total abolition of Lists II and III.[103] There were a number of reasons for this demand for a drastic overhaul of the multilateral export control programme. First, British ministers had reached the conclusion that the strategic embargo was doing little or nothing to curb Soviet military production. They thought it unwise to maintain restrictions on industrial items in East–West trade as the Soviet Union was now a powerful industrial state, and such restrictions would only create a 'reservoir of ill will' between the United States and Western Europe on economic defence issues.[104] Second, the Macmillan government believed that removing the barriers to trade between East and West would help to reduce international tensions and alleviate suspicions. Finally, ever since Churchill's speech on the expansion of

East–West trade in February 1954 Conservative governments had been under pressure to reduce export controls on sales to the Soviet bloc and the PRC. After its abandonment of the China differential in May 1957, the Macmillan government was expected to achieve a further reduction in the number of items on the international lists.[105]

The NSC greeted the British demands with much apprehension. With the exception of Eisenhower and Dulles, who were both advocates of more liberal East–West trade, the NSC members adopted a critical stance. Dulles' support for a less restrictive embargo won him strong praise from the president. He doubted that trade restrictions would have any great effect on the technologically sophisticated Soviet Union, which had produced the Sputnik programme. When Dulles stated that allied unity was more important to American security than preserving the strategic embargo on East–West trade, Eisenhower noted dryly that this was the first time in 'five long years' that someone had supported the president's position on the question. More sceptical, however, were the Commerce and Defense Departments. The latter, in particular, was keen to preserve the embargo in its present form and rejected the British proposal for further items to be removed from the international lists. Notwithstanding these dissenting voices, the NSC agreed with Dulles that the interests of the United States would be best served by liberalising the export controls on trade with the Soviet bloc and the PRC.[106]

CoCom conducted a review of the three international lists between mid March and 1 July. The United States submitted a draft proposal for International List I to be reduced from 170 items to 148. Inevitably the British delegates were far from satisfied with this proposal and clashed repeatedly with their American counterparts on a range of items, notably tankers and steel rolling mills. While approximately 70 items were deleted from the embargo, Washington managed to secure the acquiescence of other governments for the addition of 20 new exports to the list, thereby, in the words of Douglas Dillon of the State Department, producing a 'strengthened and expanded' list of strategic items. International List II was abolished and replaced with a 'watch' (surveillance) list of 35 commodities. Although Britain and the United States clashed over the scope and content of International List I, Dillon reported at a briefing for the NSC that he felt that 'the agreement would stick'.[107]

Although British Foreign Office documents on the CoCom review of 1958 were still classified at the time of writing, it is possible to discern from alternative sources the disgruntlement of ministers and officials with the extent of the review. The Macmillan government was unhappy with the State Department's refusal to consider 60 items for decontrol by CoCom in September 1959. The official responsible for American economic defence policy, Douglas Dillon, rejected the British proposal on the ground that the annual reviews of the international lists by CoCom should only involve minor amendments to the embargo.[108] This episode was known in British government circles as the 'Dillon Affair' and was especially resented by the Foreign Office.[109] No significant amendments were made to the embargo during the Eisenhower administration's final two years in office: congressional hostility, fears about the 'missile gap' and the watershed presidential election of 1960 prevented any real progress in the negotiations between London and Washington.[110] Hence at the end of 1960 Anglo-American cooperation on East–West trade remained brittle and uncertain.

Conclusion

The period 1954–60 marked a crucial turning point in the history of Anglo-American export control policy towards the Soviet bloc. In August 1954, after much prodding from Britain and France, the Eisenhower administration agreed to a substantial relaxation of the CoCom embargo. The 1954 revisions began the process of preparing the export control programme for the 'long haul'. Yet the new-look strategic embargo satisfied neither the United States, which advocated more stringent trade controls, nor Britain, which believed that the revisions were not extensive enough. The Churchill and Eden governments continued to press for further decontrol in 1955–56, but constant pressure from defence officials and Congress to retain extensive restrictions on East–West trade meant that Eisenhower and Dulles could not bring about the liberalisation of the embargo they desired.

Undoubtedly the greatest friction between London and Washington was due to the China differential. Neither government was willing to compromise on this explosive political issue, which dragged on for 18 months. Given the Eisenhower administration's strategic interests in the Far East, coupled with the potent force of the 'China Lobby' in Congress, the United States continued to insist that trade with the PRC should be more restrictive than that with the Soviet bloc. Despite numerous attempts by Dulles to settle the dispute through a series of proposals, British ministers insisted that the differential between the CoCom and ChinCom controls be abolished. It took unilateral action by Macmillan in May 1957 finally to end the differentiation between the Soviet and PRC trade controls, much to the chagrin of the United States. Continuing friction over the length and scope of the international lists marred the final years of the Eisenhower administration. Washington sought to maintain a wide-ranging embargo, while London argued that in an age of nuclear power the denial of industrial exports in East–West trade would do little to stunt the growth of Soviet military production.

9
Conflict and Conciliation: Kennedy, Macmillan and East–West Trade, 1961–63

Relations between the United States and Britain over East–West trade controls had reached a low ebb by the end of the Eisenhower administration. During the late 1950s the two countries had clashed over the abandonment of the China 'differential' and fiercely debated the criteria for restricting goods in trade with the Soviet bloc. As a result, the 1960–61 CoCom review had been fraught with friction as Washington and London attempted to pull the multilateral export control programme in different directions. American officials had wanted to add more technologically advanced products to the international lists. Conversely the British negotiators had sought to reduce considerably the scope and size of the embargo, on the basis that the Soviet Union was a highly sophisticated industrial nation and therefore would not be affected by Western trade controls.

Initially, the new Kennedy administration did little to overcome the Anglo-American differences over economic defence policy. Embroiled in a diplomatic struggle of nerves with the Kremlin over Berlin and Cuba, the government was inclined to tighten the restrictions on East–West trade, despite the efforts of the State Department to preserve the status quo, involving limited non-strategic trade. Yet by the final year of the Kennedy presidency hopes were high for closer cooperation with Britain in CoCom. This chapter charts the conflict and reconciliation that marked Anglo-American embargo policy during the 'crisis' years of the Cold War. First, a brief overview of these dramatic days is necessary to set the background to the East–West trade developments in the early 1960s.

A new Cold War?

One leading historian has described the period 1960–63 as the 'crisis years' in the Cold War era.[1] The proliferation of declassified government documents from the United States, Western Europe and the Soviet Union in the 1990s has stimulated a reassessment of the Kennedy–Khrushchev confrontation. Much of this new research has provided an enlightening insight into American and Soviet perceptions, tactics and strategy during the Berlin and Cuban missile crises. What has emerged from these newly painted portraits of policy making in Washington in Moscow was the sense of panic and urgency on the part of both powers as they reacted to a chain of international strategic developments that nearly led to the outbreak of nuclear war.

On entering the White House, John F. Kennedy was determined to take a strong stand against the Soviet Union. Despite the relative peace and stability of the Eisenhower presidency, there was a large body of opinion that the United States was losing its nuclear superiority. Critics chided Eisenhower, in his final years in office, for allowing Khrushchev to close the 'missile gap' between Washington and Moscow. Kennedy was also influenced by the Soviet leader's 'wars of liberation' speech, which was perceived by the American policy-making elite as a clarion call for cold war against the United States in the Third World. Certainly, Khrushchev was anxious to assert Soviet power in the international system in an effort to inspire a world communist revolution. Given the nuclear stalemate between the two superpowers in Europe, he sought to test the resolve of the new leader in Asia, Africa and Latin America. In response, in his legendary inaugural address Kennedy declared that the United States would 'bear any burden' and 'oppose any foe' to protect its national interests throughout the globe.[2]

The Kennedy administration placed military build-up at the top of its national security agenda. Replacing solvency with security, Kennedy increased the defence budget by 15 per cent. In close cooperation with the secretaries of state and defense, Dean Rusk and Robert McNamara, he devised a new national strategy aimed at three major objectives. Not only would the United States expand its stockpile of nuclear arms, but more emphasis would be placed on the utility of conventional weapons as a 'flexible response' to Soviet belligerency and risk-taking in Europe. Second, the Kennedy government would strive to bolster strategic alliances with non-communist nations in Europe, Africa, Asia and Latin America. Like his predecessors, Truman and Eisenhower, Kennedy saw the NATO alliance as the lynchpin of Western security. He was a strong advocate of the economic and political integration of Western Europe and lobbied on behalf of the Macmillan government for British entry into the European Economic Community (EEC).[3] As a proponent of the 'special relationship' with Britain he thought that a strong British presence in Western Europe would boost the development of closer ties between Washington and the EEC. Secretary of Defense McNamara was also keen to unify European nuclear power under the command of the United States through the creation of a Multilateral Force (MLF). While this led to friction with the two independent nuclear powers – Britain and France – in 1962, it demonstrated the Kennedy administration's realisation that in order to wage the Cold War effectively it would have to rely on the support of other Western nations. Finally, the new government would explore non-military strategies to combat the Soviet threat. These strategies took two forms: the allocation of economic assistance to less developed countries (LDC), for example the 'Alliance for Progress' with Latin America; and covert operations organised by the Central Intelligence Agency.[4] The inherent shortcomings of the latter approach surfaced in April 1961 with the ill-fated Bay of Pigs invasion, launched to overthrow the socialist regime of Fidel Castro in Cuba.[5]

Sensing that Kennedy's leadership had been undermined by the Bay of Pigs fiasco, Khrushchev attempted to take the initiative in the Cold War struggle at the Vienna conference in June 1961. The summit had been convened by the United States to discuss a range of international issues such as nuclear testing and problems to do with Berlin and Laos. Kennedy had decided to shun Dean Acheson's recommendation that he take a tough line on the division of Berlin, and went to Vienna to negotiate with the Soviet premier. Khrushchev's unwillingness to compromise rattled the young president and both leaders left the conference deeply suspicious of the motives of the other. Kennedy and his national security team were dispirited by what they saw as belligerence and nuclear brinkmanship on the part of the Soviet premier and began preparations for a period of renewed tension with Moscow. The army was increased to one million troops and an additional $6 billion was allocated to the defence budget. In a statement to the nation on 25 July, Kennedy warned the American people of an impending confrontation with the Soviet Union. Angered by the president's speech, Khrushchev forced the Berlin issue in August by erecting a wall that sealed the city into Western and Soviet zones. Thereafter American–Soviet relations deteriorated to the bleak level that had characterised the early years of the Cold War.[6]

Yet the friction over Berlin did not precipitate the worst international crisis of Kennedy's presidency and the Cold War. The earlier discovery by American reconnaissance aircraft of missile installations in Cuba brought Washington and Moscow to the brink of nuclear war. Fragmentary Soviet government records that have been recently become available point to a number of reasons why Khrushchev ordered the installation of missiles so close to the seaboard of the United States. First, the Soviet Union wanted to demonstrate to the Western world that Moscow could compete on equal terms in the Cold War struggle. Second, determined to encourage and support anticapitalist regimes in the Third World, Khrushchev sought to defend Cuba from an imminent invasion by the United States. Finally, the Soviet premier was worried that hard-line critics were undermining his leadership in the Kremlin: a show of force against the United States would enable him to retain his grip on power.[7] The Cuban missile crisis has been well documented in a number of excellent monographs that have drawn on American, Soviet, Cuban and British sources.[8] What has emerged from this research was the effectiveness and efficiency of the response by Kennedy and the NSC to Khrushchev's nuclear gambit. From October 1962 until his last days in power Kennedy held the initiative over his weakened Soviet counterpart. Humbled by the Cuban missile experience, Khrushchev shifted his Cold War strategy from nuclear brinkmanship to the policy of 'peaceful coexistence' with the West that had dominated Soviet policy making in the 1950s. Although the two leaders negotiated a test ban treaty on nuclear weapons in August 1963, suspicion and scepticism over Berlin prevented Kennedy and Khrushchev from fostering a détente in East–West relations.[9]

During these years of superpower confrontation Britain found itself very much in the background. This was an indication of London's diminished global presence and influence. But as noted above, the period 1961–63 was a time of renewal of the Anglo-American 'special relationship'. Strong personal ties were forged between Kennedy and Macmillan and the American president viewed Britain as Washington's closest and most important ally in Western Europe. The intimacy of the Kennedy–Macmillan relationship was illustrated during the Cuban missile crisis, when Kenneddy not only kept Macmillan abreast of developments but also solicited his advice.[10] Nuclear weapons, however, continued to be a source of friction in the Anglo-American alliance. McNamara's decision to cancel the Skybolt programme in the summer of 1962 threatened to strain relations between London and Washington. It took negotiations at the highest level to reach a mutually acceptable compromise at the Nassau conference in December:

Britain would forgo its nuclear independence in return for access to the technologically sophisticated Polaris missile programme.[11] Another policy area that initially produced conflict between the Kennedy administration and the Macmillan government was East–West trade. This is the subject of the remainder of this chapter.

'Recurring differences': Hodges versus Rusk, 1961–62

Prior to his election to the presidency in 1960, John F. Kennedy had often spoken out on East–West trade matters during his 14-year career in Congress. As a congressman he had condemned British trade with the People's Republic of China (PRC) in the late 1940s and had called for a general tightening of export controls against the Soviet bloc.[12] By 1957, however, Kennedy's attitude had apparently softened and as the junior senator from Massachusetts he had proposed a bill to amend the Battle Act. His bill had sought to permit the US government to grant aid to communist countries that showed a polycentric tendency. In other words, he had argued that assistance should be granted to independent-minded Eastern European governments that were anxious to sever links with the Soviet bloc. Kennedy had failed to secure the enactment of this legislation, but in the early months of his presidency he resurrected his campaign to amend the Battle Act.[13]

In his State of the Union address to Congress on 30 January 1961 Kennedy revealed his policy objectives with respect to East–West trade. He remarked that 'we must never forget our hopes for the ultimate freedom and welfare of the Eastern European peoples'. By asking the legislature to allow him more discretion in the use of economic tools 'to help re-establish ties of friendship' with the Soviet satellite states, Kennedy signalled his intention to pursue a more liberalised trade policy towards Eastern Europe. In much the same vein as Eisenhower and Dulles, he believed that the United States might be able to prise some of the more autonomous Eastern European nations, such as Poland, away from the Soviet bloc through economic inducements. Kennedy's bill authorised the president to grant economic and financial assistance 'to any nation or area, except the Union of Soviet Socialist Republics and Communist-held areas of the Far East' if such action was important to the security of the United States. Despite intense lobbying by Kennedy and the State Department, Congress failed to enact the new measure. Although the Senate passed the bill on 11 May, the legislation was not voted upon in the House of Representatives.[14]

   Despite Kennedy's personal interest in trade as an economic instrument in East–West relations, economic defence policy continued to be the responsibility of the Commerce and State Departments. Decisions on export licences for shipments to the Soviet bloc were only referred to the president when the agencies responsible for East–West trade failed to reach agreement. For this purpose, on 24 May Kennedy established the Export Control Review Board (ECRB), consisting of the secretaries of commerce, defense and state.[15] The board, which was chaired by the secretary of commerce, Luther Hodges, would discuss cases involving export licence applications where no agreement could be reached between the departments. In the event that the three secretaries could not agree on whether to deny or grant licences on particular exports to the Soviet bloc, the matter would be referred to Kennedy.[16] But the president's attempts to liberalise trade were overshadowed by a series of international crises in 1961, most notably the unsuccessful Bay of Pigs invasion and the American–Soviet confrontation over Berlin. With the renewal of East–West tensions the Kennedy administration proceeded cautiously in trade policy towards the Soviet bloc and the PRC. While determined to expand commercial contacts in non-strategic exports, Washington rigorously applied restrictions on military and advanced industrial items.

   This uncertainty over East–West relations, together with congressional pressure to increase the export controls on trade with communist nations, led to a divergence of views between the Commerce and State Departments. Since the implementation of a strategic embargo on the Soviet bloc in 1948, successive secretaries of commerce had consistently adopted a hard-line approach towards export licensing policy in respect of communist countries. Luther Hodges was no exception. Like his predecessors, Charles Sawyer and Sinclair Weeks, Hodges took a firm anticommunist line when making and executing international trade policy. In contrast to Sawyer and Weeks, however, Hodges was a proponent of 'peaceful' commerce with the Soviet bloc. This change in the Commerce Department's stance reflected the new international strategic climate and a relaxation of the Cold War tensions that had been a feature of the 1950s. It was also due to the revision of American economic strategy undertaken by the Eisenhower administration in light of the CoCom international list reviews of 1954 and 1958. Soviet technological advancement and allied demands for the expansion of trade with Eastern Europe had forced Washington to limit the embargo to items of a strictly military nature. In addition, policy planners had become convinced that trade contacts could be used not only to influence Soviet behaviour in Eastern Europe, but also as a means to bring about a détente in East–West relations.

Yet the Bay of Pigs fiasco and renewed tension with Moscow over Berlin led Hodges to pursue a restrictive policy on export licences in 1961. Concerned by the findings of congressional investigations into economic defence practices – notably the findings of the Senate Internal Security Subcommittee – Hodges was keen to tighten the existing controls on trade with the Soviet bloc and the PRC. Moreover he was adamant that export licence applications to these nations should be rigorously examined prior to approval. In fact he proposed that no further licences be approved until the international situation had greatly improved. Hodges believed that Congress and public opinion would misconstrue the Kennedy administration's commitment to increased trade in non-strategic items with the Soviet bloc. It was therefore necessary, he suggested, for the executive to appear to be taking a strong stance on the prohibition of strategic and dual-purpose commodities. Hodges also called for more pressure to be applied to Western Europe and Japan to intensify their restrictions on exports to the Soviet Union. For Hodges, 'resolute and determined action at the highest level' by Washington would act as a 'compelling influence' on NATO governments to enforce wider controls on trade with Moscow.[17]

The State Department was highly sceptical about Hodges' proposal. One official pointed out that the Commerce Department's decision to refuse export licence applications in light of the present international tensions was premature. Such action, he thought, 'would complicate our efforts to concert effective measures with the NATO countries' in matters concerning the mutual security of the Western alliance. Not only would the policy signify a hardening of the United States' attitude towards its allies and the Kremlin, it would also 'weaken the hand' of the United States in future if the West should decide to maximise the impact of the embargo on the Soviet economy. The general consensus at the State Department was to continue the policy approved by the president on 26 August for more stringent application of the licensing criteria when faced with contentious items. This flexible approach would enable the administration to refuse licenses on exports of a strategic nature while allowing the Commerce Department to approve applications for trade in non-strategic items. If Hodges' proposal were adopted, the State Department concluded, it would be 'difficult' to revert to the existing policy should international tensions abate.[18]

In reply to Hodges' memorandum, Rusk argued for the retention of the existing export licensing policy. He also informed Hodges of the State Department's view that denying export licenses for trade with the Soviet bloc would create general foreign policy problems for the United States with regard to the NATO governments and the Soviet Union. Rusk also expressed the opinion that as far as the State Department was concerned the current East–West trade controls were adequate for the protection of American national security. Hodges' fiery response to Rusk's letter took the form of a trenchant defence of his proposal for stricter controls. He charged that export controls had been 'so tightly drawn in the past as to have little real application'. Thus he aimed to make these restrictions more effective through rigorous enforcement to ensure that American exports would not be 'used abroad to frustrate the intent of the Export Control Act'. He did not intend to widen the gap between domestic and international export controls, but a more stringent embargo was required in the interests of national security.[19]

Fundamentally divided on licensing criteria, the Interdepartmental Committee of Under Secretaries on Foreign Economic Policy met to discuss the problem of trade with the Sino-Soviet bloc. The under-secretary of commerce, Jack Behrman, presented an overview of the Commerce Department's assumptions, objectives and techniques for approaching East–West trade. Behrman described the motives of the Soviet Union in respect of trade with the United States in largely negative terms. In particular, he suggested that the Kremlin sought 'co-existence on its own terms', only used trade for the purpose of exerting economic pressure on less developed countries and targeted imports of technologically advanced items in its commercial dealings with the West.

With regard to American objectives in East–West trade, Behrman argued that the Kennedy administration should continue its policy of denying strategic and dual-purpose items to the Soviet bloc. It was imperative, he noted, that the West preserve its technological advantage over the Soviet Union through a mutually agreed multilateral export control programme. Concurrently the United States could avail itself of the benefits of trade in non-strategic commodities with the Eastern European countries and the Soviet Union. This trade should be conducted on a fair and competitive basis; it should also be on American terms through the open economy.

On the question of the techniques to be applied in trade with the Soviet bloc, Behrman once more highlighted the divergent positions of the Commerce and State Departments. The Kennedy administration, he implored, should exert strong pressure on the CoCom membership to bring the international export controls into line with American domestic restrictions. Otherwise Washington would have to relax its unilateral controls at great expense to national security. Behrman also called for a review of the strategic embargo to determine whether the United States was directing its export control efforts at the 'wrong area'. He did not elaborate on this point. But given Hodges' determination to intensify the restrictions on East–West trade, the Commerce Department probably desired the incorporation of more industrial and electronic items. As well as the Sino-Soviet bloc, the Commerce Department favoured a tighter enforcement of trade controls against Cuba and other Latin American countries.

When Behrman had completed his presentation on behalf of the Commerce Department, the undersecretaries debated whether or not the United States should tighten its controls on East–West trade. The discussion centred on the contrast between the international and domestic export controls. Both Behrman and Henry Fowler of the Treasury Department advocated a more comprehensive embargo on strategic trade on the basis that this was the Soviet Union's only reason for trading with the West. They recommended that the Kennedy administration, during negotiations on economic defence policy, urge the Western Europeans and Japanese to institute more extensive restrictions on exports to the Soviet Union. On the other hand George Ball and Edwin Martin, representing the State Department, thought that any attempt to force the United States' allies to impose wider controls on East–West trade would be futile. They disagreed with Fowler's contention that the Soviet Union was only interested in obtaining strategic materials in its international trade with other nations, and pointed out that it conducted quite a large volume of commercial trade with Western Europe. Eastern European markets, moreover, were a very valuable source of imports for the Western European governments, which were heavily dependent on international trade for economic survival. In a comparison of the importance of East–West trade to Britain and the United States, Ball concluded that while the United States exported few goods to the Soviet bloc, Britain was dependent on the expansion of international commerce, of which East–West trade was an essential component. Martin commented that an increase in trade contact between the United States and the Soviet Union would not only improve political relations, but might also create a demand for Western consumer goods in the Soviet Union. The Soviet leadership would then be forced to switch attention from war production to the civilian economy, and to develop better consumer products to stave off Western competition in the domestic market.[20]

In 1962 the Cold War entered its most dangerous phase. Not since the outbreak of the Korean War in June 1950 had the United States and the Soviet Union come so close to military confrontation. During the latter months of 1961 the deterioration in American–Soviet relations over Berlin and the impending crisis over Cuba threatened to undermine the state of 'peaceful coexistence' that had characterised the Eisenhower years. It was against this backdrop that the Kennedy administration continued fiercely to debate the American economic defence strategy. While Hodges pressed for a tightening of export controls, Rusk and Ball pushed for an expansion of non-strategic trade with the Soviet bloc. Both positions clearly rested on different assumptions. The Commerce Department argued that until relations with Moscow improved, export licences for trade with the Soviet bloc should be denied. Conversely the State Department believed that trade in civilian commodities could be used to forge a détente with the Soviet Union. Robert McNamara of the Defense Department shared Hodges' view that the strategic embargo should be applied more stringently to military and dual-purpose exports. He also concurred with Rusk's argument that the channels of peaceful trade should be kept open as an economic inducement to the Soviet people and the Eastern European governments.[21]

Hodges' restrictive approach to East–West trade licensing was the subject of much debate in the State Department. Despite several attempts by officials to encourage Hodges to moderate his position, he remained resolutely hostile to any expansion of trade with the Soviet Union. The State Department maintained that if export controls were increased Washington's negotiating position *vis-à-vis* Moscow would be jeopardised. An intensified embargo would send the wrong signals to the Kremlin and the Eastern European satellites. It would exacerbate rather than alleviate the Cold War tensions between the Western alliance and the Soviet bloc. Worse still, the Eastern European governments would increase their dependence on Moscow and any attempt by the Kennedy administration to build bridges between these nations and the United States would be thwarted. Not least, diplomats were worried about the effect that Hodges' licensing policy would have on negotiations in CoCom. If Washington was perceived by Western Europe to be moving towards a more restrictive economic defence policy, this could hinder cooperation over multilateral export controls.

In short the general feeling amongst officials at the State Department was that any attempt to extend the East–West trade controls would be 'pointless' and would have a limited impact on the long-term economic and military growth of the Soviet Union.[22]

Given the conflicting policies of the Commerce and State Departments, Rusk was instructed by the NSC to review the current economic defence strategy. On 10 July he forwarded a memorandum to the NSC evaluating NSC 5704/3, the official economic defence policy statement of the American government since 1957. Rusk criticised the decision of the Commerce Department to deny export licenses to the value of $2.4 million, stating that this would 'work at cross purposes with our attempt to establish sober communications with the USSR and the Eastern European bloc'. He explained his philosophy on export policy in towards East–West trade as follows: 'trade is one of the few means of influencing the peoples of the Soviet Union towards a national attitude that will tend to make the USSR a more responsible and peaceful member of the international community'. Rusk warned that any expansion of the domestic restrictions on trade with the Soviet Union would be detrimental to Washington's relations with its partners in CoCom. As these governments would not agree to broaden the multi-lateral embargo, the United States should be under no illusion that further restrictions by the Kennedy administration 'would be effective in preventing such trade between the Soviet bloc and the rest of the free world'. Rusk concluded that NSC 5704/3 was still consistent with American economic defence policy, but recommended an expansion of non-strategic trade with the Soviet Union as a means of improving East–West relations.[23]

In response to the Rusk memorandum, Hodges prepared a policy paper for the NSC setting out the position of the Commerce Department. He concurred with Rusk's observation that the two departments had radically different views on economic defence policy objectives. While Hodges acknowledged that the 59 license applications he had decided to refuse were 'quantitatively unimportant', he thought that it was imperative for the Kennedy administration to demonstrate that it 'is not making a "qualitative" contribution to the build up of the Soviet bloc economy'. He went on to stress that the Soviet Union was not interested in commercial trade in the usual sense; just in the acquisition of machinery, technical data and technically advanced commodities from the Western industrialised nations. With these considerations in mind, Hodges urged against breaking down the barriers to commercial trade with the Soviet Union. The United States should wait, he recommended, until the international situation improved and there was clear evidence that the Soviet Union would adopt a 'responsible' and 'peaceful' attitude. Now that Congress had amended and passed the Export Control Act, Hodges argued, the domestic controls should be more extensive than the international East–West trade restrictions. In its attempts to reach an agreement with CoCom on the scope and size of the multilateral embargo, the United States should not set its domestic controls at the 'lowest level represented by the allies'.[24]

At the NSC meeting of 17 July President Kennedy attempted to resolve the dispute over export licensing between the Commerce and State Departments, but despite his intervention economic defence policy remained confused and lacking in direction. Rusk led the assault against an expansion of the present export controls by commenting that the Western European nations would not endorse any further additions to the multilateral embargo. The United States and Western Europe already held contrasting views on economic defence policy, and extension of the domestic controls would only accentuate these differences in CoCom. He added that despite the tensions over Berlin, the Kennedy administration should not abandon trade as a flexible economic instrument to improve American–Soviet relations. Rusk was supported by Ball, the undersecretary of state for economic affairs, who declared that if Washington rejected the pending export license applications for East–West trade, the Kremlin might conclude that the United States did not want to trade with the Soviet Union. This would heighten the Soviet mistrust of and suspicion about American trade policy towards Eastern Europe. Hodges dissented, but Kennedy appeared to support the State Department's position. He ordered that the economic defence policy agreed in August 1961 be maintained for the following two months pending the outcome of the Berlin crisis.[25]

Despite Kennedy's decision, Hodges was unrelenting in his campaign to widen the strategic embargo.[26] In response to Hodges' proposal of 17 August to expand the multilateral export controls, Rusk asserted that this would be 'fruitless' given the prevailing attitude in Western Europe and Japan against any additions to the international lists. From the standpoint of negotiations with Moscow, it was Rusk's opinion that further restrictions on East–West trade would have an adverse effect on East–West relations as well as creating disharmony in CoCom. Despite this, if tensions worsened over Berlin the United States would have to take 'selected economic countermeasures' against Moscow under the auspices of NATO.[27]

'Waiting and seeing': the search for a new economic defence policy, 1963

The Cuban missile crisis of October 1962 had a profound effect on American export control policy for the remainder of Kennedy's presidency. Kennedy extended the embargo on trade with Cuba to include 'offence weapons', and limited exports to non-subsidised foodstuffs and medical supplies on humanitarian grounds.[28] In response to the crisis, Henry Fowler sent a memorandum to the president's assistant for national security affairs, McGeorge Bundy, calling for an immediate expansion of the controls on exports to the Soviet Union. However Kennedy and Rusk preferred to await the outcome of the Cuban crisis before taking further action in the area of economic defence policy. Their decision not to tighten the trade controls against Moscow was probably due to the intensity of the American–Soviet confrontation over Cuba, which paralysed the Washington government for almost two weeks in October.

The improvement in American–Soviet relations after the Cuban missile crisis encouraged the State Department to urge the president to relax the trade controls against Moscow. One State Department official argued that any attempt by the United States to increase the multilateral controls was bound to fail 'in the absence of a very much worsened international climate'. He told Bundy that with the apparent abatement of the threat of nuclear war, Washington would be less likely to gain support in CoCom for economic warfare than in the months preceding the confrontation over Cuba.[29]

Significantly, the president was receptive to the liberalisation of East–West trade. In May he ordered the ECRB to advise him on how to deal with the question of exports of technically advanced machinery and equipment to the Soviet bloc. More specifically, he asked the ECRB whether the United States should rethink its trading relationship with the Soviet Union and Eastern Europe.[30] Walt Rostow of the Policy Planning Staff at the State Department prepared an independent report that offered possible answers to the president's questions. Rostow's lengthy paper reviewed the economic defence policy of the Kennedy administration and concluded that trade with the Soviet bloc was essentially a political issue rather than an economic, commercial or strategic one. For this reason he recommended that the Kennedy administration embrace trade in non-strategic exports to the Soviet bloc. While little would be gained in economic terms, trading contact might enable Washington to push 'the USSR towards policies and

conduct more compatible with US interests'. Similarly, if trading rela-
tionships were developed with some of the Eastern European governments the United States could find itself in the position of being able
to 'influence the course of events and evolution of policies' within the
Soviet bloc.[31] Rostow did not offer a new approach to export control
policy, rather he merely recommended that the existing economic
defence strategy be preserved.[32]

The ECRB met on 15 August to discuss the ramifications of the president's questions about American East–West trade policy. After much
debate Hodges, Rusk and McNamara unanimously concluded that 'no
significant change should be made in our export control policy with
the USSR – either over goods or technical data'. While the Commerce
Department would remain vigilant in respect of licensing applications, decisions about individual cases would be taken in a manner
that would not undermine the 'negotiating posture' of the United
States with respect to the Soviet Union. The ECRB considered that
nothing meaningful would be gained from a 'serious extension of the
controls or serious relaxation of them on a unilateral basis'. Moreover,
in line with the existing export licensing procedures and congressional legislation, they urged the president to use his discretionary
authority to explore the possibility of establishing bilateral trading
agreements with certain Eastern European countries. Finally, on the
issue of multilateral trade controls the ECRB informed Kennedy that a
closer understanding must be forged with the allies in CoCom: multilateral policy should be coordinated so that the member governments
could 'collectively restrict or cut-off trade as a response to Soviet-
initiated crises'.[33]

Kennedy responded positively to the findings of the ECRB. In a
memorandum to the board he declared his support for increased
trading contact with the Soviet Union and Eastern Europe. With the
signing of the test ban treaty in August 1963, Kennedy was anxious to
press for a détente in American–Soviet relations. He was therefore
'strongly in favour of pressing forward more energetically [in East–West
trade] than this report and its recommendations imply'. Evidence that
the Western European governments had stepped up trade with the
Soviet bloc also convinced Kennedy of the necessity of pressing
forward with the liberalisation of embargo policy.[34] While the United
States would preserve its restrictions on military and technologically
advanced exports, the president asserted that the United States 'must
not be left behind' the other CoCom members in the area of commercial trade. Yet Kennedy would not live to see the liberalisation of

East–West trade for which he enthusiastically campaigned in the final months of his presidency.

Different policies, divergent views: Anglo-American disagreement over East–West trade, 1961–62

At the end of the Eisenhower administration Britain and the United States were still divided over the strategic criteria that should be applied to trade with the Sino-Soviet bloc. British officials argued that the multilateral embargo should be limited to items of a strictly military nature, while American government representatives stressed that heavy industrial and technologically advanced items should also be denied to Eastern Europe, as these commodities could contribute to the development of the Soviet war economy. During the 1960–61 CoCom review the two governments remained bitterly divided our the issue: Washington wanted to increase the number of exports under embargo; London sought a substantial relaxation of East–West trade controls.

At a meeting of CoCom in January 1961 the British delegation expressed the view that the embargo should be limited to strategic materials and equipment – trade in 'peaceful goods' was 'advantageous' to the West and therefore, should not be prohibited. Any attempt to impose restrictions on non-military exports to Eastern Europe would not only be 'wrong' but also futile. Since the Soviet Union was now a technologically sophisticated industrial nation, the British delegation concluded, export controls would have little effect on Moscow's ability to produce heavy machinery and military materials. For these reasons the Macmillan government would 'firmly oppose' an extension of the embargo to include commodities that might become the subject of commercial trade with the Soviet bloc in the near future. In other words the government would not support controls on industrial and technological items that could be procured from non-CoCom countries or be developed by the Soviet Union, if these items were of commercial value to the British economy. Restrictions could only be justified if such items were deemed by CoCom to be of military benefit to Moscow.[35]

The American delegates were greatly alarmed by the British statement. In a telegram to Rusk one if the delegates, Frederick Nolting, suggested that the unilateral nature of the statement had grave implications for the spirit of multilateral cooperation in export control policy. Targeting his criticism at the Macmillan government, Nolting charged Britain with being clearly unwilling to apply the criteria to which it was bound as a member of CoCom. Furthermore Britain's intransigence demonstrated that it put commercial interests ahead of strategic priorities. He believed that British government ministers had not properly considered the security implications of the proposed American additions to the embargo. According to Nolting, Whitehall continued to demand a further relaxation of controls despite obtaining 'whole and partial deletions' from the embargo during the review.[36]

In an effort to avert a crisis with the Macmillan government, a meeting was convened in Washington between representatives of the State Department and the British embassy. Edwin Martin of the Economic Affairs Bureau informed the British diplomats of his government's concern about Britain's posture in CoCom. He admitted to being 'puzzled by British reluctance to get involved in [a] realistic consideration of advanced technological factors when they are involved in questions of addition to the embargo list'. He added that Britain did not appear 'to apply the CoCom criteria with an even hand' when proposals to extend or reduce the embargo were made. In Martin's eyes it seemed that British policy was geared towards promoting a relaxation of export controls and opposing attempts to increase the numbers of items on the international lists. Defending the British statement in CoCom, embassy officials emphasised that the Macmillan government was under constant parliamentary pressure to reduce the restrictions on East–West trade. They stated that the general feeling of British policy makers was that the application of stringent export controls was merely forcing the Kremlin to develop 'its own strategic industries, while cutting off East–West trade'. Ministers also complained that once an item had been placed on an international list it never came off. Both delegations agreed that further talks at a higher level were required to prevent a breakdown in Anglo-American cooperation on economic defence policy. As a prelude to these bilateral discussions an *aide mémoire* was prepared by the State Department and forwarded to the British embassy on 5 March for consideration by the Macmillan government.[37]

The *aide mémoire* reiterated many of the issues that had been raised by Nolting and Martin. It expressed the Kennedy administration's disappointment with London's decision to push for extensive revisions during an annual review designed merely 'to canvass technical advances of possible strategic significance and to bring them under early control'. In the opinion of the United States, the Macmillan government had decided to resist any additions to the embargo without regard for the strategic merits of individual cases. Such an approach was inconsistent with the criteria approved by CoCom and to which London had agreed to adhere. Challenging Britain's contention that the export control programme was an impediment to trade with Eastern Europe, the State Department stated that the multilateral embargo was currently of a 'highly selective nature' that did not hinder access to Soviet bloc markets. The *aide mémoire* also underscored the view of the Kennedy administration that CoCom was 'an essential part of the system safeguarding the security of the free world'.[38]

In a telegram to the British embassy in Washington the Foreign Office outlined the position of Whitehall on the matter. Sir Patrick Reilly, who was responsible for conducting negotiations on behalf of the Macmillan government, was to make senior State Department officials aware of Britain's 'disquiet' about the criticisms levelled against it by Washington. He was to emphasise that Britain did not perceive the embargo as an impediment to East–West trade, but that ministers were worried about the 'political damage' that would be caused to Anglo-American relations as a result of conflict over export control policy. Most importantly, Reilly was to adopt a flexible approach on contentious items in his discussions with the State Department. He was instructed to forge a compromise with the American negotiators, even if this might be contrary to British interests.[39]

On 14 March Reilly met Martin in Washington for talks on the Anglo-American differences over the scope and length of CoCom International List I. He told Martin that the State Department's *aide mémoire* had caused him much concern. Reilly explained that the Foreign Office wanted to avoid disunity with Washington over economic defence policy and was anxious to find a compromise between the American and British positions on the multilateral embargo on East–West trade. He patiently described the philosophy behind British thinking on export control policy. From Britain's perspective, a comprehensive programme of trade restrictions against the Soviet bloc would not stunt the Soviet Union's military and industrial development. Reilly pointed out that the Soviet Union's large stockpile of nuclear weapons and Sputnik space programme suggested that Western trade controls had not prevented the Soviet Union from becoming a technologically advanced superpower. Notwithstanding British scepticism about the value of restricting technology transfer from the West to the Soviet bloc, Reilly pointed out that the Macmillan government was under intense domestic pressure to liberalise trade with Eastern Europe. While nothing concrete was achieved at the Reilly–Martin talks with regard to overcoming the problem of strategic definition, the two men agreed that differences over embargo policy should not jeopardise Anglo-American relations in wider and more important international issues. In particular London wished to 'avoid political friction between the United Kingdom and the United States in the CoCom forum'. To this end, both Reilly and Martin concluded that high-level talks should be convened so that the two governments could coordinate their economic defence policies in advance of the 1962 CoCom review.[40]

Yet British ministers were not willing to compromise their policy of pursuing a substantial relaxation of International List I, a sentiment that was shared by all the departments responsible for export control policy.[41] The president of the Board of Trade, Reginald Maudling, advised Macmillan that bilateral discussions would not be very productive unless they took place 'at a sufficiently high level to ensure that broad political, rather than technical considerations are taken into account'. Pressing for a meeting between Kennedy and Macmillan, Maudling thought that the United States should be made aware of London's view that the 'CoCom 1 list has outlived its usefulness and should now be abandoned or very drastically pruned'.[42]

Foreign Office officials echoed the president of the Board of Trade's convictions. A wide-ranging embargo on East–West trade, they concluded, would not weaken the capacity of the Soviet Union to wage war; instead it would have a negative impact on Western relations with the Kremlin. A more limited export control programme confined to key items of military importance would not only allow Western nations to benefit economically from increased trade with the Soviet Union, but might also help to alleviate Cold War tensions. Pressure from opposition parties in parliament, moreover, rendered extensive trade controls indefensible. According to the Foreign Office, in the long run the government would not be able to defend the current embargo 'logically and sensibly' in the face of increasing Soviet technological sophistication.[43]

Because of the Berlin crisis, bilateral talks between Washington and London did take place in October 1961 as planned, and by early 1962 British policy makers began to detect a hardening of the American attitude to wards the expansion of commerce with the Soviet Union. Cabinet ministers began to express doubt about the continuation of the multilateral system of export controls. Home pointed out to Macmillan the 'sharp differences' between the Kennedy administration's proposal to increase the number of items under embargo and Britain's belief that export controls should be relaxed. He warned that the United States was likely to reject any British request for a reduction of the items on International List I.[44]

In response Macmillan urged the Foreign Office to push for a liberalisation of trade controls in its negotiations with the State Department. As far as Macmillan was concerned, 'the whole CoCom concept is absurd' and he welcomed the opportunity to discuss the issue with Kennedy in April.[45] Five days later he sent a minute to Home inquiring whether there really was 'any purpose in CoCom'.[46] Home agreed that CoCom was 'not much use and particularly its International List'. The foreign secretary remarked that the Atomic Energy and Munitions Lists adequately denied strategic exports to the Soviet bloc.[47] Yet the British ambassador to Washington, David Ormsby-Gore, cautioned against demanding a substantial relaxation of the strategic trade controls, as this might antagonise American officials and weaken Anglo-American relations. Ormsby-Gore added that ministers 'seeking to reduce the embargo list' should be made aware of the wider implications of conflict between the two governments in CoCom.[48]

Reconciliation: the 1962 CoCom review

During 19–23 March American and British officials met in Washington in a determined effort to avoid disunity at the impending CoCom review. The talks highlighted the wide differences between the two governments over economic defence policy. The British delegation, headed by Reilly, opened the discussions by confirming the Macmillan government's commitment to an embargo on certain strategic items, especially items contained on the Atomic Energy and Munitions Lists.[49] Moving swiftly to the crux of the matter, Reilly stated that export controls should reflect current strategic assumptions about nuclear war. With this in mind, he continued, Whitehall had concluded that International List I was 'out of date', given the rapid development of Soviet technology. As the embargo appeared to to be having no adverse effect on the Soviet economy it was not possible to defend the restriction of a large number of the items controlled by CoCom. He proposed that the embargo list be reduced by 50 per cent in light of the new strategic realities, insisting that a 'healthy economy is the cornerstone of our defences'.

In a more detailed presentation of British thinking on East–West trade controls, Reilly outlined the three principles that underpinned the Macmillan government's argument that the embargo list should be drastically reduced. First, when making an objective judgement about whether to control an item, CoCom should endeavour to determine the 'pattern of use' of the product by the Soviet bloc. For example, with respect to electronic computers technical experts should refer to the pattern of use of this product in Western industrialised countries when deciding whether or not it could be construed as a strategic good. Second, policy planners in Whitehall believed that the importance of certain goods to Moscow should be taken into account before evaluating these items against the strategic criteria set by CoCom. Finally, commodities contained on the international embargo list should be released for export 'when such equipment has been in normal commercial use for so long that the "know how" could be considered common property' and would not be beneficial to Soviet military production. In short, London wanted to restrict the export controls to items of a solely strategic nature, plus technologically advanced materials that were not available to the Soviet bloc through normal commercial channels. Since the Soviet Union was generally perceived by British officials to be at a technologically advanced stage of industrial development, they contended that the embargo should be limited to atomic and conventional military materials.

Surprisingly, the American delegation did not object to the second and third principles. They did object, however, to the first one, remarking that the strategic value of an export should not be judged on the basis of its Western pattern of use but on its pattern of use in the Soviet Union and Eastern Europe. More positively, State Department officials concurred with the British contention that CoCom 'should avoid listing items, which while meeting the criteria, are of minimal strategic importance to the Soviet bloc'. They also assured the British delegation that the Kennedy administration was committed to a periodic review of the CoCom criteria to establish whether items should be removed from or retained on the embargo in light of Soviet technological advancement.[50]

While the two delegations seemed to move towards common ground on the subject of strategic criteria, they remained divided on the length and structure of the embargo list. Edwin Martin rejected outright the Macmillan government's proposal to reduce the list by 50 per cent on the ground that a substantial relaxation of the international trade controls would spark a hostile reaction from Congress and the American public.[51] According to Martin the United States would be prepared to consider the deletion of approximately 28 items from the CoCom list in return for London's acceptance of 34 new additions to the embargo. Convinced that a 'possible package deal' was beginning to emerge, the British delegation did not reject the American offer, viewing the proposed additions as mostly 'minor and not likely to be seriously controversial'. When the talks, described by one Foreign Office official as 'amicable throughout', ended on 23 March the two governments appeared to have reached a common position in advance of the CoCom review, which was scheduled to begin on 1 May.[52]

In contrast to previous multilateral negotiations the CoCom review of 1962 did not involve a clash of views between the United States and the Western European nations. From the viewpoint of Anglo-American relations in CoCom, the absence of conflict and confrontation over East–West trade was welcomed on both sides of the Atlantic.[53] Yet on balance it was the Kennedy administration that profited most from the strategic embargo adjustments.

The CoCom members agreed to a slight revision of International List I, but in effect any deletions from the embargo were cancelled out by a reciprocal number of trade controls on new items. A major part of the review was devoted to technologically advanced exports, especially items used in the fields of electronics, rocketry and space exploration.[54] A British proposal to relax the control on telecommunication and aviation equipment, in particular the sale of Viscount aircraft to China, received a mixed reaction. While the French, German, Dutch and Italian delegations supported the deletion of a large number of items pertaining to aircraft equipment, they were less enthusiastic about Britain's request for a reduction in telecommunication controls. The United States agreed to some concessions on telecommunication, electronic and aircraft equipment, but according to a senior Foreign Office official 'not as much as we asked for'.[55] Significantly the British delegation reported that not only was a clash with the Americans avoided, but also the European members were more sympathetic to Britain's proposals than during the 1960–61 review.[56]

The important question of why the British delegation did not press for a more extensive relaxation of the embargo during the 1962 review must be considered. Although the British archival evidence is sketchy, it seems that the decision not to table a request to reduce the embargo by half was taken by the cabinet. The advice of David Ormsby-Gore to place the health of the Anglo-American 'special relationship' above squabbles between the two countries over East–West trade had a profound impact on ministerial thinking. What is more, McNamara's determination to bring European nuclear power under American command and the subsequent cancellation of the Skybolt missile programme had soured relations between London and Washington somewhat. Hence Whitehall was perhaps prepared to make some concessions on economic defence policy. Certainly the differences over strategic criteria that had marred cooperation between the two government at the end of the Eisenhower administration and the beginning of Kennedy's presidency were not visible during the three-month review in Paris in 1962.[57]

One aspect of East–West trade that did cause friction between the two countries in the final year of the Kennedy administration was the exportation by Western European nations of large-diameter oil pipe to the Soviet Union.[58] CoCom had once embargoed the sale of oil pipe to Eastern Europe, but this item had been removed from the international lists in the late 1950s. The development of the Soviet oil industry, coupled with the Berlin crisis in the early 1960s, led to calls by Washington for the restriction of oil pipes in East–West trade. This was followed by the North Atlantic Council's request on 21 November 1962 that members should 'to the extent possible' prevent the delivery of large-diameter pipe to the Soviet Union.[59] Efforts by the Kennedy administration, however, to place oil pipe back on the multilateral export control programme met firm resistance from Whitehall.[60]

As Alan Dobson has argued, Britain's opposition to the embargo was based on a matter of principle since Britain was not a large exporter of large-diameter pipe to the Soviet bloc.[61] But clearly economic considerations in other areas of East–West trade played a key role in the Macmillan government's decision to resist the United States' demands. In March 1963 the cabinet, led by Home and the new president of the Board of Trade, Frederick Erroll, signified its intention to oppose not only an embargo on oil pipes to the Soviet Union, but also multilateral export controls on trade with Cuba and restrictions on the sale of Viscount aircraft to China.[62] During meetings with officials in the Kennedy administration and senior American politicians, British ministers emphasised the necessity of expanding East–West trade, given the precarious state of the British economy.[63] By the time that the Kennedy presidency reached its premature end in November 1963, it appeared that the two governments had reached more of an understanding on economic defence policy than had been the case in the late 1950s, notwithstanding their very different perceptions of the value and objectives of the multilateral strategic embargo.

Conclusion

While President Kennedy announced his determination to liberalise East–West trade in his State of the Union address to Congress in January 1961, it was not until the summer of 1963 that the United

States committed itself to the expansion of commerce with the Soviet bloc. Even then the Kennedy administration confined its trade policy to items of non-strategic value, preferring to maintain the restrictions on industrial and technologically advanced commodities. There were three reasons for this: the series of Cold War crises with the Soviet Union over Berlin and Cuba during 1961–62; divisions within the administration over export licenses for trade with the Soviet bloc and China, which paralysed effective decision making and policy planning in economic defence; and Kennedy's poor relationship with Congress with respect to the enactment of domestic legislation extended into foreign policy when the House of Representatives rejected his proposed amendment to the Battle Act in May 1961.

Kennedy built up a close working relationship with Macmillan in a diverse range of international issues, including nuclear weapons, Britain's attempt to join the EEC and the Cuban missile crisis. After an uncertain beginning, Anglo-American relations in respect of economic defence policy improved, reaching a high point during the CoCom review of 1962. Yet the two governments continued to disagree about the shape and scope of the East–West trade embargo. While London desired a limited export control programme covering just atomic and military materials, Washington favoured more restrictive trade controls and the inclusion of industrial and electronic exports. Moreover they clashed over the sale of oil pipe to the Soviet Union in 1963. Whereas the Macmillan government was opposed to an embargo on this item on commercial grounds, the Kennedy administration demanded that oil pipe equipment be placed on the international control lists.

10
Conclusion

With the implementation of a strategic embargo on East–West trade in March 1948, the Truman administration added an economic dimension to its strategy of containment against the Soviet Union. Much like political containment, economic defence policy evolved in a piecemeal fashion. Whereas American policy makers had been prodded by Winston Churchill and Ernest Bevin to take a firm stand against the global communist threat in the late 1940s, the Truman government was pushed by Congress to restrict exports to the Soviet Union and Eastern Europe. Forced to respond constructively to the strong anticommunist feeling in the legislature, the State and Commerce Departments began to debate the utility of economic sanctions against Moscow.

During the period 1948–63 successive administrations grappled with three interlocking problems. The first of these concerned the type of embargo to be employed in East–West trade. In effect the number of items under export control was conditioned by strategic considerations. Thus at the height of the Cold War the embargo embraced a wide range of industrial and strategic commodities. From the mid 1950s to the early 1960s, however, trade controls were confined to goods of strategic and advanced technological value to the Kremlin. Second, successive administrations had to consider public and congressional opinion when making trade policy towards the Soviet bloc. Attitudes in Congress towards commercial contact with the Soviet Union did not change over the 15-year period under study, and policy makers were subject to scathing criticism in appearances before congressional committees on export control practices, especially during the McCarthy investigations in the early 1950s. Finally, American diplomats had to strive constantly to gain the support of Western allies for a strategic embargo. They realised that domestic export restrictions would be largely ineffectual if Western European governments and Japan did not impose similar controls on trade with the Sino-Soviet bloc. This was never an easy task for the State Department. From 1950–63 the Western European participants in CoCom, led by Britain, consistently opposed the United States' demands for a comprehensive embargo on East–West trade. British ministers successfully negotiated a limited multilateral export control programme in 1950–51, secured the relaxation of approximately 50 per cent of all items under embargo in 1954 and ended the China trade differential in 1957.

American economic defence policy from Truman to Kennedy

While economic defence policy was essentially the preserve of cabinet secretaries and senior officials at the State, Commerce and Defense Departments, American presidents took a keen interest in East–West trade matters. Of the three presidents under consideration, Harry S. Truman played the least influential role in economic defence policy. Although Truman was a proponent of limited export controls on trade with the Soviet bloc, he tended to leave policy planning and execution in the hands of his secretaries of state: George Marshall and Dean Acheson. When faced with the conflicting policy positions of the State Department and the staunchly anticommunist Commerce Department, Truman sided with the more liberal stance of the former. Truman also condemned the restrictive Kem Amendment of June 1951, on the basis that the measure threatened to strain relations between Washington and the Western European members of CoCom.

Dwight Eisenhower brought to the presidency a clear understanding of the issues confronting the United States in trade policy towards communist nations. In much the same vein as his predecessor, Eisenhower was anxious to ensure that economic defence considerations did not undermine close cooperation with Western Europe in CoCom. The new president believed that the controls on exports to the Soviet bloc were too restrictive. Unlike Truman, Eisenhower used the NSC as an important, high-level forum for discussions on economic defence strategy. The president's extensive pronouncements on East–West trade, contained in the minutes of the NSC, reveal his understanding of the embargo problem and his exasperation with the hard-line position adopted by the Commerce and Defense Departments. Ultimately, however, Eisenhower was not able to convince the majority of the members of the NSC radically to revise export control policy. The administration's blueprint document on economic defence, NSC

152/3, did not fully reflect the views of either the president or the secretaries of commerce and defense (Sinclair Weeks and Charles Wilson). However the substantial relaxation of international controls by CoCom in August 1954 was the result of personal negotiations between Eisenhower and Prime Minister Winston Churchill. During the remainder of his presidency Eisenhower, together with Secretary of State John Foster Dulles, continued to advocate a less restrictive East–West trade policy than Weeks, Wilson and the chairman of the Joint Chiefs of Staff, Admiral Arthur Radford. Despite the liberal views of the president, the Eisenhower administration clashed with the other CoCom governments over the strategic criteria to be applied to trade with communist nations.

John F. Kennedy had adopted a liberal attitude towards East–West trade before entering the White House in January 1961. As a senator he had attempted unsuccessfully to amend the Battle Act to allow Eastern European governments seeking autonomy from the Soviet bloc to receive economic assistance from the United States. A series of Cold War crises with Khrushchev over Berlin and Cuba, however, prevented Kennedy from developing closer economic ties with some of these Eastern European governments. Efforts to liberalise East–West trade were thwarted, moreover, by a clash over the export licensing procedure between Luther Hodges of the Commerce Department and Dean Rusk of the State Department. It was not until the partial alleviation of American–Soviet tensions in 1963 that Kennedy could begin to use trade as an economic instrument to improve relations between East and West. Two months after the president encouraged the ECRB to take swift steps towards expanding commercial contact with the Soviet Union, he was assassinated in Dallas. Building on Kennedy's legacy, the Johnson and Nixon administrations began to remove the remaining barriers to non-strategic trade with Moscow and Beijing.

One of the most striking themes in the history of the East–West trade embargo was the lack of consensus on economic defence policy within American government circles from 1948–63. In particular the views of the Commerce and State Departments diverged over export control objectives from the inception of the embargo in 1947 to the debate on licensing policy that paralysed effective decision making during the Kennedy administration. Ironically the Commerce Department – a strong proponent of free trade and enterprise in the early post-war period – was perhaps the fiercest critic of trade contact with the Soviet Union and Eastern Europe.

Successive secretaries of commerce consistently called for extensive and stringent restrictions on exports to the Soviet bloc. It should be noted that each of the three most prominent secretaries of commerce in the first 15 years of the strategic embargo – Sawyer, Weeks and Hodges – were virulently anticommunist. They persistently demanded that international export controls be brought into line with the American domestic restrictions. Moreover the Commerce Department complained that American exporters suffered unjust discrimination in Eastern European markets because their CoCom counterparts were subject to less restrictive controls. By contrast the State Department proffered a narrower multilateral trade control programme that would allow the Western European governments to acquire essential imports from vital Soviet bloc sources. For Marshall, Acheson, Dulles and Rusk mutual security and unity within the Western alliance always took preference over disagreements in CoCom about embargo policy.

Conflict also characterised executive–legislative relations in respect of trade with the Soviet bloc and China in the formative decades of the Cold War. In the immediate aftermath of the Second World War, Congress, influenced by American public opinion, condemned the practice of East–West trade. There were two reasons for this hostility. First, many congressional representatives and senators were fearful that communism might spread throughout the globe. They were therefore anxious to sever all commercial, cultural and diplomatic links with the Soviet Union. Second, a large section of the public was concerned that if the United States continued to export military and industrial products to Eastern Europe, this would benefit Soviet military power at the expense of national security.

Through a series of legislative initiatives in the 1940s and 1950s, anti-communist congressional representatives sought to prevent the shipment of strategic materials to the Soviet Union. In March 1948 Congressman Karl Mundt succeeded in passing an amendment to the Economic Assistance Act that prohibited the reshipment of Marshall aid from Western European governments to the Soviet bloc. The Export Control Act of 1949, moreover, declared trade with communist nations to be a national security issue. But the most contentious piece of legislation was the Battle Act, which not only strained executive–legislative relations but also caused friction in CoCom. Significantly, the Act bestowed on the president the power to withdraw economic and military assistance from nations that engaged in strategic trade with communist governments. The Battle Act, which was signed into law in October 1951, enabled Congress to monitor international export control policy through reports every six months from the mutual security administrator. While the measure provided the legislature with a significant role in economic defence, the Truman and Eisenhower administrations were consistently able to secure waivers from the legislation for key allies that had large volumes of trade with the Soviet bloc.

The Anglo-American nexus: cooperation and constraint

When negotiating a multilateral export control programme, American policy planners looked to Britain to lead the Western European response. Drawing on the close relationship that existed between Washington and London in the early years of the Cold War, State Department officials sought to build an Anglo-American partnership in economic defence policy. By and large the Attlee government responded positively to the Truman administration's initiative. From the perspective of national security, British policy makers, especially at the Foreign Office and the Ministry of Defence, supported restrictions on strategic trade with the Soviet bloc. Nevertheless some government departments, notably the Board of Trade and the Ministry of Supply, feared that a comprehensive East–West trade embargo would hamper traditional imports of raw materials and foodstuffs from Eastern European markets during the period of economic recovery and readjustment. Despite these reservations, Britain assumed the responsibility of obtaining the support of the other OEEC member governments for a multilateral trade control system. In January 1950 the Anglo-American collaboration yielded an international export control advisory group and agreement on a list of strategic exports that would be restricted in trade with the Soviet bloc.

Disturbed by the determination of American negotiators to extend the strategic embargo into the field of industrial exports, the Attlee government, in conjunction with France, mounted an effective campaign to limit the export control programme to strategic and 'dual-purpose' commodities. After almost a year of conflict Britain, the United States and France agreed upon a partial expansion of the embargo in light of the Korean War. While a compromise was reached in December 1950 on the content and scope of the international export control lists, congressional attempts to link assistance to the denial of East–West trade precipitated a further outbreak of conflict between the United States and Britain in CoCom. Realising the importance of Anglo-American unity to mutual security, Truman and Acheson had no alternative but to grant exceptions under the Battle Act legislation to the Western European participants in CoCom. Again, the ability of London to marshal opposition to the demands of the United States in CoCom demonstrated the moderating influence of Britain on American economic defence policy. The lessening of Cold War tensions inspired a radical review of the multilateral embargo in 1953–54. Both the United States and Britain concluded that the international export control lists should be revised in content and scope for the 'long haul'. Contrary to the opinion of some scholars, it was Churchill and not Eisenhower who provided the necessary leadership to obtain a substantial relaxation of trade controls in August 1954. Constrained by his own administration and Congress, Eisenhower was consigned to the sidelines and Churchill provided the high-level impetus that was required to keep the decontrol process moving in the early months of 1954. Following the triumphs of their illustrious predecessor, Anthony Eden and Harold Macmillan continued to press for further reductions of the international lists, despite opposition from the United States. Macmillan's unilateral decision to end the China trade differential in May 1957, while straining relations with Washington, underscored Britain's influence in international economic defence matters. The Kennedy years were also marked by a phase of conflict and reconciliation in Anglo-American export control policy. Although the American and British governments had very different views on the efficacy of the embargo, they endeavoured to avert a breakdown in cooperation over East–West trade.

Despite frequent confrontation over economic defence policy during 1948–63, it could be argued that the United States and Britain always placed the health of the Anglo-American 'special relationship' ahead of differences over policy in CoCom. This perhaps explains why successive presidents did not attempt, through hegemonic coercion, to force Britain to comply with American demands for a strategy of economic warfare against the Sino-Soviet bloc. What is more, when waging the Cold War against Moscow, Washington drew heavily on British support and influence on a global scale. Thus disunity over East–West trade might have jeopardised more significant issues confronting the Western alliance.

Implications

This study challenges the conclusions of previous scholars of Western economic defence policy in the early Cold War years. Recently declassified official documents in the United States and Britain shed a very different light on policy making in CoCom during the 1940s and 1950s. For the most part, the traditional interpretations of the strategic embargo endorsed Gunnar Adler-Karlsson's view that the United States used the threat of aid denial to force Western European governments to adopt controls on East–West trade. But exhaustive research by scholars on the history CoCom in the 1980s and 1990s has largely refuted the findings of Adler-Karlsson, provided an important reinterpretation of Western embargo policy towards communist nations in the first decade of the Cold War, and demonstrated the vital role played by Britain and other Western European powers in shaping policy in CoCom. What this new research has shown is the extent to which Britain, in particular, moderated American demands within the Paris Group for a comprehensive export control programme on East–West trade. Moreover the Churchill and Macmillan governments were highly influential in stimulating the relaxation of trade controls on a substantial number of exports that had been placed under embargo in 1950–51.

The present work draws on these new interpretations. Significantly, it presents the first detailed account of Anglo-American relations in CoCom during the period 1948–63. As this book has shown, it is possible to study the dynamics of the Anglo-American 'special relationship' by focusing on the interaction between Britain and the United States in the making of international embargo policy. In line with recent findings on other aspects of Anglo-American relations in the post-1945 era, this study asserts that Britain was not merely a reliable junior partner to the United States. In fact an analysis of Western economic defence strategy in the early decades of the Cold War suggests that successive British governments had a moderating influence on American policy in CoCom.

This work makes a significant contribution to the economic dimension of Cold War studies. Most monographs and scholarly articles have dealt exclusively with the political and military events that defined international relations for over 40 years; few have examined the issue of trade as a source of conflict in East–West relations. An analysis of East–West trade not only aids understanding of the clash of ideologies between capitalism and communism, it also provides further insight into Western strategies for containing the Soviet 'threat'. Despite fundamental disagreements over policy, American and British planners were convinced that a strategic embargo could prevent the outbreak of an East–West military conflict by denying military and atomic materials to the Soviet Union. However economic containment failed to curb Soviet military growth. Ultimately, international export controls, which contradicted the American objective of creating a liberal world economy based on free trade, were a constant source of friction within the Western alliance.

Notes and References

Introduction

1. Gunnar Adler-Karlsson, *Western Economic Warfare, 1947–67: A Case Study in Foreign Economic Policy* (Stockholm: Almquist and Wiksell, 1968).
2. Yoko Yasuhara, 'The Myth of Free Trade: The Origins of CoCom, 1945–50', *Japanese Journal of American Studies*, vol. 4 (1991), pp. 127–148; Vibeke Sørensen, 'Economic Recovery versus Containment: The Anglo-American Controversy over East–West Trade, 1947–51', *Co-operation and Conflict*, vol. 24 (June 1989), pp. 69–97.
3. Alan P. Dobson, *The Politics of the Anglo-American Economic Special Relationship, 1940–87* (Brighton: Wheatsheaf, 1988), pp. 127–34.
4. Michael Mastanduno, 'Trade as a strategic weapon: American and alliance export control policy in the early post-war period', *International Organisation*, vol. 42 (Winter 1988), pp. 121–50.
5. Michael Mastanduno, *Economic Containment: CoCom and The Politics of East–West Trade*, (Ithaca, NY: Cornell University Press, 1992), pp. 39–63; Tor Egil Førland, '"Economic Warfare" and "Strategic Goods": A Conceptual Framework for Analysing CoCom', *Journal of Peace Research*, vol. 28, no. 2 (1991), pp. 191–204.
6. The term 'economic containment' used in this study is borrowed from Michael Mastanduno, 'Strategies of Economic Containment: US Trade Relations with the Soviet Union', *World Politics*, vol. 37 (July 1985), pp. 503–31.
7. G. John Ikenberry, 'Rethinking the Origins of American Hegemony', *Political Science Quarterly*, vol. 104, no. 3 (1989), pp. 375–400.
8. Alan P. Dobson, *Anglo-American Relations in the Twentieth Century: of friendship, conflict and the rise and decline of superpowers* (London: Routledge, 1995), p. 121.

1 The Orgins of Economic Containment

1. Philip J. Funigiello, *American–Soviet Trade in the Cold War* (Chapel Hill: University of North Carolina Press, 1988), pp. 17–23.
2. Wilson D. Miscamble, 'The Foreign Policy of the Truman Administration: A Post-Cold War Appraisal', *Presidential Studies Quarterly*, vol. XXIV, No. 3 (Summer 1994), pp. 481–3.
3. Melvyn P. Leffler, *A Preponderance of Power: National Security, the Truman Administration, and the Cold War* (Stanford, CA: Stanford University Press, 1992), pp. 94–140.
4. See, in particular, Anne Deighton, *The Impossible Peace: Britain, the Division of Germany and the Origins of the Cold War* (Oxford: Oxford University Press, 1990).

5. The best account of Churchill's 'Iron Curtain' speech is Fraser Harbutt's *The Iron Curtain: Churchill, America, and the Origins of the Cold War* (New York: Oxford University Press, 1986).
6. George F. Kennan ['X'], 'The Sources of Soviet Conduct', *Foreign Affairs*, vol. 25 (July 1947), pp. 566–82.
7. Miscamble, 'The Foreign Policy of the Truman Administration', op. cit., p. 481.
8. John Lewis Gaddis, *The Long Peace: Inquiries into the History of the Cold War* (New York: Oxford University Press, 1987), pp. 48–103.
9. Justus D. Doenecke, *Not to the Swift: The Old Isolationists in the Cold War Era* (Lewisburg, PA: Bucknell University Press, 1979), pp. 19–72.
10. National Archives and Records Administration, Washington, DC [hereafter NARA], RG 59 661.119/11-2547, letter from Senator Guy Cordon to the secretary of state, 25 November 1947.
11. NARA RG 59 661.119/3-2448, letter from Congressman John F. Kennedy to Charles Bohlen, State Department, 24 March 1948.
12. NARA RG 59 661.119/-2547, letter from an unidentified employee at Brown Brothers Harriman to Robert A. Lovett, State Department, 25 September 1947.
13. NARA RG 59 661.119/3-2648, letter from the Consolidated War Veterans Councils of Michigan Inc. to the secretary of state, 26 March 1948.
14. For example see NARA RG 59 661.119/12-748, letter from the president of Westinghouse International to the secretary of commerce, 7 December 1948.
15. Speech by Congressman Robert T. Ross on East–West trade, *Congressional Record: House Proceedings and Debates 80th Congress, 1st Session*, vol. 93, pt 9 (Washington, DC: Government Printing Office, 1947), p. 11 635.
16. Speech by Congressman Karl Mundt introducing Section 117(d) of the Economic Co-operation Act 1948, *Congressional Record: House Proceedings and Debates 80th Congress, 1st Session*, vol. 93, pt 3 (Washington, DC: Government Printing Office, 1948), pp. 3755–6.
17. Vladislav Zubok and Constantine Pleshakov, *Inside the Kremlin's Cold War: From Stalin to Khrushchev* (Cambridge, MA: Harvard University Press), pp. 46–54; Vojtech Mastny, *The Cold War and Soviet Insecurity: The Stalin Years* (New York: Oxford University Press, 1996), pp. 11–30.
18. On this point see Funigiello, *American-Soviet Trade*, op. cit., pp. 33–4.
19. *Foreign Relations of the United States* [hereafter *FRUS*], vol. IV (1948), p. 512, report by the National Security Council on the control of exports to the Soviet Union and Eastern Europe, 17 December 1947.
20. *FRUS*, vol. IV (1948), pp. 513–4, press release by the Commerce Department, 15 January 1948.
21. See *FRUS*, vol. IV (1948), pp. 499–503, paper prepared by the Policy Planning Staff entitled 'US Economic Policy Towards the Soviet Sphere, 19 November 1947.
22. The Policy Planning Staff's role in the making of policy in the State Department is discussed in Wilson D. Miscamble, *George F. Kennan and the Making of American Foreign Policy, 1947–50* (Princeton, NJ: Princeton University Press, 1992), pp. 3–40, and David Mayers, *George F. Kennan and the Dilemmas of US Foreign Policy* (Oxford University Press: New York, 1988), pp. 105–60.

23. *FRUS*, vol. IV (1948), pp. 489–97, paper prepared by the Policy Planning Staff entitled 'US Exports to the USSR and the Satellite States', 26 November 1947.

24. Marshall's opposition to a strategy of economic warfare is documented in Edwin M. Martin's oral history interview transcript housed in the Harry S. Truman Library, Independence, Missouri.

25. *FRUS*, vol. IV (1948), pp. 527–8, memorandum by Marshall to Truman's cabinet on the control of exports to the Soviet bloc, 26 March 1948.

26. It is interesting to note that James Forrestal, the staunchly anticommunist secretary of defense, appeared to support the position of the State Department at the cabinet meeting of 25 June. See Harry S. Truman Library, Matthew J. Connelly Papers, box 1, minutes of the cabinet meeting, Friday, 25 June 1948.

27. *FRUS*, vol. IV (1948), pp. 536–42, report by the ad hoc subcommittee of the advisory committee of the secretary of commerce, 4 May 1948.

28. *FRUS*, vol. IV (1948), p. 544, letter from Sawyer to Marshall, 20 May 1948.

29. NARA RG 59 661.119/6-1948, letter from Marshall to Sawyer, 25 June 1948.

30. NARA RG 330 CD 39-1-1, report by the Munitions Board on the national security aspects of export controls, 1 January 1949.

31. *FRUS*, vol. IV (1950), p. 147, the secretary of state to certain diplomatic offices, 12 January 1950.

32. Tor Egil Førland, 'Cold Economic Warfare: The Creation and Prime of CoCom, 1948–54', unpublished D.Phil. thesis, University of Oslo, 1991, pp. 46–50.

33. NARA RG 59 660.509/8-1048, memorandum sent to desk officers handling negotiations with participating countries, undated.

34. For two excellent interpretations see Michael J. Hogan, *The Marshall Plan: America, Britain and the reconstruction of Western Europe, 1947–52* (Cambridge: Cambridge University Press, 1987), and Melvyn P. Leffler, 'The United States and the Strategic Dimensions of the Marshall Plan', *Diplomatic History*, vol. 12 (Summer 1988), pp. 277–306.

35. Robert Mark Spaulding, *Osthandel and Ostpolitik: German Trade Policies in Eastern Europe from Bismarck to Adenauer* (Providence, RI: Berghahn Books, 1997), pp. 349–53.

36. *FRUS*, vol. IV (1948), pp. 564–8, telegram from Marshall and Hoffman to Harriman, Paris, 27 August 1948.

37. Førland, 'Cold Economic Warfare', op. cit., pp. 50–1.

2   Britain, Western Europe and East–West Trade

1. Melvyn P. Leffler, *A Preponderance of Power: The Truman Administration, National Security and the Cold War* (Stanford, CA: Stanford University Press, 1992), pp. 62–3.

2. Alec Cairncross, *Years of Recovery: British Economic Policy, 1945–51* (London: Methuen, 1985), pp. 61–83.

3. David Reynolds, 'Great Britain', in David Reynolds (ed.), *The Origins of the Cold War in Europe: International Perspectives* (New Haven, CT: Yale University Press, 1994), p. 79.

4. D. Cameron Watt, 'Britain, the United States and the Opening of the Cold War', in Ritchie Ovendale (ed.), *The Foreign Policy of the Labour Governments, 1945–51* (Leicester: Leicester University Press, 1984), pp. 43–60.
5. For example see Richard A. Best Jr, '*Co-operation with Like-Minded Peoples*': *British Influences on American Security Policy, 1945–49* (Westport, CT: Greenwood, 1986), p. 159.
6. National Archives and Records Administration, Washington, DC [hereafter NARA] RG 489, file S-13123, box 118 (USSR), copy of 'The United Kingdom and East–West Trade' by the Central Office of Information, 6 May 1954.
7. Public Record Office, Kew, London [hereafter PRO], FO 371/71923, memorandum of conversation between Makins, Foreign Office, and Bliss, American embassy, London, 29 May 1948.
8. PRO FO 371/71923, letter from Welch, Board of Trade, to Makins, 6 August 1948.
9. PRO FO 371/71923, note of meeting in the Foreign Office to discuss Section 117(d), 10 August 1948.
10. PRO FO 371/71926/ UR 7793, EPC (48) 93, report of the Economic Policy Committee meeting, 20 November 1948.
11. PRO CAB 134 (216) 40, minutes of cabinet meeting, 14 December 1948.
12. PRO CAB (216), memorandum of meeting of Economic Policy Committee on UK position with respect to US proposals, 23 November 1948.
13. PRO 371/77789/ UR 462, report of OEEC meeting by British delegation, Paris, 17 January 1949.
14. France's role in the origins of the Cold War is treated extensively in John W. Young, *France, the Western Alliance and the Cold War, 1944–49* (Leicester: Leicester University Press, 1990), especially pp. 134–75. For an excellent recent account of French foreign policy in the first decade of the Cold War see William I. Hitchcock, *France Restored: Cold War Diplomacy and the Quest for Leadership in Europe, 1944–54* (Chapel Hill, NC: University of North Carolina Press, 1998).
15. On this point see John W. Young, *Britain, France and the Unity of Europe* (Leicester: Leicester University Press, 1984).
16. PRO FO 371/77789, telegram from the British delegation, OEEC, to Foreign Office, 14 January 1949.
17. PRO FO 371/77790/ UR 820, report by British representatives on the discussions with France on the restriction of exports to Eastern Europe under the British list corresponding to the American 1-A list, 7 February 1949.
18. Hitchcock, *France Restored*, op. cit., pp. 41–98.
19. PRO FO 371/77790, telegram from the British delegation, OEEC, to Foreign Office, undated.
20. PRO FO 371/77791, letter from Berthoud, Foreign Office, to Coulson, British delegation, OEEC, 19 February.
21. *Foreign Relations of the United States* [hereafter FRUS], vol. v (1949), pp. 77–78, telegram from Caffery to Acheson, 5 February 1949.
22. *FRUS*, vol. v (1949), p. 79, telegram from Hoffman to Harriman, 9 February 1949.
23. PRO FO 371/77789/ UR 727/45/48, telegram from Gore-Booth, Foreign Office, to Coulson, British delegation, OEEC, 25 January 1949.

24. PRO FO 371/77792, EPC (49) 17, 'Economic Policy towards Europe', 10 March 1949; PRO FO 371/77793, brief for the foreign secretary, 14 March 1949.
25. PRO FO 371/77791, memorandum for the president of the Board of Trade on Section 117(d) for presentation at EPC meeting, undated; PRO FO371/77792, telegram from Foreign Office to British delegation, OEEC, 31 March 1949; PRO FO 371/77794, telegram from Commonwealth Relations Office to Commonwealth countries, 31 March 1949.
26. PRO FO 371/77793, note sent by British delegation, OEEC, to Brussels Treaty Permanent Commission, 16 March 1949.
27. PRO FO 371/77797, report by C. B. Duke of London Committee meeting, 1 June 1949.
28. PRO FO 371/77797, report by the 117D Working Group, Ministry of Defence, 25 May 1949.
29. PRO FO 371/77793, telegram from Coulson, British delegation, OEEC, to Robb, Foreign Office, 21 March 1949.
30. PRO FO 371/77797, report by the Economic Intelligence Department, Foreign Office, 8 June 1949.
31. PRO FO 371/77801, note by H. Gwyn Jones, Ministry of Defence, on the effects on British trade of the security restrictions on exports to Eastern Europe, 22 July 1949.
32. Tor Egil Førland, 'Cold Economic Warfare: The Creation and Prime of CoCom, 1948–54', unpublished D.Phil. thesis, University of Oslo, 1991, p. 68.
33. PRO FO 371/77803, memorandum by the 117D Working Party on the effect on British trade of the security restrictions on exports to Eastern Europe, 13 August 1949; PRO FO 371 77801, paper by Working Party, JWPS (WP)/P (49) 20, 28 July 1949; PRO FO 371/77803, telegram from Foreign Office to Chanceries of Moscow, Bucharest, Warsaw, Helsinki, Belgrade, Prague and Sofia, 17 August 1949.
34. PRO FO 371/77804, telegram from Foreign Office to British delegation, OEEC, 3 September 1949.
35. PRO FO 371/77799, paper submitted to EPC by Berthoud, Foreign Office, undated.
36. PRO FO 371/77800, memorandum by the Economic Intelligence Department, Foreign Office, undated; PRO FO 371/77814, paper on East–West trade by Gaydon, Foreign Office, 31 October 1949.
37. PRO FO 371/77801, note by Aiers on meeting of US–UK technicians on East–West trade, 28 July 1949; PRO FO 371/77802, telegram from Foreign Office to British embassy, Washington DC, on technical talks with the United State, 29 July 1949.
38. *FRUS*, vol. v (1949), p. 123, telegram from Webb to Harriman, 1 June 1949.
39. PRO FO 371 77794, paper by Robb on possible East–West trade group, 13 April 1949.
40. PRO FO 371/77806, E. R. London (49) 252, European Co-operation Committee on East–West trade, 12 September 1949.
41. PRO FO 371/77808, telegram from British delegation, OEEC, to Foreign Office, 26 September 1949; PRO FO 371/77808, telegram from British delegation, OEEC, to Foreign Office, 30 September 1949.

42. PRO FO 371/809, telegram no. 1084 from Duke, British delegation, OEEC, to Foreign Office, 6 October 1949.
43. *FRUS*, vol. v (1949), pp. 150–2, telegram from Harriman to Hoffman, 15 October 1949; PRO FO 371/77811, telegram from British delegation, OEEC, to Foreign Office, 17 October 1949.
44. *FRUS*, vol. v (1949), pp. 163–4, telegram from Harriman to Hoffman, 28 October 1949.
45. National Archives and Records Administration, Washington DC [hereafter NARA] RG 59, File 661.119/11-1049, telegram Webb to Harriman, 10 November 1949.
46. *FRUS*, vol. v (1949), p. 168, telegram from Foster, ECA, to Harriman, 4 November 1949.
47. PRO FO 371/77815, report by the British delegation, OEEC, on the meetings in Paris from 14–21 November 1949 and 29 November 1949.
48. *FRUS*, vol. v (1949), pp. 174–5, telegram from Katz, Paris, to Hoffman, 25 November 1949; PRO FO 371/77816, report on list of production for export control to Eastern Europe, 21 November 1949.
49. PRO FO 371/77817, report by British delegation, OEEC, on advisory group, 24 November 1949; *FRUS*, vol. v (1949), p. 178, telegram from Acheson to Harriman, 13 December 1949.
50. *FRUS*, vol. v (1949), pp. 178–9, telegram from Acheson to Harriman, 7 December 1949.
51. NARA RG 59 File: 661.119/9-2649, memorandum of conversation between Armstrong, State Department, and officials from French embassy, Washington DC, 26 September 1949.
52. *FRUS*, vol. v (1949), pp. 136–7, letter from Sawyer to Acheson, 15 August 1949.
53. See in particular Yoko Yasuhara, 'The Myth of Free Trade: The Origins of CoCom, 1945–50', *The Japanese Journal of American Studies*, no. 4 (1991), pp. 139–40.

3   American and British Economic Defence Policies

1. John Lewis Gaddis, *Strategies of Containment: A Critical Appraisal of Post-War American National Security* (New York: Oxford University Press, 1982), p. 90.
2. James Chace, *Acheson: The Secretary of State who created the American World* (New York: Simon and Schuster, 1998), pp. 146–90.
3. For an excellent account of Acheson's strategic thinking see Melvyn P. Leffler, 'Negotiating from Strength: Acheson, the Russians and American Power', in Douglas Brinkley (ed.), *Dean Acheson and the Making of US Foreign Policy* (New York: St. Martin's Press, 1993), pp. 176–210.
4. Vladislav Zubok and Constantine Pleshakov, *Inside the Kremlin's Cold War: From Stalin to Khrushchev* (Cambridge, MA: Harvard University Press, 1996), pp. 52–72; Vojtech Mastny, *The Cold War and Soviet Insecurity: The Stalin Years* (New York: Oxford University Press, 1996), pp. 63–97.
5. Steven L. Reardon, 'Frustrating the Kremlin Design: Acheson and NSC-68', in Brinkley, *Dean Acheson*, op. cit., pp. 169–72.
6. For good discussions of NSC-68 see Melvyn P. Leffler, *A Preponderance of Power: National Security, the Truman Administration and the Cold War*

(Stanford, CA: Stanford University Press, 1992), pp. 355–60, and Michael J. Hogan, *A Cross of Iron: Harry S. Truman and the Origins of the National Security State, 1945–54* (Cambridge: Cambridge University Press, 1998), pp. 265–315.

7. Chace, *Acheson*, op. cit., pp. 270–80.

8. Leffler, *A Preponderance of Power*, op cit., p. 358.

9. National Archives and Records Administration, Washington, DC [hereafter NARA], RG 489, file S-131123, box 117 (USSR), telegram no. 237 from US embassy, Moscow, to State Department, 3 March 1950.

10. *Foreign Relations of the United States* [hereafter *FRUS*], vol. 1 (1950), p. 285, National Security Policy Paper 68 (NSC-68), 7 April 1950.

11. NARA, RG 59 460.509/4–2150, office memorandum by Howard J. Hilton, State Department, 21 April 1950.

12. See, for example, Acheson's testimony on the Wherry Resolution before the Senate Foreign Relations Committee, 16 February 1951, copy in Harry S. Truman Library, Independence, Missouri [hereafter HSTL], Dean Acheson Papers, box 84.

13. NARA RG 59 460.509/5–2350, report on US economic programmes, 23 May 1950.

14. NARA RG 59 460.509/5–550, report of Foreign Military Assistance Co-ordinating Committee, 5 May 1950.

15. NARA RG 59 460.509/5–550, telegram from Thorp to Acheson, 5 May 1950; NARA RG 489 S-S13123, box 117 (USSR), subject paper by L. C. Boocherer Jr, 'The Significance and development of East–West Trade', undated.

16. *FRUS*, vol. IV (1950), p. 151, paper on East–West trade prepared by the State Department, undated.

17. *FRUS*, vol. IV (1950), p. 87, telegram from Acheson to certain diplomatic offices, 26 April 1950.

18. *FRUS*, vol. IV (1950), pp. 81–2, telegram from Acheson to Bruce, 13 April 1950.

19. Ibid., pp. 158–9, telegram from Acheson to Bruce, 14 July 1950.

20. NARA RG 269 NSC Files: NSC 91, report by the secretary of state on East–West trade, 30 October 1950.

21. *FRUS*, vol. 1 (1951), pp. 1026–33, report by Acheson to the president on US policies in the economic field that might affect the war potential of the Soviet bloc, 9 February 1951.

22. Charles Sawyer, *Concerns of a Conservative Democrat* (Carbondale, Ill.: Southern Illinois University Press, 1968).

23. *FRUS*, vol. IV (1950), p. 83, letter from Sawyer to McLay (NSC), 25 April 1950.

24. Ibid., pp. 84–5, memorandum (NSC-69) from Sawyer to NSC, 25 April 1950.

25. See the statement by Sawyer to the Special Subcommittee on Defence Activities House Interstate and Foreign Commerce Committee, 6 September 1950, copy in HSTL, Charles Sawyer Papers, box 102.

26. *FRUS*, vol. IV (1950), p. 100, memorandum from the acting assistant secretary of state for European Affairs to the secretary of state, 2 May 1950.

27. Ibid., pp. 95–6, telegram from Acheson to Douglas, 28 April 1950.

28. Ibid., pp. 98–9, telegram from Douglas to Acheson, 2 May 1950.

29. Ibid., pp. 95–6, telegram from Douglas to Acheson, 1 May 1950.

30. Ibid., p. 101, position paper prepared by the State Department, 2 May 1950.

31. NARA RG 59 460.509/4-2150, report by R. J. Hilton on export control negotiations, undated.
32. NARA RG 59 460.509/5-350, comments by the State Department on Sawyer's NSC memorandum, undated.
33. Philip J. Funigiello, *American–Soviet Trade in the Cold War* (Chapel Hill, NC: University of North Carolina Press, 1988), pp. 57–8.
34. *FRUS*, vol. IV (1950), pp. 194–5, Webb to Bruce, 23 September 1950; Ibid., pp. 196–7, Webb to Holmes, 27 September 1950.
35. NARA RG 59 460.509/9-2650, Holmes to Acheson, 26 September 1950.
36. Tor Egil Førland, 'Cold Economic Warfare: The Creation and Prime of CoCom, 1948–54', D.Phil. thesis, University of Oslo, 1991, p. 129.
37. *FRUS*, vol. IV (1950), p. 201, memorandum of conversation between Acheson, Sawyer and Blaisdell, 11 October 1950; Ibid., p. 215, memorandum of conversation between Acheson and Sawyer, 30 October 1950.
38. *FRUS*, vol. 1 (1951), pp. 1026–33, report by Acheson to Truman on US policies and programmes that might affect the war potential of the Soviet bloc, 9 February 1951.
39. Funigiello, *American–Soviet Trade*, op. cit., p. 58.
40. A good overview can be found in Bradford Perkins, 'Unequal Partners: The Truman Administration and Great Britain', in William Roger Louis and Hedley Bull (eds), *The 'Special Relationship': Anglo–American Relations since 1945* (Oxford: Clarendon Press, 1986), pp. 43–64.
41. David Reynolds, 'Great Britain', in David Reynolds (ed.), *The Origins of the Cold War in Europe: International Perspectives* (New Haven, CT: Yale University Press, 1994), pp. 92–3.
42. Alan P. Dobson, *The Politics of the Anglo-American Economic Special Relationship, 1940–87* (Brighton: Wheatsheaf, 1988), pp. 113–25.
43. Alan P. Dobson, *Anglo-American Relations in the Twentieth Century: of friendship, conflict and the decline of superpowers* (London: Routledge, 1995), pp. 90–100; Ritchie Ovendale, *Anglo-American Relations in the Twentieth Century* (London: Macmillan, 1998), pp. 58–80.
44. Førland, 'Cold Economic Warfare', op. cit., p. 126.
45. Public Record Office, Kew, London [hereafter PRO], FO 371/87197, telegram from US embassy, London, to Foreign Office, undated.
46. PRO FO 371/87197, telegram from British delegation, OEEC, to Foreign Office, 20 April 1950.
47. PRO FO 371/87197, record of an informal meeting between Roger Makins, Foreign Office, and French representatives on East–West trade, 30 March 1950.
48. PRO FO 371/87197, memorandum by Ministry of Defence on security restrictions, 20 March 1950; PRO FO 371/87197, letter from Marshall, Ministry of Supply to Aiers, Foreign Office, 2 March 1950.
49. PRO FO 371/87197, telegram from British delegation, OEEC, to Foreign Office, 10 June 1950.
50. PRO FO 371/87197, *aide mémoire* by His Majesty's Government on British extension of the 1-b List, 1 August 1950.
51. PRO FO 371/87197, telegram from Foreign Office to British embassy, Washington DC, 15 August 1950.
52. For a discussion of this point see Alec Cairncross, *Years of Recovery: British Economic Policy, 1945–51* (London: Methuen, 1985), p. 214.

53. PRO FO 371/87198, telegram from British embassy, Washington DC, to Foreign Office, 29 August 1950.
54. Førland, 'Cold Economic Warfare', op. cit., pp. 33–4, 115–16; Vibeke Sørensen, 'Economic Recovery versus Containment: The Anglo-American controversy over East–West Trade, 1947–51', *Co-operation and Conflict*, vol. XXIV (1989), pp. 79–82.
55. Michael Mastanduno, *Economic Containment: CoCom and the Politics of East–West Trade* (New York: Cornell University Press, 1992), pp. 86–91.
56. See, for example, William Stueck, *The Korean War: An International History* (Princeton, NJ: Princeton University Press, 1995), pp. 70–5.
57. PRO FO 371/87199, report of Security Export Controls Working Party on the US *aide mémoire* of 25 August, undated.

4 America, CoCom and the Extension of the East–West

1. William I. Hitchcock, *France Restored: Cold War Diplomacy and the Quest for Leadership in Europe, 1944–1954* (Chapel Hill, NC: University of North Carolina Press, 1998), pp. 116–32.
2. Melvyn P. Leffler, *A Preponderance of Power: National Security, The Truman Administration and the Cold War* (Stanford, CA: Stanford University Press, 1992), pp. 383–91.
3. Tor Egil Førland, 'Cold Economic Warfare: The Creation and Prime of CoCom, 1948–54', D. Phil. thesis, University of Oslo, 1991, pp. 125–6.
4. For details see Dean Acheson, *Present at the Creation: My Years in the State Department* (New York: Norton, 1969), pp. 393–6.
5. Peter Lowe, *Containing the Cold War in East Asia: British policies towards Japan, China and Korea, 1948–53* (Manchester: Manchester University Press, 1997), p. 170.
6. National Archives and Records Administration, Washington DC [hereafter NARA], RG 59 460.509/6-550, Foreign Ministers Meetings: Position Paper on East–West Trade Discussion, 6 May 1950.
7. NARA RG 59 460.509/5-450, Foreign Ministers Meetings: Paper on Economic Situation, 20 April 1950.
8. *Foreign Relations of the United States* [hereafter *FRUS*], vol. IV (1950), pp. 116–22, memorandum by the associate chief of economic resources and security staff on tripartite meeting, undated.
9. Ibid., pp. 123–4, memorandum by Martin, undated.
10. NARA RG 59 460.509/5-2550, telegram from Bruce to Acheson, 2 May 1950; *FRUS* vol. IV (1950), p. 127, telegram from Bruce to Acheson, 17 May 1950.
11. *FRUS*, vol. IV (1950), pp. 128–30, telegram from Bruce to Webb, 17 May 1950.
12. Ibid., pp. 132–3, telegram from Webb to Bruce, 20 May 1950.
13. Ibid., p. 133, telegram from Douglas, London, to Webb, 22 May 1950.
14. Ibid., pp. 134–5, telegram from Bruce to Webb, 24 May 1950.
15. Ibid., p. 161, Douglas to Acheson, 2 August 1950.
16. Vibeke Sørensen, 'Economic Recovery versus Containment: The Anglo-American Controversy over East–West Trade, 1947–51', *Co-operation and Conflict*, vol. XXIV (1989), p. 79.
17. Førland, 'Cold Economic Warfare', op. cit., pp. 129–30.

18. James Chace, *Acheson: The Secretary of State who created the American World* (New York: Simon and Schuster, 1998), pp. 242–3.
19. NARA RG 59 460.509/8-550, telegram from Acheson to Bruce, 5 August 1950.
20. NARA RG 59 460.509/509/8-1750, paper for September Foreign Ministers' Meeting, 16 August 1950.
21. *FRUS*, vol. IV (1950), pp. 174–5, telegram from Acheson to Douglas, 22 August 1950.
22. Public Record Office [hereafter PRO] CAB 129/42, CP (50) 201, paper by Shinwell, 31 August 1950.
23. *Parliamentary Debates: House of Commons, July 24–October 26 1950*, vol. 478 (London: HMSO, 1950), pp. 982–3.
24. Førland, 'Cold Economic Warfare', op. cit., pp. 137–9.
25. For detail see Saki Dockrill, *Britain's Policy for West German Rearmament, 1950–55* (Cambridge: Cambridge University Press, 1991), pp. 21–40.
26. NARA RG 59 460.509/9-1150, telegram from Acheson to American embassy, London, 11 September 1950.
27. For Acheson's perceptions of Western security see Melvyn P. Leffler, 'Negotiating from Strength: Acheson, the Russians and American Power', in Douglas Brinkley (ed.), *Dean Acheson and the Making of US Foreign Policy* (London: Macmillan, 1993), pp. 187–205.
28. Harry S. Truman Library, Independence, Missouri, Dean Acheson Papers, box 181, telegram from Acheson to Bruce, 18 September 1950.
29. NARA RG 59 460.509/9-2750, telegram from Bruce to Acheson, 27 September 1950.
30. Michael Mastanduno, *Economic Containment: CoCom and the Politics of East–West Trade* (New York, Cornell University Press, 1992), p. 92.
31. Førland, 'Cold Economic Warfare', op. cit., pp. 147–8; Yoko Yasuhara, 'Myth of Free Trade: COCOM and CHINCOM, 1945–52', Ph.D. dissertation, University of Wisconsin-Madison, 1984, pp. 135–6.
32. Førland, 'Cold Economic Warfare', op. cit., p. 148.
33. Alec Cairncross, *Years of Recovery: British Economic Policy, 1945–51* (London: Methuen, 1985), pp. 214–32; Kenneth Harris, *Attlee* (London: Weidenfeld and Nicolson, 1982), pp. 454–6; Jerry Brookshire, *Clement Attlee* (Manchester: Manchester University Press, 1995), p. 222; Geoffrey Warner, 'The British Labour Governments and the Atlantic Alliance', in Olav Riste (ed.), *Western Security the Formative Years* (Oslo: Norwegian University Press, 1986), pp. 249–57.
34. NARA RG 59 460.509/10-1350, position paper for Charles E. Bohlen, chairman of the delegation of the United States to the tripartite conversations on security export controls in London, 13 October 1950.
35. Acheson, *Present at the Creation*, op. cit., pp. 371–401.
36. NARA RG 59 460.509/10-1350, telegram from Acheson to Bohlen, 13 October 1950.
37. PRO FO 371/87200, telegram from Foreign Office to British embassy, Washington DC, 5 October 1950.
38. PRO FO 371/87200, memorandum on East–West trade prepared by Mutual Aid Department, Foreign Office, 30 October 1950.
39. PRO FO 371/87201, interpretation and implementation of agreed minute of London tripartite talks, 17 October 1950.

40. See for example PRO FO 371/87203, memorandum by Foreign Office on British trade with the Soviet bloc, 23 November 1950.
41. PRO FO 371/87204, EPC (50) 123, London tripartite talks on East–West trade, 23 November 1950.
42. PRO FO 371/87202, telegram from Ministry of Defence to British embassy, Washington DC, 28 October 1950.
43. *FRUS*, vol. IV (1950), p. 240, agreed report of the London tripartite conversations on security export control, 17 October–20 November 1950; NARA RG 59 460.429/11-2950, American embassy, Ottawa, to Acheson, 29 November 1950.
44. Sørensen, 'Economic Recovery versus Containment', op. cit., pp. 83–4.
45. *FRUS*, vol. IV (1950), p. 240, telegram from Holmes, London, to Acheson, 21 November 1950.
46. Ibid., p. 243, telegram from Acheson to Bruce, 22 November 1950.
47. PRO FO 371/87205, communiqué from American embassy, London, to Foreign Office, 28 November 1950.
48. NARA RG 59 460.509/12-450, telegram from Bohlen to Acheson, 4 December 1950.
49. *FRUS*, vol. 1 (1951), p. 1012, editorial note.
50. NARA RG 59 460.509/2-1451, paper entitled 'Questions of Economic Impact Arising from International Control of Exports to the Soviet Bloc and the Relationship between the Consultative Group/Co-ordinating Committee, NATO and other International Organisations', 14 February 1951.
51. NARA RG 59 460.509/2-1451, paper on British trade with the Soviet bloc, undated; PRO FO 371/94291, telegram from British embassy, Lisbon, to Foreign Office, 30 March 1951.

5 Amerian Isolationists and East–West Trade

1. For a good overview see Justus D. Doenecke, *Not to the Swift: The Old Isolationists in the Cold War Era* (Lewisberg, PA: Bucknell University Press, 1979), pp. 153–211.
2. Robert J. Donovan, *Tumultuous Years: The Presidency of Harry S. Truman, 1949–53* (New York: Norton, 1982), pp. 322–8; Thomas G. Paterson, *Meeting the Communist Threat* (New York: Oxford University Press), pp. 78–81.
3. Melvyn P. Leffler, *A Preponderance of Power: National Security, the Truman Administration, and the Cold War* (Stanford, CA: Stanford University Press, 1992), pp. 398–445.
4. Michael J. Hogan, *A Cross of Iron: Harry S. Truman and the Origins of the National Security State, 1945–1954* (Cambridge: Cambridge University Press, 1998), pp. 315–66.
5. Doenecke, *Not to the Swift*, op. cit., pp. 196–201.
6. Michael J. Hogan, *The Marshall Plan: America, Britain and the reconstruction of Western Europe, 1947–52* (Cambridge: Cambridge University Press, 1987), pp. 385–7.
7. Philip J. Funigiello, *American-Soviet Trade in the Cold War* (Chapel Hill, NC: University of North Carolina Press, 1988), pp. 50–73.
8. *Congressional Record, 81st Congress, 2nd Session, Vol. 96, Pt. II* (Washington, DC: Government Printing Office, 1951), pp. 14794–809.

9. Harry S. Truman Library [hereafter HSTL], Independence, Missouri, Matthew J. Connelly Papers, box 1, Minutes of Cabinet Meeting, Friday 15 September 1950.
10. The details of this letter are discussed in Funigiello, *American–Soviet Trade*, op. cit., p. 52.
11. *Foreign Relations of the United States* [hereafter *FRUS*], vol. iv (1950), p. 190, telegram from Bruce to Acheson, 20 September 1950.
12. Ibid., pp. 192–3, telegram from Webb to Bruce, 23 September 1950.
13. Funigiello, *American–Soviet Trade*, op. cit., p. 53.
14. *US Statutes at Large, 81ˢᵗ Congress, 2ⁿᵈ Session, Vol. 64, 1950–51, Public Law 843* (Washington, DC: Government Printing Office, 1951), p. 1044.
15. Funigiello, *American–Soviet Trade*, op. cit., p. 65.
16. *US Statutes at Large, 82ⁿᵈ Congress, 1ˢᵗ Session, Vol. 65, 1952, Public Law 45* (Washington, DC: Government Printing Office, 1952), pp. 62–3.
17. *FRUS*, vol. 1 (1951), p. 1074, telegram from Acheson to certain diplomatic offices, 10 May 1951; Gaddis Smith, *Acheson* (New York: Cooper Square, 1972), p. 323.
18. *FRUS*, vol. 1 (1951), p. 1081, 'Estimate of the Probable Economic and Political Consequences of the Kem Amendment' prepared by the Estimates Group of the Office of Intelligence Research in the Department of State, 25 May 1951.
19. National Archives and Records Administration, Washington DC [hereafter NARA], RG 59 460.509/6-1451, report by the National Security Council regarding an interim general exception to 1302 of the Third Supplemental Appropriation Act of 1951, 14 June 1951.
20. HSTL, Harry S. Truman Papers, Records of the National Security Council, 'A report by the National Security Council on trade between Western European members of the National Atlantic Treaty Organisation and the Soviet bloc, in light of Section 1302 of the Third supplemental Appropriation Act of 1951'.
21. *FRUS*, vol. 1 (1951), p. 1105, telegram from Acheson to Bruce, 16 June 1951.
22. Ibid., pp. 1109–11, memorandum by Linder, 20 June 1951.
23. HSTL, Thomas Blaisdell Jr, papers, box 8, memorandum by Thomas Blaisdell Jr entitled 'The Problem of Trade with the Soviet Bloc', 5 July 1951.
24. *Public Papers of the Presidents: Harry S. Truman*, statement to Congress on the Kem Rider to the Third Supplemental Appropriation Bill of 1951 (Washington, DC: Government Printing Office, 1960), pp. 641–2.
25. *FRUS*, vol. 1 (1951), p. 1109, telegram from Acheson to Bruce, 14 June 1951.
26. Ibid., pp. 1117–8, memorandum of conversation between Moline (acting chief of Economic Defence Staff) and Bullock, 19 June 1951.
27. *Congressional Record, 82ⁿᵈ Congress, 1ˢᵗ Session, Vol. 97, Pt. 7* (Washington, DC: Government Printing Office, 1951), pp. 9443–4.
28. NARA RG 460.509/11-651, memorandum by Harry S. Truman, 6 November 1951.
29. Funigiello, *American–Soviet Trade*, op. cit., p. 70.
30. Vibeke Sørensen, 'Economic Recovery versus Containment: The Anglo-American Controversy over East–West Trade, 1947–51', *Co-operation and Conflict*, vol. 24 (1989), p. 89.

31. For an enlightening account of the response of the West German government see Robert Mark Spaulding, *Osthandel and Ostpolitik: German Trade Policies in Eastern Europe from Bismarck to Adenauer* (Providence, RI: Berghahn Books, 1997), pp. 351–9.

32. Public Record Office, Kew, London [hereafter PRO], FO 371 94308, telegram from British embassy, Washington DC, to Foreign Office, 18 May 1951.

33. *FRUS*, vol. 1 (1951), pp. 1085–6, memorandum of conversation between Linder and Franks, 5 June 1951.

34. PRO FO 371 94308, telegram from Franks to Foreign Office, 11 May 1951.

35. PRO FO 371 94310, telegram from Franks to Foreign Office, 30 June 1951.

36. PRO FO 371 94308, report by Franks to Foreign Office on Western European security export controls to the Soviet bloc (including China), 15 March 1951.

37. PRO FO 371 94308, telegram from Foreign Office to British embassy, Washington DC, 25 May 1951.

38. PRO FO 371 94309, telegram from Foreign Office to Commerce Department, Washington DC, 10 July 1951.

39. *FRUS*, vol. 1 (1951), p. 1115, telegram from Bruce to Acheson, 16 June 1951.

40. NARA RG 59 460.509/6-2251, memorandum prepared by State Department on approach to CoCom countries regarding the Kem Amendment, 22 June 1951.

41. *FRUS*, vol. 1 (1951), pp. 1128–30, telegram from Acheson to Douglas, American embassy, London, 22 June 1951.

42. NARA RG 59 460.509/7-851, telegram from Gifford, London, to Acheson, 10 July 1951.

43. *FRUS*, vol. 1 (1951), p. 1145, telegram from Acheson to Gifford, 9 July 1951.

44. NARA RG 59 460.509/7-1051, telegram from Gifford to Acheson, 10 July 1951.

45. *FRUS*, vol. 1 (1951), pp. 1151–3, telegram from Gifford to Acheson, 17 July 1951; Ibid., p. 1153, telegram from Bruce to Acheson, 18 July 1951.

46. NARA RG 59 460.509/7-1751, telegram from Acheson to Bruce, 17 July 1951.

47. HSTL, Dean Acheson Papers, box 181, telegram from Acheson to Bruce.

48. NARA RG 59 460.509/7-1851, telegram from Acheson to Bruce, 18 July 1951.

49. PRO FO 371 94298, statement of chairman of American delegation at CoCom, 19 July 1951.

50. PRO FO 371 94297, telegram from Foreign Office to British embassy, Copenhagen, 21 July 1951.

51. *FRUS*, vol. 1 (1951), p. 1158, telegram from Bruce to Acheson, 20 July 1951.

52. NARA RG 59 460.509/7-2351, telegram from Jacques, Paris, to Acheson, 23 July 1951.

53. NARA RG 59 460.509/7-2851, telegram from Bruce to Acheson, 28 July 1951.

54. *FRUS*, vol. 1 (1951), p. 1164, telegram from Gifford to Acheson, 31 July 1951.

55. PRO FO 371 94299, brief for Berthoud on the position to be taken by Britain at the Consultative Group meeting on 1 August 1951, undated.

56. *FRUS*, vol. 1 (1951), pp. 1164–6, telegram from Bonsal, Paris, to Acheson, 2 August 1951.

57. NARA RG 59 460.509/8-251, telegram from Linder to Acheson, 2 August 1951, HSTL, Dean Acheson Papers, box 181, telegram from Bruce to Acheson, 3 August 1951.

6   Anglo–American Relations and the Battle Act

1. For a representative sample of recent works on Churchill and Anglo-American relations in the 1950s see Peter Boyle, 'The "Special Relationship" with Washington', in John W. Young, *The Foreign Policy of Churchill's Peacetime Administration, 1951–55* (Leicester: Leicester University Press, 1988), pp. 39–42; Alan P. Dobson, *Anglo-American Relations in the Twentieth Century: of friendship, conflict and the rise and decline of superpowers* (London: Routledge, 1995), pp. 101–4; John Charmley, *Churchill's Grand Alliance: The Anglo-American Special Relationship* (London: Hodder and Stoughton, 1995).

2. A. P. Dobson, 'Informally special? The Churchill–Truman talks of January 1952 and the state of Anglo-American relations', *Review of International Studies*, vol. 23 (1997), pp. 27–47.

3. Charmley, *Churchill's Grand Alliance*, op. cit., pp. 254–5.

4. Dobson, 'Informally Special', op. cit., pp. 36–44.

5. William I. Hitchcock, *France Restored: Cold War Diplomacy and the Quest for Leadership in Europe, 1944–54* (Chapel Hill, NC: University of North Carolina Press, 1998), pp. 133–68.

6. John W. Young, *Winston Churchill's Last Campaign: Britain and the Cold War, 1951–55* (Oxford: Clarendon Press, 1996), pp. 58–63.

7. Charmley, *Churchill's Grand Alliance*, op. cit., p. 255.

8. Alan P. Dobson, *The Politics of the Anglo-American Economic Special Relationship, 1940–87* (Brighton: Wheatsheaf, 1988), pp. 134–6.

9. Public Record Office, Kew, London [hereafter PRO], FO 371/94326, telegram from Foreign Office to British embassy, Washington DC, 27 July 1951; PRO FO 371/94310, telegram from British embassy, Washington DC, to State Department, 6 August 1951.

10. National Archives and Records Administration, Washington DC [hereafter NARA], RG 59 460.509/8-251, telegram from Bonsal to Acheson, 2 August 1951.

11. PRO FO 371/94310, telegram from Franks, Washington DC, to Foreign Office, 23 July 1951.

12. PRO FO 371/94294, telegram from Pink, British delegation to the OEEC, to Everson, Foreign Office, 22 June 1951.

13. PRO FO 371/94322, notes for the president of the Board of Trade's speech at Truro, Cornwall, 15 August 1951.

14. PRO FO 371/94323, brief for the secretary of state for his meeting with Dean Acheson, 3 September 1951.

15. *Foreign Relations of the United States* [hereafter *FRUS*], vol. 1 (1951), pp. 1183–5, minutes of the second meeting of the American and British foreign ministers in Washington DC, 11 September 1951.

16. Vibeke Sørensen, 'Economic Recovery versus Containment: The Anglo-American Controversy over East–West Trade, 1947–51', *Co-operation and Conflict*, vol. XXIV (1989), pp. 69–97.
17. For context, see Melvyn P. Leffler, *The Spectre of Communism: The United States and the Origins of the Cold War, 1917–1953* (New York: Hill and Wang, 1994), pp. 119–26.
18. *FRUS*, vol. 1 (1951), p. 1218, telegram from Webb, State Department to Bruce, Paris, 22 November 1951; Ibid., p. 1218, telegram from Bonsal to Webb, 23 November 1951; Ibid., pp. 873–5, telegram from Dunn to Acheson, 22 September 1952; NARA RG 59 460.509/10-1752, *aide mémoire* from the State Department to the French embassy, Washington DC, 17 October 1952.
19. *FRUS*, vol. 1 (1951), pp. 1221–2, telegram from Webb, State Department, to Bruce, Paris, 5 December 1951.
20. NARA RG 59 460.509/10-351, memorandum by R. B. Wright of conversation at the State Department, 3 October 1951.
21. PRO FO 371/100213, Pink, British delegation to the OEEC, to Foreign Office, 8 January 1952.
22. *FRUS*, vol. 1 (1951), pp. 1223–4, telegram from Bruce to Webb, 22 December 1951.
23. PRO FO 371/100213, record of conversation at the Foreign Office by R. M. K. Slater, 29 December 1951.
24. PRO FO 371/100218, minutes of meeting of Joint War Production Committee Export Controls Working Party at the Ministry of Defence, 28 December 1951.
25. *FRUS*, vol. 1 (1952–54), p. 817, telegram from Penfold, London, to Acheson, 4 January 1952.
26. PRO FO 371/100218, memorandum by Todd, American embassy, London, on action desired by the British government in connection with the Battle Act, 1 February 1952.
27. PRO FO 371/100213, paper by Slater on Britain's objections to the Battle Act, 28 December 1951.
28. PRO FO 371/94326, note by the secretariat of the Joint War Production Committee Security Export Controls Working Party at the Ministry of Defence, 8 December 1951.
29. Gunnar Adler-Karlsson, *Western Economic Warfare, 1947–67: A Case Study in Foreign Economic Policy* (Stockholm: Almquist and Wicksell, 1968), pp. 34–7; Sørensen, 'Economic Recovery versus Containment', op. cit., pp. 90–1.
30. Dobson, 'Informally Special', op. cit., pp. 37; Helen Leigh-Phippard, 'US Strategic Export Controls and Aid to Britain', *Diplomacy and Statecraft*, vol. 6, no. 3 (November 1995), pp. 735–45.
31. *FRUS*, vol. 1 (1952–54), p. 818, memorandum of conversation by Godley, 5 January 1952.
32. PRO FO 371/100213, telegram from Foreign Office to British embassy, Copenhagen, 6 January 1952.
33. PRO FO 371/100213, telegram no. 99 from Franks to Foreign Office, 10 January 1952.
34. PRO FO 371/100213, telegram no. 100 from Franks to Foreign Office, 10 January 1952.

35. PRO FO 371/100213, record of meeting between the British and American delegations at the Foreign Office on the implications of the Battle Act, 12 January 1952.
36. PRO FO 371/100214, draft notes for the leader of British delegation for the discussions on the Battle Act in CoCom, undated.
37. PRO FO 371/100214, statement by the British delegation, 15 January 1952.
38. PRO FO 371/100214, speech by the leader of French delegation, Schuman, at the Paris Group meetings, 15–16 January 1952.
39. *FRUS*, vol. 1 (1952–54), pp. 819–21, telegram from Bruce to Acheson, 17 January 1952.
40. PRO FO 371/100213, telegram from Foreign Office to British delegation, 18 January 1952.
41. NARA RG 59/460.509/2-2652, telegram from Ainsworth, Paris, to Camp, State Department, 26 February 1952.
42. PRO FO 371/100213, telegram no. 35 from Patch-Hall, British delegation to the OEEC, to Foreign Office, 21 January 1952.
43. PRO FO 371/100213, telegram no. 34 from British delegation to the OEEC to Foreign Office, 21 January 1952.
44. Philip J. Funigiello, *American–Soviet Trade in the Cold War* (Chapel Hill, NC: University of North Carolina Press, 1988), pp. 72–3.
45. *FRUS*, vol. 1 (1952–54), pp. 847–9, letter from Acheson to Connolly, 9 June 1952.
46. Harry S. Truman Library, Dean Acheson Papers, box 75, memorandum by Linder of conversations between Acheson and certain Western European ambassadors, 12 June 1952.
47. *FRUS*, vol. 1 (1952–54), pp. 852–3, memorandum by Linder of conversation between Acheson and Franks, 12 June 1952.
48. PRO FO 371/100215, note by Garvey, Foreign Office, on the revival of the Kem Amendment, 26 June 1952.
49. PRO FO 371/100225, draft British proposal on East–West trade, 28 May 1952.
50. PRO FO 371/100223, record of the meeting of the Consultative Group from the British delegation to the OEEC to Foreign Office, 21 June 1952.
51. PRO FO 371/100225, telegram from Franks to Foreign Office, 15 June 1952.
52. PRO FO 371/100225, record of meeting at the Foreign Office between the British and American delegations prior to the Consultative Group meeting of 20 June 1952.
53. PRO FO 371/100227, statement by the American delegation to the Consultative Group on outstanding commitments to export embargoed items to the Soviet bloc, 24 June 1952.
54. PRO FO 371/100225, telegram from the British delegation to the Foreign Office, 26 June 1952; PRO FO 371/100227, summary record of the Consultative Group meetings, 27 June 1952; PRO FO 371/100225, note by Garvey on prior commitments, 19 June 1952.
55. PRO FO 371/100225, minute of meeting at the Foreign Office between Eden, Acheson and Schuman, 27 June 1952.
56. PRO FO 371/100228, note on prior East–West trade commitments by Garvey, 11 July 1952; NARA RG 59 461.119/7-1152, telegram from Gifford to Acheson, 11 July 1952.

57. PRO FO 371/100233, Consultative Group discussion on American proposals for exceptions under the Battle Act, CoCom document no. 877, undated.
58. PRO FO 371/100231, CoCom report on Britain's proposals for exceptions to the Battle Act, telegram from British delegation to the OEEC to Foreign Office, 31 July 1952.
59. PRO FO 371/100237, telegram from Cazelet, Paris, to Arculus, Foreign Office, 13 November 1952.
60. PRO FO 371/100216, telegram from Pink, Paris, to Berthoud, Foreign Office, 15 August 1952.
61. PRO FO 371/100216, letter from Gresswell to Berthoud, 5 September 1952.
62. PRO FO 371/100216, Foreign Office note for discussion with Congressman Battle, 18 September 1952.
63. PRO FO 371/100216, telegram from Hoyer-Millar, Paris, to Foreign Office, 18 September 1952.
64. PRO FO 371/100216, telegram from McCall-Judson, Washington DC, to Berthoud, Foreign Office, 19 September 1952; PRO FO 371/100217, telegram from McCall-Judson, Washington DC, to Berthoud, Foreign Office, 10 October 1952.
65. PRO FO 371/100216, note of meeting between British officials and Battle at the Ministry of Defence on East–West trade controls, 19 September 1952.
66. PRO FO 371/100216, record of conversation between Makins and Battle at the Foreign Office, 22 September 1952.
67. *FRUS*, vol. 1 (1952–54), pp. 896–900, letter from Battle to Harriman, 29 September 1952.
68. PRO FO 371/100232, letter from Arculus to Shepherd, 15 September 1952.
69. PRO FO 371/105846, copy of President Truman's letter to six congressional committees on Britain's exception to the Battle Act, 31 December 1952.
70. PRO FO 371/100283, telegram from Pink, Paris, to Coulson, Foreign Office, 23 December 1952.
71. PRO FO 371/105865, covering memorandum to the report by the British study team on the American system of security export controls, 9 January 1953.
72. PRO FO 371/105865, minutes of conversation between Gresswell, Ministry of Defence, and Coulson, Foreign Office, 13 January 1952.

7 Eisenhower, Churchill and East–West Trade

1. Robert Mark Spaulding, '"A Gradual and Moderate Relaxation": Eisenhower and the Revision of American Export Control Policy, 1953–55', *Diplomatic History*, vol. 17, no. 2 (Spring 1993), pp. 223–49.
2. John W. Young, 'Winston Churchill's Peacetime Administration and the Relaxation of East–West Trade Controls, 1953–54', *Diplomacy and Statecraft*, vol. 7, no. 1 (March 1996), pp. 125–40.
3. For context see Stephen E. Ambrose, *Eisenhower: The President, 1952–69* (New York: Simon and Schuster, 1984), pp. 13–44, and Herbert S. Parmet, *Eisenhower and the American Crusades* (New Brunswick: Transaction, 1999), pp. 3–63.

206 Notes and References

4. The 'solvency and security' approach to national security policy is discussed in Michael J. Hogan, *A Cross of Iron: Harry S. Truman and the Origins of the National Security State, 1945–54* (Cambridge: Cambridge University Press, 1998), pp. 366–418.

5. John Lewis Gaddis, *We Now Know: Rethinking Cold War History* (New York: Oxford University Press, 1997), pp. 230–4.

6. Saki Dockrill, *Eisenhower's New-Look National Security Policy, 1953–61* (London: Macmillan, 1996), pp. 72–115.

7. John Lewis Gaddis, *The United States and the End of the Cold War: Implications, Reconsiderations, Provocations* (New York: Oxford University Press, 1992), pp. 73–7; Frederick Marks III, *Power and Peace: The Diplomacy of John Foster Dulles* (Westport, CT: Praeger, 1993), pp. 25–40.

8. An important new account of the Eisenhower administration's national security policy is Robert R. Bowie and Richard H. Immerman, *Waging Peace: How Eisenhower Shaped an Enduring Cold War Strategy* (New York: Oxford University Press, 1998), pp. 202–21.

9. Pascaline Winand, *Eisenhower, Kennedy, and the United States of Europe* (London: Macmillan, 1993), pp. 65–82.

10. Anne-Marie Burley, 'Restoration and Reunification: Eisenhower's German Policy', in Richard Melanson and David Mayers (eds), *Re-evaluating Eisenhower: American Foreign Policy in the Fifties* (Chicago, Ill.: University of Illinois Press, 1987), pp. 220–41.

11. Saki Dockrill, 'Co-operation and Suspicion: The United States' Alliance Diplomacy for the Security of Western Europe', *Diplomacy and Statecraft*, vol. 5, no. 1 (March 1994), pp. 153–4.

12. John W. Young, *Winston Churchill's Last Campaign: Britain and the Cold War, 1951–55* (Oxford: Oxford University Press, 1996), pp. 117–31.

13. Alan P. Dobson, *Anglo-American Relations in the Twentieth Century: of friendship, conflict and the rise and demise of superpowers* (London: Routledge, 1995), pp. 108–10.

14. Bowie and Immerman, *Waging Peace*, op. cit., pp. 215–19.

15. Stephen G. Rabe, 'Eisenhower Revisionism: The Scholarly Debate', in Michael Hogan (ed.), *America in the World: The Historiography of American Foreign Relations Since 1941* (Cambridge: Cambridge University Press, 1995), pp. 300–25.

16. Tor Egil Førland, '"Selling Firearms to the Indians": Eisenhower's Export Control Policy, 1953–54', *Diplomatic History*, vol. 15, no. 2 (Spring 1991), pp. 221–44.

17. The NSC during the Eisenhower years is examined in Anna Kasten Nelson, 'The Top of the Policy Hill: President Eisenhower and the National Security Council', *Diplomatic History*, vol. 7, no. 4 (Fall 1983), pp. 307–26; Fred I. Greenstein, *The Hidden-Hand Presidency: Eisenhower as Leader* (Baltimore, MD: The Johns Hopkins University Press, 1982), pp. 124–36; Cecil V. Crabb and Kevin V. Mulcahy, *American National Security: A Presidential Perspective* (Pacific Grove, CA: Brook/Cole, 1991), pp. 89–105.

18. See Alan P. Dobson, *The USA and Economic Warfare: Selected Perspectives on Economic Statecraft, 1933–1990* (London: Routledge, forthcoming).

19. *Foreign Relations of the United States* [hereafter *FRUS*], vol. 1 (1952–54), pp. 1006–7, memorandum of discussion at the 157th meeting of the National Security Council, 30 July 1953.
20. *FRUS*, vol. 1 (1952–54), pp. 940–1, memorandum of discussion at the 137th meeting of the National Security Council, 18 March 1953.
21. Ibid., pp. 1161–4, memorandum of discussion at the 197th meeting of the National Security Council, 13 May 1954.
22. Ibid., p. 1169, memorandum of discussion at the 198th meeting of the National Security Council, 20 May 1954.
23. Ibid., p. 1220, memorandum of discussion at the 205th meeting of the National Security Council, 1 July 1954.
24. Ibid., pp. 1109–15, memorandum of discussion at the 188th meeting of the National Security Council, 11 March 1954; Ibid., pp. 1219–20, memorandum of discussion at the 205th meeting of the National Security Council, 1 July 1954.
25. Ibid., p. 1169, memorandum of discussion at the 198th meeting of the National Security Council, 20 May 1954.
26. Public Record Office, Kew, London [hereafter PRO], FO 371/105866, copy of letter from Eisenhower to Bridges, 1 August 1953.
27. *FRUS*, vol. 1 (1952–54), p. 940, memorandum of discussion at the 137th meeting of the National Security Council, 18 March 1953.
28. Ibid., p. 1219, memorandum of discussion at the 205th meeting of the National Security Council, 1 July 1954.
29. Spaulding, 'A Gradual and moderate Relaxation', op. cit., p. 237, Philip J. Funigiello, *American–Soviet Trade in the Cold War* (Chapel Hill, NC: University of North Carolina Press, 1988), pp. 76–96.
30. Ambrose, *Eisenhower*, op. cit., p. 39.
31. *FRUS*, vol. 1 (1952–54), pp. 1112–15, memorandum of discussion at the 188th meeting of the National Security Council, 11 March 1954.
32. Ibid., pp. 1201–3, memorandum of discussion at the 202nd meeting of the National Security Council, 17 June 1954.
33. Ibid., pp. 1112–15, memorandum of discussion at the 188th meeting of the National Security Council, 11 March 1954.
34. Ibid., p. 1162, memorandum of discussion at the 197th meeting of the National Security Council, 13 May 1954.
35. National Archives and Records Administration, Washington DC [hereafter NARA], RG 59 460.509/5–2154, letter from Weeks to Dulles, 21 May 1954.
36. *FRUS*, vol. 1 (1952–54), pp. 1219–20, memorandum of discussion at the 205th meeting of the National Security Council, 1 July 1954.
37. Ibid., pp. 1112–15, memorandum of discussion at the 188th meeting of the National Security Council, 11 March 1954.
38. Ibid., pp. 1219–20, memorandum of discussion at the 205th meeting of the National Security Council, 1 July 1954.
39. Ibid., pp. 1219–20, memorandum of discussion at the 205th meeting of the National Security Council, 1 July 1954.
40. Ibid., p. 1007, memorandum of discussion at the 157th meeting of the National Security Council, 30 July 1953.
41. Funigiello, *American–Soviet Trade*, op. cit., pp. 76–7; Burton I. Kaufman, *Trade and Aid: Eisenhower's Foreign Economic Policy, 1953–61* (Baltimore, MD:

The Johns Hopkins University Press, 1982), pp. 60–1; Gunnar Adler–Karlsson, *Western Economic Warfare, 1947–67: A Case-Study in Foreign Economic Policy* (Stockholm: Almquist and Wiksell, 1968), pp. 83–4.

42. Dockrill, *Eisenhower's New-Look National Security Policy*, op. cit., pp. 19–49.
43. For discussion see Tor Egil Førland, 'Cold Economic Warfare; The Creation and Prime of CoCom, 1948–54', unpublished D.Phil. thesis, University of Oslo, 1991.
44. *FRUS*, vol. 1 (1952–54), pp. 1009–14, NSC 152/2, 31 July 1953.
45. PRO FO 371/105865, brief for the foreign secretary for talks with Dulles on the security control of East–West trade, 4 March 1953.
46. PRO FO 371/105866, letter from Arculus to Dunnett, British delegation to the OEEC, Paris, 7 September 1953.
47. PRO FO 371/105867, report of CoCom meeting on the *Third Battle Report to Congress*, CoCom document no. 1327, 8 September 1953.
48. Young, *Churchill's Last Campaign*, op. cit., pp. 247–51.
49. PRO CAB 134 887, ES (53), note on East–West trade by the secretary of the Economic Steering Committee, 25 August 1953.
50. PRO CAB 134 885 ES (53), memorandum of the seventh meeting of the Economic Steering Committee, 2 September 1953.
51. PRO CAB 134 849 EA (54) 133, memorandum by the president of the Board of Trade on East–West trade, 13 November 1953.
52. PRO CAB 134 EA (54), third meeting of the Economic policy committee, 18 February 1954; PRO CAB 134 848 EA (53) 113, report on East–West trade by the Mutual Aid Committee of the Economic Policy Committee.

8   Economic Containment for the 'Long Haul'

1. National Archives and Records Administration, Washington DC [hereafter NARA], RG 59 460.509/10-653, *aide mémoire* from the State Department to the British embassy, Washington DC, 6 October 1953.
2. NARA RG 460.509/9-1653, telegram from Smith to all American diplomatic posts and FOA missions and certain consular posts, 11 September 1953.
3. Public Record Office, Kew, London [hereafter PRO], FO 371/105867, telegram no. 2127 from Makins to Foreign Office, 6 October 1953.
4. PRO FO 371/105867, telegram no. 2126 from Makins to Foreign Office, 6 October 1953.
5. PRO FO 371/105867, memorandum of a conversation at the Foreign Office on the new American attitude towards strategic export controls, 9 October 1953.
6. PRO FO 371/105867, note from Crawford to Coulson, 10 October 1953; PRO FO 371/105867, letter from Baylis, Board of Trade, to Crawford, 15 October 1953; PRO FO 371/105867, report by Security Export Control Working Party of the Joint War Production Committee, Ministry of Defence, on the forthcoming Anglo-American talks on East–West trade, 15 October 1953.
7. NARA RG 59 461.419/11-753, telegram from Aldrich to Dulles, 7 November 1953.

8. *Foreign Relations of the United States* [hereafter *FRUS*], vol. 1 (1952–54), pp. 1040–3, report of the prebilateral meetings of 3–6 November, 10 November 1953.
9. PRO FO 371/105867, note of meeting between American and British officials, 5 November 1953; PRO FO 371/105867, record of the first meeting of the Anglo-American talks on East–West trade, 3 November 1953.
10. PRO FO 371/105868, report by the Mutual Committee of the cabinet on the Anglo-American talks on security export controls on trade with the Soviet bloc and the PRC, undated.
11. PRO FO 371/105867, statement by the British delegation at the Anglo-American discussions on East–West trade, 20 November 1953.
12. PRO FO 371/105867, statement by the American delegation at the Anglo-American discussions on East–West trade, 21 November 1953.
13. *FRUS*, vol. 1 (1952–54), pp. 1063–4, letter from Aldrich to British government, 3 December 1953.
14. Ibid., p. 1065, memorandum from Stassen to Dulles, 9 December 1953.
15. Ibid., pp. 1070–1, letter from Dulles to Stassen, 21 January 1954.
16. PRO CAB 128/26, CC (53) 67, minutes of cabinet meeting, 17 November 1953.
17. For details see John W. Young, 'Winston Churchill's Peacetime Administration and the Relaxation of East–West Trade Controls, 1953–54, *Diplomacy and Statecraft*, vol. 7, no. 1 (March 1996), pp. 130–3.
18. PRO CAB 128/27, CC (54) 3, minutes of cabinet meeting, 18 January 1954.
19. PRO CAB 130/99, Gen. 454, 1, minutes of the ad hoc ministerial committee on security export controls, 25 January 1954.
20. PRO CAB 128/27, CC (54) 9, minutes of cabinet meeting, 17 February 1954.
21. NARA RG 59 460.509/2-2654; Churchill's speech is quoted in a telegram from Aldrich to Dulles, 26 February 1954.
22. Robert Mark Spaulding, '"A Gradual and Moderate Relaxation": Eisenhower and the Revision of American Export Control Policy, 1953–55', *Diplomatic History*, vol. 17, no. 2 (Spring 1993), p. 242.
23. NARA RG 59 460.419/2-454, telegram from Brown, London, to Dulles, 4 February 1954.
24. *FRUS*, vol. 1 (1952–54), p. 1081, telegram from Aldrich to Dulles, 26 February 1954.
25. PRO FO 371/111293, memorandum from the British government to the American embassy-London, 1 March 1954.
26. *FRUS*, vol. 1 (1952–54), pp. 1083–4, telegram from Aldrich to Dulles, 1 March 1954.
27. NARA RG 59 460.509/3-554, telegram from Hughes to Dulles, 1 March 1954.
28. NARA RG 59 460.509/3-454, telegram from Smith to Aldrich, 5 March 1954; NARA RG 59 460.509/3-554, Smith to Dillon, Paris, 6 March 1954.
29. NARA RG 59 460.509/3-954, telegram from Hughes to Dulles, 9 March 1954; NARA RG 59 460.509/3-1054, telegram from Hughes to Dulles, 10 March 1954.
30. NARA RG 59 460.509/3-1154, memorandum by the Planning Board of the NSC, 9 March 1954; NARA RG 59 460.509/1654, memorandum by the State Department on East–West trade, 16 March 1954.

31. NARA RG 59 460.509/3-1954, letter from Eisenhower to Churchill, 19 March 1954.
32. *FRUS*, vol. 1 (1952–54), pp. 1132–3, telegram from Dulles to Aldrich containing Churchill's reply to Eisenhower, 27 March 1954.
33. PRO FO 371/111304, record of the first plenary meeting of the British/American/French talks on East–West trade, 29 March 1954; PRO FO 371111304, record of the second plenary meeting of the tripartite talks on East–West trade, 30 March 1954.
34. PRO FO 371/111304, record of the third plenary meeting of the tripartite talks on East–West trade, 30 March 1954.
35. PRO FO 371/111304, communiqué by the United States, Britain and France on East–West trade, 30 March 1954.
36. PRO FO 371/111211, telegram no. 277 from British delegation, Paris, to Foreign Office, 15 April 1954.
37. NARA RG 59 460.509/5-2454, telegram from Dulles to certain diplomatic posts, FOA missions and consular posts, 24 May 1954.
38. *FRUS*, vol. 1 (1952–54), pp. 1183–4, report on the trilateral and CoCom meetings in Paris, 24 May 1954.
39. Ibid., pp. 1151–3, telegram from Dillon to Dulles, 29 April 1954.
40. Ibid., pp. 1148–9, telegram from Aldrich to Dulles, 22 April 1954.
41. Tor Egil Førland, 'Cold Economic Warfare: The Creation and Prime of CoCom, 1948–54', D.Phil. thesis, University of Oslo, 1991, pp. 290–2.
42. *FRUS*, vol. 1 (1952–54), pp. 1223–5, telegram from Dulles to Dillon, 7 July 1954; NARA RG 59 460.509/7-954, Anglo-American East–West trade talks: 'package settlement plan', 7 July 1954.
43. *FRUS*, vol. 1 (1952–54), pp. 1229–30, telegram from Aldrich to Dulles, 16 July 1954.
44. NARA RG 59 460.509/7-2454, telegram from Hughes to Dulles, 24 July 1954; PRO FO 371/111213, telegram from British delegation, Paris, to Foreign Office, 20 July 1954; NARA RG 59 460.509/8-2454, advance press release by the foreign operations administrator, 26 August 1954.
45. *FRUS*, vol. 1 (1952–54), pp. 1230–1, telegram from Hughes to Dulles, 22 July 1954; Ibid., p. 1244, report from Dulles and Stassen to the NSC, 30 August 1954.
46. Dwight D. Eisenhower Library, Abilene, Kansas [hereafter DDEL], US Council on Foreign Economic Relations Reports Series, box 2, 'Economic Defence Policy Review', 20 January 1955.
47. PRO FO 371/116076, CP (55) 122, memorandum on security export controls and East–West trade by the Ministry of Defence, report by A. J. Edden, 20 September 1955; PRO FO 371/116076, report on discussions between representatives from the Foreign Office, Ministry of Defence, the American embassy, London, and the State Department, 27 September 1955.
48. *FRUS*, vol. x (1955–57), pp. 203–4, telegram from Dulles to American embassy, London, containing note for Eden, 7 January 1955.
49. Ibid., pp. 223–4, telegram from Hoover to American embassy, London, 23 February 1955; PRO FO 371/116071, telegram from Foreign Office to British embassy, Washington, containing message from Thorneycroft to Stassen, 10 January 1955; PRO FO 371/116071, telegram from British embassy, Washington, to Foreign Office, 13 January 1955.

50. *FRUS*, vol. x (1955–57), pp. 224–5, letter from Murphy, State Department, to Wilson, 28 February 1955.
51. PRO FO 371/ 116072, telegram from Foreign Office to British embassy, Washington, 2 March 1955; PRO FO 371/116072, brief on East–West trade for New York meeting, prepared by Edden, 11 June 1955.
52. *FRUS*, vol. x (1955–57), pp. 238–9, telegram from Aldrich to State Department, 28 June 1955.
53. Ibid., pp. 269–70, letter from Weeks to Hoover, 23 November 1955; Ibid., pp. 270–1, letter from Hoover to Weeks, 3 December 1955.
54. Gunnar Adler-Karlsson, *Western Economic Warfare, 1947–67: A Case Study in Foreign Economic Policy* (Stockholm: Almquist and Wiksell, 1968), pp. 93–4; PRO FO 371/116077, telegram from Foreign Office to British embassy, Washington, 27 October 1955.
55. Chester J. Pach Jr and Elmo Richardson, *The Presidency of Dwight D. Eisenhower* (Kansas: University of Kansas Press, 1991), pp. 108–12.
56. *FRUS*, vol. x (1955–57), p. 236, memorandum from the chief of division of functional intelligence (Doherty) to the special assistant to the secretary of state for intelligence (Armstrong), 24 June 1955.
57. Ibid., pp. 239–41, memorandum of discussion at the 254th meeting of the National Security Council, 7 July 1955.
58. Ibid., p. 245, editorial note.
59. DDEL, Dwight D. Eisenhower Papers, Ann Whitman File, International Series, box 2, memorandum on psychological strategy at Geneva no. 3, 'Expansion of Trade Proposal', by Nelson A. Rockefeller, 11 July 1955.
60. Eden's statement reflected the belief held by ministers and officials that trade was an important issue to be addressed in East–West relations and that the expansion of commerce could help to alleviate international tensions. See PRO FO 371/116072, brief by Coulson on East–West trade and the Four Power talks, 31 May 1955; PRO FO 371/116072, note by Macmillan on East–West trade, 8 June 1955; PRO FO 371/116072, brief for Macmillan on East–West trade for New York talks, 16 June 1955; PRO FO 371/116072, record of comments by Thorneycroft on East–West trade, 15 June 1955.
61. NARA RG 59 460.509/8-955, enclosure containing text of Eden's speech in instruction from State Department to certain diplomatic posts on East–West trade and the Geneva Conference, 9 August 1955.
62. DDLE, Dwight D. Eisenhower Papers, Confidential File, box 61, memorandum for the secretary of state entitled 'Study of Psychological Aspects of US Strategy', by Nelson A. Rockefeller, 9 August 1955; DDE, C. D. Jackson Papers, box 91, letter from C. D. Jackson to Nelson A. Rockefeller, 7 February 1955.
63. *FRUS*, vol. x (1955), p. 252, memorandum of conversation in the State Department, 11 August 1955.
64. NARA RG 489 S-S 13123, box 118 (Soviet Union), Economic Advisory Committee, tripartite statement on the Geneva Foreign Ministers' Meeting, October–November 1955, 29 November 1955; NARA RG 59 460.509/12-655, letter from Gray, Defense Department, to Hoover, 16 December 1955; NARA RG 59 460.509/12-655, letter from Hoover to Gray, 30 December 1955.

65. Yoko Yasuhara, 'Japan, Communist China, and Export Controls in Asia, 1948–52', *Diplomatic History*, vol. 10, no. 1 (Winter 1986), pp. 74–89; Frank Cain, 'The US–led Trade Embargo on China: the Origins of ChinCom, 1947–52', *Journal of Strategic Studies*, vol. 18, no. 4 (December 1995), pp. 33–55; Rosemary Foot, *The Practice of Power: US Relations with China since 1949* (Oxford: Clarendon Press, 1995), pp. 52–60.

66. DDEL, US Council on Foreign Economic Policy Reports Series, box 2, 'Economic Defence Policy Review', undated.

67. *FRUS*, vol. x (1955–57), pp. 247–8, memorandum from deputy director of operations, International Co-operation Administration, to director of the International Co-operation Administration, 8 August 1955; Ibid., p. 249, telegram from State Department to American embassy, Paris, 10 August 1955.

68. NARA RG 59 460.509/10-2555, CS/RA, office memorandum from Robertson to McConaughy, 25 October 1955.

69. NARA RG 59 460.509/10-55, telegram from State Department to embassies in Bonn, London and Tokyo, 5 October 1955.

70. *FRUS*, vol. x (1955–57), pp. 275–6, letter from Dulles to Eisenhower, 8 December 1955.

71. Ibid., pp. 275–6, telegram from State Department to American embassy, London, containing note from Dulles to Macmillan, 10 December 1955.

72. Ibid., pp. 278–9, letter from Gray to Hoover, 12 December 1955.

73. Ibid., pp. 286–7, minutes of the 36th meeting of the CFEP, 12 January 1956.

74. Ibid., pp. 304–8, memorandum of conversation between Dulles and Lloyd, 31 January 1956.

75. Ibid., pp. 309–11, memorandum of conversation between Eisenhower and Eden at the White House, 31 January 1956.

76. Ibid., p. 320, memorandum of a conversation at the State Department, 7 March 1956.

77. Ibid., pp. 331–3, memorandum of discussion at the 281st meeting of the National Security Council, 5 April 1956; Ibid., pp. 338–9, memorandum of conversation with the president, White House, 18 April 1956.

78. Ibid., pp. 339–40, memorandum of conversation between Dulles and Ambassador Roger Makins, 13 April 1956; Ibid., pp. 342–43, memorandum by Hoover for the record, 19 April 1956.

79. Ibid., pp. 343–4, letter from Dulles to Lloyd, 19 April 1956.

80. Ibid., p. 357, letter from Eisenhower to Eden, 27 April 1956.

81. Ibid., p. 358, memorandum of conversation between Dulles and Makins, 1 May 1956.

82. Ibid., p. 359, letter from Eden to Eisenhower, 2 May 1956.

83. Ibid., pp. 362–3, telegram from American delegation at the North Atlantic Council meeting, Paris, 4 May 1956; Ibid., p. 364, letter from Dulles to Eisenhower containing a note from Lloyd, 14 May 1956.

84. Ibid., pp. 371–2, letter from Wilson to Dulles, 22 June 1956.

85. Ibid., pp. 373–4, letter from Dulles to Wilson, 28 June 1956.

86. For the effect of the Suez Crisis on Anglo-American relations see W. Scott Lucas, *Divided We Stand: Britain, the US and the Suez Crisis* (London: Sceptre, 1996), pp. 276–330; Alan P. Dobson, *Anglo-American*

Relations in the Twentieth Century: of friendship, conflict and the rise and decline of superpowers (London: Routledge, 1995), pp. 117–20.

87. Alistair Horne, *Macmillan, 1957–86: Volume II of the Official Biography* (London: Macmillan, 1989), pp. 21–7.

88. *FRUS*, vol. x (1955–57), pp. 418–19, telegram from American embassy, London, to State Department, containing note from British government, 1 March 1957.

89. Ibid., pp. 434–5, memorandum of conversation between Dulles and Lloyd, Bermuda, 22 March 1957.

90. Ibid., pp. 436–7, note from Lloyd to Dulles, 23 March 1957.

91. Ibid., p. 437, note from Dulles to Lloyd, 23 March 1957.

92. Ibid., pp. 438–9, letter from Ambassador Caccia to Dillon, 7 April 1957.

93. Ibid., pp. 450–1, telegram from Dulles to State Department, 3 May 1957.

94. Ibid., p. 451, editorial note.

95. Ibid., pp. 451–2, telegram from American embassy, London, to State Department, 14 May 1957.

96. Ibid., p. 457, telegram from State Department to American embassy, London, containing message from Eisenhower to Macmillan, 17 May 1957.

97. Ibid., pp. 458–9, editorial note.

98. Ibid., pp. 460–1, letter from Macmillan to Eisenhower, 21 May 1957.

99. Ibid., pp. 464–7, letter from Lloyd to Dulles, 25 May 1957.

100. Ibid., p. 466, editorial note.

101. Ibid., p. 467, letter from Macmillan to Eisenhower, 29 May 1957.

102. *FRUS*, vol. iv (1958–60), pp. 680–5, memorandum of conversation with British and Canadian representatives on trade control criteria, 15 January 1958.

103. Ibid., pp. 689–90, memorandum of discussion at the 353rd meeting of the National Security Council, 30 January 1958.

104. Ibid., pp. 692–3, memorandum of discussion at the 354th meeting of the National Security Council, 6 February 1958.

105. Ibid., pp. 688–9, memorandum on conversation on strategic export controls between Dulles and Lloyd in Ankara, 30 January 1958; Ibid., pp. 697–701, memorandum of conversation between American and British representatives on strategic export controls, 8 February 1958.

106. Ibid., pp. 704–10, memorandum of discussion at the 356th meeting of the National Security Council, 27 February 1958.

107. Ibid., pp. 725–8, minutes of 78th meeting of the Council on Foreign Economic Policy, 7 August 1958; Ibid., pp. 730–4, memorandum of discussion at the 377th meeting of the National Security Council, 21 April 1958.

108. Ibid., pp. 771–4, memorandum of conversation between British and American representatives on CoCom list review, 15 September 1959; Ibid., p. 775, editorial note.

109. PRO FO 371/158074/ M 341/24, outline of Foreign Office's contribution to the brief on Anglo-American talks on strategic export controls, 10 May 1961.

110. *FRUS*, vol. iv (1958–60), p. 776, editorial note; Herbert S. Parmet, *Eisenhower and the American Crusades* (New Jersey: Transaction Editions, 1999), pp. 524–70.

9   Kennedy, Macmillan and East–West Trade

1. Michael R. Beschloss, *Kennedy V. Khrushchev: The Crisis Years, 1960–63* (London: Faber and Faber, 1991).
2. James N. Giglio, *The Presidency of John F. Kennedy* (Kansas: University Press of Kansas, 1991), pp. 45–50.
3. Pascaline Winand, *Eisenhower, Kennedy and the United States of Europe* (London: Macmillan, 1993), pp. 139–60.
4. Diane B. Kunz, *Butter and Guns: America's Cold War Diplomacy* (New York: The Free Press, 1997), pp. 120–48.
5. John Lewis Gaddis, *Strategies of Containment: A Critical Appraisal of Post-War American National Security Policy* (New York: Oxford University Press, 1982), pp. 198–237.
6. Arthur M. Schlesinger Jr, *A Thousand Days: John F. Kennedy in the White House* (New York: Fawcett Edition, 1971), pp. 319–76; Theodore C. Sorensen, *Kennedy* (London: Pan, 1966), pp. 644–700.
7. For an excellent account of Khrushchev 's Cold War policies based on Soviet government sources, see Vladislav Zubok and Constantine Pleshakov, *Inside the Kremlin's Cold War: From Stalin to Khrushchev* (Cambridge, Mass.: Harvard University Press, 1996), pp. 236–75.
8. Beschloss, *Kennedy V. Khrushchev*, op cit., pp. 431–576; Aleksandr Fursenko and Timothy Naftali, *'One Hell of A Gamble': Khrushchev, Castro, Kennedy and the Cuban Missile Crisis, 1958–64* (London: Pimlico 1999), pp. 216–90; John Lewis Gaddis, *We Now Know: Rethinking Cold War History* (New York: Oxford University Press, 1996), pp. 260–81; Ernest R. May and Philip D. Zelikow (eds), *The Kennedy Tapes: Inside the White House During the Cuban Missiles Crisis* (Cambridge, Mass.: Harvard University Press, 1997).
9. Giglio, *The Presidency of John F. Kennedy*, op cit., pp. 218–20.
10. Alistair Horne, *Macmillan, 1957–1986: Volume II of the Official Biography* (London, Macmillan, 1989), pp. 361–87.
11. Alan P. Dobson, *Anglo-American Relations in the Twentieth Century: of friendship, conflict and the rise and decline of superpowers* (London: Routledge, 1995), pp. 124–131.
12. Christopher J. Matthews, *Kennedy and Nixon: The Rivalry that Shaped Postwar America* (New York: Simon and Schuster, 1996), p. 75.
13. For details of Kennedy's attempt to amend the Battle Act in 1957 see Philip J. Funigiello, *American–Soviet Trade in the Cold War* (Chapel Hill, NC, University of North Carolina Press, 1988), pp. 124–5.
14. *Foreign Relations of the United States* [hereafter *FRUS*], vol. IX (1961–63), p. 648, editorial note.
15. Ibid., p. 656, editorial note.
16. Ibid., pp. 651–2, memorandum from Bohlen to Bowles, 7 April 1961; Ibid., pp. 653–6, memorandum of conversation on Commerce Advisory Export Board, 18 May 1961.
17. Ibid., pp. 658–60, letter from Hodges to Rusk and McNamara, 18 September 1961.
18. National Archives and Records Administration, Washington DC [hereafter NARA], RG 59 460.509/9-2061, memorandum by State Department on Hodges' letter to Rusk and McNamara, 20 September 1961.

19. *FRUS*, vol. ix (1961–63), pp. 661–3, letter from Hodges to Rusk, 20 October 1961.
20. Ibid., pp. 663–8, summary of minutes of the meeting of the Interdepartmental Committee of Under Secretaries on Foreign Economic Policy, 10 January 1962.
21. Ibid., pp. 670–1, letter from Hodges to Ball, 14 February 1962.
22. Ibid., pp. 675–6, memorandum from Trezise to Rusk, 20 April 1962.
23. Ibid., pp. 678–83, memorandum from Rusk to the NSC, 10 July 1962.
24. Ibid., pp. 689–94, memorandum from Hodges to the NSC, 16 July 1962.
25. Ibid., pp. 695–7, summary record of the 503rd meeting of the National Security Council, 17 July 1962.
26. Ibid., p. 699, National Security Council Record of Action No. 2455, 17 July 1962.
27. Ibid., p. 703, letter from Rusk to Hodges, 5 September 1962.
28. Ibid., p. 705, editorial note.
29. Ibid., pp. 707–8, memorandum from Brubeck, State Department, to Bundy, 4 December 1962.
30. Ibid., p. 711–2, memorandum from Kennedy to the Export Control Review Board, 16 May 1963.
31. Ibid., pp. 718–25, report prepared by the Policy Planning Council, State Department, 26 July 1963.
32. Ibid., pp. 725–7, memorandum from Klein, National Security Council, to Bundy, 14 August 1963.
33. Ibid., pp. 729–32, minutes of Export Control Review Board meeting, 15 August 1963; Ibid., pp. 733–7, memorandum from the Export Control Review Board to Kennedy, 15 August 1963.
34. Ibid., p. 740, memorandum from Kennedy to the Export Control Review Board, 19 September 1963.
35. NARA RG 59 460.509/2-161, telegram from American embassy, Paris, to State Department, 1 February 1961; NARA RG 59 460.509/2-1661, telegram from the American embassy, London, to Rusk, 16 February 1961.
36. NARA RG 59 460.509/2-2161, telegram (section two) from Nolting, Paris, to Rusk, 21 February 1961.
37. NARA RG 59 460.509/3-361, memorandum of conversation between representatives of the State Department and the British embassy, London, 3 March 1961.
38. NARA RG 59 460.509/2-2161, telegram from Nolting, Paris, to Rusk, 21 February 1961; Public Record Office, Kew, London [hereafter PRO], FO 371/158073/ M 341/3A, copy of *aide mémoire* from State Department to Foreign Office, 5 March 1961.
39. PRO FO 371/158073/ M 341/3A, telegram from Foreign Office to Reilly, Washington DC, 9 March 1961.
40. *FRUS*, vol. ix (1961–63), pp. 649–50, memorandum of conversation between American and British representatives in Washington DC, 14 March 1961; PRO FO 371/158073/ M 341/3A, telegram from Reilly, Washington DC, to Foreign Office, 14 March 1961; PRO FO 371/158073/ M 341/6, Foreign Office minute on Reilly–Martin conversation, 14 March 1961.
41. PRO FO 371/158073/ M 341/2, letter from Parker, Board of Trade, to Gallagher, Foreign Office, 30 December 1960.

42. PRO FO 371/158073/ M 341/9, letter from Maudling to Macmillan, 23 March 1961.

43. PRO FO 371/158074/ M 341/24, outline of Foreign Office contribution to brief on Anglo-American talks on strategic controls, 10 May 1961; PRO FO 371/158075/ M 341/39, briefing paper prepared by Foreign Office for Home entitled 'United Kingdom and United States views on Economic Relations with the Bloc', 30 June 1961

44. PRO FO 371/164505/ UEE 10419/102, minute (PM/62/18) from Home to Macmillan on CoCom and East–West trade, 8 February 1962.

45. PRO FO 371/164505/ UUE 10419/102, minute from Macmillan to Home, 9 February 1962.

46. PRO FO 371/164507/ UUE 10419/137, minute (M39/62) from Macmillan to Home, 14 February 1962.

47. PRO FO 371/164507/ UUE 10419/137, minute from Home to Macmillan, 22 February 1962.

48. PRO FO 371/164507/ UUE 10419/137, letter from Ormsby-Gore to Home, 27 February 1962.

49. PRO FO 371/158075/ M 341/60, letter from Mills, paymaster general, to Macmillan on results of ministerial committee on strategic exports, 4 August 1961.

50. *FRUS*, vol. IX (1961–63), pp. 671–4, current economic development circular on Anglo-American East–West trade talks, State Department, 27 February 1962.

51. PRO FO 371/164509/ UEE 10419/172, minute of Reilly's conversation with Martin, State Department, 2 March 1962.

52. PRO FO 371/164511/ UEE 10419/310, minute from fielding on Anglo-American discussions on strategic controls, 23 March 1962; PRO FO 371/164511/ UEE 10419/210, telegram no. 2026 from Foreign Office to British delegation, Paris, 6 April 1962.

53. PRO FO 371/164523/ UEE 10419/392, internal Foreign Office minute from Hale to Fielding, 30 May 1962.

54. NARA RG 59 460.509/7-2662, telegram from Finletter, Paris, to State Department, 23 July 1962; *FRUS*, vol. IX (1961–63), pp. 700–1, current economic developments, 'CoCom completes 1962 List Review', 31 July 1962; NARA RG 59 460.509/7-3162, telegram from American delegation, Paris, to State Department, 31 July 1962; NARA RG 59 460.509/9-2762, letter from Rusk to Lyndon Johnson, 27 September 1962.

55. PRO FO 371/164524/ UEE 10419/404, minute from Mason on CoCom review, 6 June 1962.

56. PRO FO 371/164524/ UEE 10419/404, minute from Mason on the termination of the 1962 CoCom review, 23 July 1962.

57. PRO FO 371/164526/ UEE 10419/441, letter from Hale to Fielding, 11 July 1962.

58. See Bruce W. Jentleson, 'From consensus to conflict: the domestic political economy of East–West energy trade policy', *International Organisation*, vol. 38, no. 4 (Autumn 1984), pp. 637–44; Michael Mastanduno, *Economic Containment: CoCom and the Politics of East–West Trade* (Ithaca, NY: Cornell University Press, 1992), pp. 128–31.

59. PRO FO 371/172413/ UEE 10415/14, minute from Mason on exports of large-diameter pipe to the Soviet Union, 24 January 1963.

60. PRO FO 371/172413/ UEE 10415/14, minute from Reilly on East–West trade differences with the Americans, 1 February 1963.
61. Alan P. Dobson, 'The Kennedy administration and economic warfare against communism', *International Affairs*, Vol. 64 (Autumn 1988), pp. 606–10.
62. PRO FO 371/172414/ UEE 10415/21, cabinet memorandum on East–West trade, prepared by Mason, 4 February 1963; CAB C (63) 45, memorandum on proposal to increase exports to the Soviet bloc, 14 February 1963.
63. PRO FO 371/172414/ UEE 10415/22, memorandum of meeting between Home and Christian Herter in Foreign Office, 1 February 1962; PRO FO 371/172415/ UEE 10415/44, telegram no. 686 from Ormsby-Gore to Foreign Office, 4 March 1963; PRO FO 371/172415/ UEE 10415/53, memorandum of meeting between Erroll and Hodges, 5 March 1963.

Bibliography

Primary sources

National Archives, College Park, Maryland, USA

Record Group 59: general records of the Department of State.
Record Group 269: general records of the National Security Council (policy papers series).
Record Group 330: general records of the Department of Defense.
Record Group 489: general records of the International Trade Administration, Bureau of Foreign Commerce.

Harry S. Truman Library, Independence, Missouri, USA

Papers of Dean Acheson.
Papers of Thomas C. Blaisdell.
Papers of Mathew J. Connelly.
Papers of Charles Sawyer.
Papers of Harry S. Truman: President's Official File.
Papers of Harry S. Truman: Secretary's File.

Dwight D. Eisenhower Library, Abilene, Kansas, USA

Papers of John Foster Dulles.
Papers of Dwight D. Eisenhower: Ann Whitman File.
Papers of C. D. Jackson.
Papers of Clarence B. Randall.
US President's Commission on Foreign Economic Policy Papers.

Public Record Office, Kew, London, UK

CAB 128: cabinet minutes.
CAB 129: cabinet papers.
CAB 134: cabinet committees: general series.
FO 371: general records of the Foreign Office.

Published primary sources

Foreign Relations of the United States 1948: Volume IV (Washington, DC: Government Printing Office, 1974).
Foreign Relations of the United States, 1949: Volume V (Washington, DC: Government Printing Office, 1976).
Foreign Relations of the United States, 1950: Volume IV (Washington, DC: Government Printing Office, 1980).
Foreign Relations of the United States, 1951: Volume I (Washington, DC: Government Printing Office, 1979).

Foreign Relations of the United States, 1952–1954: Volume I (Washington, DC: Government Printing Office, 1983).

Foreign Relations of the United States, 1955–1957: Volume X (Washington, DC: Government Printing Office, 1989).

Foreign Relations of the United States, 1958–60: Volume IV (Washington, DC: Government Printing Office, 1992).

Foreign Relations of the United States, 1961–63: Volume IX (Washington, DC: Government Printing Office, 1995).

Congressional Record (Washington, DC: Government Printing Office).

US Statutes At Large (Washington, DC: Government Printing Office).

Parliamentary Debates (London: HMSO).

Secondary sources

Memoirs and biographies

Acheson, Dean (1969) *Present at the Creation: My Years in the State Department* (New York: Norton).

Ambrose, Stephen E. (1984) *Eisenhower Vol.2: The President, 1953–69* (New York, Simon and Schuster).

Brookshire, Jerry (1995) *Clement Attlee* (Manchester: Manchester University Press).

Bullock, Alan (1983) *Ernest Bevin Vol.III: Foreign Secretary, 1945–51* (London: Heinemann).

Chace, James (1998) *Acheson: The Secretary of State Who Created the American World* (New York: Simon and Schuster).

Charmley, John (1995) *Churchill's Grand Alliance: The Anglo-American Special Relationship, 1940–57* (London: Hodder and Stoughton).

Dutton, David (1997) *Anthony Eden: A Life and a Reputation* (London: Arnold).

Eden, Anthony (1960) *Memoirs Vol.III: Full Circle* (London: Cassell).

Eisenhower, Dwight D. (1963) *Mandate for Change: The White House Years, 1953–56* (New York: Doubleday).

Eisenhower, Dwight D. (1965) *Waging Peace: The White House Years, 1956–61* (New York: Doubleday).

Ferrell, Robert H. (1994) *Harry S. Truman: A Life* (Missouri: University of Missouri Press).

Gilbert, Martin (1988) *'Never Despair': Winston S. Churchill, 1945–65* (London: Heinemann).

Hamby, Alonzo L. (1995) *Man of the People: A Life of Harry S. Truman* (New York: Oxford University Press).

Harris, Kenneth (1982) *Attlee* (London: Weidenfeld and Nicolson).

Hoopes, Townsend (1974) *The Devil and John Foster Dulles* (Boston, Ill.: Little, Brown).

Horne, Alistair (1989) *Macmillan, 1957–86: Volume II of the Official Biography* (London: Macmillan).

Kennan, George F. (1967) *Memoirs Vol. I: 1925–50* (Boston, Ill.: Little, Brown).

Kissinger, Henry A. (1979) *White House Years* (Boston, Ill.: Little, Brown).

McCullough, David (1992) *Truman* (New York: Simon and Schuster).

McLellan, David S. (1976) *Dean Acheson: The State Department Years* (New York: Dodd, Mead).

Rothwell, Victor (1992) *Anthony Eden: A Political Biography, 1931–57* (Manchester: Manchester University Press).

Schlesinger, Arthur M. Jr (1971) *A Thousand Days: John F. Kennedy in the White House* (New York: Fawcett).

Smith, Gaddis (1972) *Dean Acheson* (New York: Cooper Square).

Sorensen, Theodore C. (1966) *Kennedy* (London: Pan).

Truman, Harry S. (1956) *Memoirs Vol. II: Years of Trial and Hope, 1946–53* (New York: Doubleday).

Weiler, Peter (1993) *Ernest Bevin* (Manchester: Manchester University Press).

Academic studies

Adler-Karlsson, Gunnar (1968) *Western Economic Warfare, 1947–67: A Case Study in Foreign Economic Policy* (Stockholm: Almquist and Wiksell).

Baldwin, David A. (1985) *Economic Statecraft* (Princeton, NJ: Princeton University Press).

Bertsch, Gary K. (1988) *Controlling East–West Trade and Technology Transfer: Power, Politics and Policies* (Durham, NC: Duke University Press).

Beschloss, Michael R. (1991) *Kennedy V. Khrushchev: The Crisis Years, 1960–63* (London: Faber and Faber).

Bowie, Robert R. and Richard Immerman (1998) *Waging Peace: How Eisenhower Shaped an Enduring Cold War Strategy* (New York: Oxford University Press).

Boyle, Peter (1988) 'The Special Relationship with Washington', in John W. Young (ed.), *The Foreign Policy of Churchill's Peace-time Administration, 1951–55* (Leicester: Leicester University Press), pp. 29–53.

Cairncross, Alec (1985) *Years of Recovery: British Economic Policy, 1945–51* (London: Methuen).

Crabb, Cecil V. Jr and Kevin V. Mulcahy (1991) *American National Security: A Presidential Perspective* (Pacific Grove, CA: Brook/Cole).

Croft, Stuart (1991) 'British Policy Towards Western Europe, 1945–51', in Peter M. R. Stirk and David Willis (eds), *Shaping Post-war Europe: European Unity and Disunity* (London: Pinter), pp. 77–89.

Croft, Stuart (1994) *The End of Superpower: British Foreign Office Conceptions of a Changing World, 1945–51* (Aldershot: Dartmouth).

Cumings, Bruce (1981) *The Origins of the Korean War Vol. I: Liberation and the Emergence of Separate Regimes, 1945–47* (Princeton, NJ: Princeton University Press).

Cumings, Bruce (1990) *The Origins of the Korean War Vol. II: The Roaring of the Cataract, 1947–50* (Princeton, NJ: Princeton University Press).

Divine, Robert A. (1981) *Eisenhower and the Cold War* (New York: Oxford University Press).

Dobson, Alan P. (1988) *The Politics of the Anglo-American Economic Special Relationship, 1940–87* (Brighton: Wheatsheaf).

Dobson, Alan P. (1995) *Anglo-American Relations in the Twentieth Century: Of Friendship, Conflict and the Rise and Decline of Superpowers* (London: Routledge).

Dockrill, Saki (1991) *Britain's Policy for West German Rearmament, 1950–55* (Cambridge: Cambridge University Press).

Dockrill, Saki (1996) *Eisenhower's New-Look National Security Policy, 1953–61* (London: Macmillan).

Doenecke, Justus D. (1979) *Not to the Swift: The Old Isolationists in the Cold War Era* (Lewisberg, PA: Bucknell University Press).

Folts, David W. (1986) 'The Development of Economic Warfare Against the Soviet Union in the Truman Administration', in William F. Levantrosser (ed.), *Harry S. Truman: The Man from Independence* (New York: Greenwood), pp. 111–27.

Foot, Peter (1992) 'Britain, European Unity and NATO, 1947–50', in Francis H. Heller and John R. Gillingham (eds), *NATO: The Founding of the Atlantic Alliance and the Integration of Europe* (New York: St. Martin's Press), pp. 57–69.

Foot, Rosemary (1995) *The Practice of Power: US Relations with China since 1949* (Oxford: Clarendon Press).

Funigiello, Philip J. (1988) *American Soviet Trade in the Cold War* (Chapel Hill, NC: University of North Carolina Press).

Fursenko, Aleksandr and Timothy Naftali (1999) *'One Hell of a Gamble': Khrushchev, Castro, Kennedy and the Cuban Missile Crisis, 1958–64* (London: Pimlico).

Gaddis, John Lewis (1982) *Strategies of Containment: A Critical Appraisal of Post-war American National Security Policy* (New York: Oxford University Press).

Gaddis, John Lewis (1987) *The Long Peace: Inquiries into the History of the Cold War* (New York: Oxford University Press).

Gaddis, John Lewis (1990) *Russia, the Soviet Union and the United States: An Interpretative History*, 2nd edn (New York: McGraw-Hill).

Gaddis, John Lewis (1992) *The United States and the End of the Cold War: Implications, Reconsiderations, Provocations* (New York: Oxford University Press).

Gaddis, John Lewis (1997) *We Now Know: Rethinking Cold War History* (New York: Oxford University Press).

Giglio, James N. (1991) *The Presidency of John F. Kennedy* (Kansas: University of Kansas Press).

Gonchrov, Sergi N., John W. Lewis and Xue Litai (1993) *Uncertain Partners: Stalin, Mao and the Korean War* (Stanford, CA: Stanford University Press).

Greenstein, Fred I. (1994) *The Hidden-Hand Presidency: Eisenhower as Leader*, revised edn (Baltimore, MD: The John Hopkins University Press).

Greenwood, Sean (1993) 'The Third Force in the Late 1940s', in Brian Brivati and Harriet Jones (eds), *From Reconstruction to Integration: Britain and Europe since 1945* (Leicester: Leicester University Press), pp. 59–69.

Heuser, Beatrice (1998) *NATO, Britain, France and the FRG: Nuclear Strategies and Forces for Europe, 1949–2000* (London: Macmillan).

Hitchcock, William I. (1998) *France Restored: Cold War Diplomacy, and the Quest for Leadership in Europe, 1944–54* (Chapel Hill, NC: University of North Carolina Press).

Hogan, Michael J. (1987) *The Marshall Plan: America, Britain and the reconstruction of Western Europe* (Cambridge: Cambridge University Press).

Hogan, Michael J. (1991) 'European Integration and German Reintegration: Marshall Planners and the Search for Recovery and Security in Western Europe', in Charles S. Maier (ed.), *The Marshall Plan and Germany: West German Development Within the Framework of the European Recovery Programme* (New York: Berg), pp. 115–70.

Hogan, Michael J. (ed.) (1995) *America in the World: The Historiography of American Foreign Relations since 1941* (Cambridge: Cambridge University Press).

Hogan, Michael J. (1998) *A Cross of Iron: Harry S. Truman and the Origins of the National Security State, 1945–54* (Cambridge: Cambridge University Press).

Ireland, Timothy P. (1981) *Creating the Entangling Alliance: The Origins of the North Atlantic Treaty Organisation* (London: Aldwych).

Kaplan, Lawrence S. (1984) *The United States and NATO: The Formative Years* (Lexington, KY: University Press of Kentucky).

Kaufman, Burton I. (1982) *Trade and Aid: Eisenhower's Foreign Economic Policy, 1953–61* (Baltimore, MD: The Johns Hopkins Press).

Kent, John and John W. Young (1992) 'British Policy Overseas: The Third Force and the Origins of NATO – In Search of a New Perspective', in Beatrice Heuser and Robert O'Neill (eds), *Securing Peace in Europe: Thoughts for the Post-Cold War Era* (London: Macmillan), pp. 41–61.

Kolko, Joyce and Gabriel Kolko (1972) *The Limits of Power: The World and United States Foreign Policy, 1945–54* (New York: Harper and Row).

Kunz, Diane B. (1997) *Butter and Guns: America's Cold War Cold War Economic Diplomacy* (New York: The Free Press).

Lacey, Michael J. (ed.) (1989) *The Truman Presidency* (Cambridge: Cambridge University Press).

LaFeber, Walter (1993) *America, Russia and the Cold War, 1945–92*, 7th edn (New York: McGraw-Hill).

Leffler, Melvyn P. (1992) *A Preponderance of Power: National Security, the Truman Administration and the Cold War* (Stanford, CA: Stanford University Press).

Leffler, Melvyn P. (1992) 'Negotiating from Strength: Acheson, the Russians and American Power', in Douglas Brinkley (ed.), *Dean Acheson and the Making of US Foreign Policy* (New York: St. Martin's Press), pp. 176–210.

Leffler, Melvyn P. (1994) *The Spectre of Communism: The United States and the Origins of the Cold War, 1917–53* (New York: Hill and Wang).

Louis, William Roger, and Hedley Bull (eds) (1986) *The Special Relationship: Anglo-American Relations since 1945* (Oxford: Clarendon Press).

Lucas, W. Scott (1996) *Divided We Stand: Britain, the US and the Suez Crisis* (London: Sceptre).

Lundestad, Geir (1990) *The American Empire* (Oslo: Norwegian University Press).

Maier, Charles S. (1989) 'Alliance and Autonomy: European Identity and US Foreign Policy Objectives in the Truman Years', in Michael J. Lacey (ed.), *The Truman Presidency* (Cambridge: Cambridge University Press), pp. 273–98.

Marks III, Frederick W. (1993) *Power and Peace: The Diplomacy of John Foster Dulles* (Westport,: Praeger).

Mastanduno, Michael (1992) *Economic Containment: CoCom and the Politics of East–West Trade* (Ithaca, NY: Cornell University Press).

Mastny, Vojtech (1996) *The Cold War and Soviet Insecurity: The Stalin Years* (New York: Oxford University Press).

Matthews, Christopher J. (1996) *Kennedy and Nixon: The Rivalry that Shaped Post-war America* (New York: Simon and Schuster).

Mayers, David (1988) *George Kennan and the Dilemmas of US Foreign Policy* (New York: Oxford University Press).

McCormick, Thomas J. (1995) *America's Half-Century: United States Foreign Policy in the Cold War and After*, 2nd edn (Baltimore, MD: The Johns Hopkins University Press).

McGlothlen, Ronald (1993) *Controlling the Waves: Dean Acheson and US Foreign Policy in Asia* (New York: Norton).

Milward, Alan S. (1984) *The Reconstruction of Western Europe, 1945–51* (London: Methuen).

Miscamble, Wilson D. (1992) *George F. Kennan and the Making of American Foreign Policy, 1947–50* (Princetor, NJ: Princeton University Press).

Morgan, Kenneth O. (1984) *Labour in Power, 1945–51* (Oxford: Clarendon Press).

Ovendale, Ritchie (ed.) (1984) *The Foreign Policy of the British Labour Governments, 1945–51* (Leicester: Leicester University Press).

Ovendale, Ritchie (1998) *Anglo-American Relations in the Twentieth Century* (London: Macmillan).

Pach, Chester J. (1991) *Arming the Free World: The Origins of the United States Military Assistance Programme, 1945–51* (Chapel Hill, NC: University of North Carolina Press).

Pach, Chester J. and Elmo R. Richardson (1991) *The Presidency of Dwight D. Eisenhower* (Kansas: University of Kansas Press).

Paterson, Thomas G. (1988) *Meeting the Communist Threat: Truman to Reagan* (New York: Oxford University Press).

Paterson, Thomas G. (1992) *On Every Front: The Making and Unmaking of the Cold War*, revised edn (New York: Norton).

Pollard, Robert A. (1985) *Economic Security Origins of the Cold War, 1945–50* (New York: Colombia Press).

Rabe, Stephen G. (1995) 'Eisenhower Revisionism: The Scholarly Debate', in Michael J. Hogan (ed.), *America in the World: The Historiography of America Foreign Relations Since 1941* (Cambridge: Cambridge University Press).

Rearden, Steven L. (1992) 'Frustrating the Kremlin Design: Acheson and NSC 68', in Douglas Brinkley (ed.), *Dean Acheson and the Making of US Foreign Policy* (New York: St. Martin's Press), pp. 157–75.

Reynolds, David (ed.) (1994) *The Origins of the Cold War in Europe: New Perspectives* (New Haven, CT: Yale University Press).

Schwabe, Klaus (1992) 'The Origins of the United States' Entanglement in Europe, 1946–52', in Francis H. Heller and John R. Gillingham (eds), *NATO: The Founding of the Atlantic Alliance and the Integration of Europe* (New York: St. Martin's Press), pp. 161–82.

Small, Melvin (1996) *Democracy and Diplomacy: The Impact of Domestic Politics on US Foreign Policy, 1789–1994* (Baltimore, MD: The Johns Hopkins University Press).

Sørensen, Vibeke (1992) 'Defence Without Tears: US Embargo Policy and Economic Security in Western Europe, 1947–51', in Francis H. Heller and John R. Gillingham (eds), *NATO: The Founding of the Atlantic Alliance and the Integration of Europe* (New York: St. Martin's Press), pp. 253–81.

Spaulding, Robert M. (1997) *Osthandel and Ostpolitik: German Foreign Trade Policies in Eastern Europe from Bismarck to Adenauer* (Providence, RI: Berghahn Books).

Steininger, Rolf (1990) 'John Foster Dulles, the European Defence Community and the German Question', in Richard H. Immerman (ed.), *John Foster Dulles and the Diplomacy of the Cold War* (Princeton, NJ: Princeton University Press), pp. 79–108.

Stueck, William (1995) *The Korean War: An International History* (Princeton, NJ: Princeton University Press).

Warner, Geoffrey (1984) 'The Labour Governments and the Unity of Western Europe, 1945–51', in Ritchie Ovendale (ed.), *The Foreign Policy of the British Labour Governments, 1945–51* (Leicester: Leicester University Press), pp. 61–82.

Warner, Geoffrey (1985) 'The British Labour Government and the Atlantic Alliance, 1949–51', in Olav Riste (ed.), *Western Security: The Formative Years* (Oslo: Norwegian University Press), pp. 247–65.

Warner, Geoffrey (1996) 'From Ally to Enemy: Britain's Relations with the Soviet Union, 1941–48', in Michael Dockrill and Brian McKercher (eds), *Diplomacy and World Power: Studies in British Foreign Policy, 1890–1950* (Cambridge: Cambridge University Press), pp. 221–43.

Watt, D. Cameron (1984) 'Britain, the United States and the Opening of the Cold War', in Ritchie Ovendale (ed.), *The Foreign Policy of the British Labour Governments, 1945–51* (Leicester: Leicester University Press), pp. 43–60.

Watt, Donald Cameron (1984) *Succeeding John Bull: America in Britain's Place, 1900–1975* (Cambridge: Cambridge University Press).

Winand, Pascaline (1993) *Eisenhower, Kennedy, and the United States of Europe* (London: Macmillan).

Woods, Randall B. and Howard Jones (1991) *Dawning of the Cold War: The United States' Quest for Order* (Athens, GA: University of Georgia Press).

Yergin, Daniel (1977) *Shattered Peace* (London: Penguin).

Young, John W. (1984) *Britain, France and the Unity of Europe, 1945–51* (Leicester: Leicester University Press).

Young, John W. (ed.) (1988) *The Foreign Policy of Churchill's Peace-time Administration, 1951–55* (Leicester: Leicester University Press).

Young, John W. (1996) *Winston Churchill's Last Campaign: Britain and the Cold War, 1951–55* (Oxford: Clarendon Press).

Zubok, Vladislav and Constantine Pleshakov (1996) *Inside the Kremlin's Cold War: From Stalin to Khrushchev* (Cambridge, Mass.: Harvard University Press).

Journal articles

Adamthwaite, Anthony (1985) 'Britain and the World: The View from the Foreign Office, 1945–49', *International Affairs*, vol. 61 (Spring), pp. 223–36.

Adamthwaite, Anthony (1988) 'Overstretched and Overstrung: Eden, the Foreign Office and the making of policy, 1951–55', *International Affairs*, vol. 64 (Spring), pp. 241–59.

Baylis, John (1984) 'Britain, the Brussels Pact and the Continental Commitment', *International Affairs*, vol. 60 (Autumn), pp. 615–29.

Boyle, Peter G. (1982) 'The British Foreign Office and American Foreign Policy, 1947–48', *Journal of American Studies*, vol. 16, no. 3, pp. 373–89.

Boyle, Peter G. (1987) 'Britain, America and the Transition from Economic to Military Assistance, 1948–51', *Journal of Contemporary History*, vol. 22, pp. 521–38.

Brands, H. W. (1989) 'The Age of Vulnerability: Eisenhower and the National Insecurity State', *The American Historical Review*, vol. 94 (October), pp. 963–89.

Cain, Frank M. (1994) 'Exporting the Cold War: British Responses to the USA's Establishment of COCOM, 1947–51', *Journal of Contemporary History*, vol. 29, pp. 501–22.

Cain, Frank M. (1995) 'The US-led Trade Embargo on China: The Origins of ChinCom, 1947–52', *Journal of Strategic Studies*, vol. 18, no. 4 (December), pp. 33–55.

Croft, Stuart (1988) 'British Policy Towards Western Europe, 1947–49: The Best of Possible Worlds', *International Affairs*, vol. 64 (Autumn), pp. 617–29.

Cromwell, William C. (1982) 'The Marshall Plan, Britain and the Cold War', *Review of International Studies*, vol. 8, pp. 233–49.

Dobson, Alan P. (1988) 'The Kennedy administration and economic warfare against communism', *International Affairs*, vol. 64 (Autumn), pp. 606–10.

Dobson, A. P. (1997) 'Informally Special? The Churchill–Truman Talks of January 1952 and the State of Anglo-American Relations', *Review of International Studies*, vol. 23, pp. 27–47.

Dockrill, M. L. (1986) 'The Foreign Office, Anglo-American Relations and the Korean War, June 1950–June 1951', *International Affairs*, vol. 62 (Summer), pp. 459–76.

Dockrill, Saki (1994) 'Co-operation and Suspicion: The United States' Alliance Diplomacy for the Security of Western Europe, 1953–54', *Diplomacy and Statecraft*, vol. 5, (March), pp. 138–82.

Førland, Tor Egil (1990) 'An Act of Economic Warfare? The Dispute over NATO's Embargo Resolution, 1950–51', *The International History Review*, vol. 12, no. 3, (August), pp. 490–513.

Førland, Tor Egil (1991) 'Selling Firearms to the Indians: Eisenhower's Export Control Policy, 1953–54', *Diplomatic History*, vol. 15 (Spring), pp. 221–44.

Førland, Tor Egil (1991) '"Economic Warfare" and "Strategic Goods": A Conceptual Framework for Analysing COCOM', *Journal of Peace Research*, vol. 28 (May), pp. 191–204.

Heuser, Beatrice (1991) 'NSC 68 and the Soviet Threat: A New Perspective on Western Threat Perception and Policy Making', *Review of International Studies*, vol. 17, pp. 17–40.

Hogan, Michael J. (1982) 'The Search for a Creative Peace: The United States, European Unity and the Origins of the Marshall Plan', *Diplomatic History*, vol. 6 (Summer), pp. 267–85.

Hogan, Michael J. (1985) 'American Marshall Planners and the Search for a European Neocapitalism', *The American Historical Review*, vol. 90 (February), pp. 44–72.

Ikenberry, G. John (1989) 'Rethinking the Origins of American Hegemony', *Political Science Quarterly*, vol. 104, no. 3, pp. 375–400.

Jentleson, Bruce W. (1984) 'From consensus to conflict: the domestic political economy of East–West energy trade policy', *International Organisation*, vol. 38, no. 4 (Autumn), pp. 637–44.

Kaufman, Robert G. (1992) 'Winston Churchill and the Art of Statecraft: The Legacy of Principled Internationalism', *Diplomacy and Statecraft*, vol. 3, pp. 159–87.

Larres, Klaus (1995) 'Eisenhower and the First Forty Days after Stalin's Death: The Incompatibility of Détente and Political Warfare', *Diplomacy and Statecraft*, vol. 6 (July), pp. 431–69.

Larres, Klaus (1996) 'Integrating Europe or Ending the Cold War? Churchill's Post-war Foreign Policy', *Journal of European Integration History*, vol. 2, no. 1, pp. 15–49.

Leffler, Melvyn P. (1984) 'The American Conception of National Security and the Beginnings of the Cold War', *The American History Review*, vol. 89 (April), pp. 346–81.

Leffler, Melvyn P. (1985) 'Strategy, Diplomacy, and the Cold War: The United States, Turkey and NATO, 1945–52', *Journal of American History*, vol. 71 (March), pp. 807–25.

Leffler, Melvyn P. (1988) 'The United States and the Strategic Dimensions of the Marshall Plan', *Diplomatic History* (Summer), pp. 277–306.

Lundestad, Geir (1986) 'Empire by Invitation? The United States and Western Europe, 1945–52', *Journal of Peace Research*, vol. 23, no. 3, pp. 263–77.

Mastanduno, Michael (1985) 'Strategies of Economic Containment: US Trade Relations with the Soviet Union', *World Politics*, vol. 37 (April), pp. 503–31.

Mastanduno, Michael (1988) 'Trade as a Strategic Weapon: American and Alliance Export Control Policy in the Early Post-war Period', *International Organisation*, vol. 42, (Winter), pp. 121–50.

Miscamble, Wilson D. (1994) 'The Foreign Policy of the Truman Administration: A Post-Cold War Appraisal', *Presidential Studies Quarterly*, vol. 24 (Summer), pp. 479–94.

Nelson, Anna K. (1983) 'The Top of the Policy Hill: President Eisenhower and the National Security Council', *Diplomatic History*, vol. 7 (Fall), pp. 307–26.

Nelson, Anna K. (1985) 'President Truman and the Evolution of the National Security Council', *Journal of American History*, vol. 72 (September), pp. 360–78.

Ovendale, Ritchie (1982) 'Britain, the USA and the European Cold War, 1945–48', *History*, vol. 67, pp. 217–35.

Reynolds, David (1985–86) 'A Special Relationship? America, Britain and the International Order since the Second World War', *International Affairs*, vol. 62 (Winter), pp. 1–20.

Reynolds, David (1988–89) 'Rethinking Anglo-American Relations', *International Affairs*, vol. 65 (Winter), pp. 89–111.

Shlaim, Avi (1983–84) 'Britain, the Berlin Blockade and the Cold War', *International Affairs*, vol. 60 (Winter), pp. 1–14.

Sloan, John W. (1990) 'The Management and Decision-Making Style of President Eisenhower', *Presidential Studies Quarterly*, vol. 20 (Spring), pp. 295–313.

Sørensen, Vibeke (1989) 'Economic Recovery versus Containment: The Anglo-American Controversy over East–West Trade, 1947–51', *Co-operation and Conflict*, vol. 24, (June), pp. 69–97.

Spaulding, Robert M. (1993) 'A Gradual and Moderate Relaxation: Eisenhower and the Revision of American Export Control Policy, 1953–54', *Diplomatic History*, vol. 17, (Spring), pp. 223–49.

Warner, Geoffrey (1989) 'The Anglo-American Special Relationship', *Diplomatic History*, vol. 13 (Fall), pp. 479–99.

Yasuhara, Yoko (1986) 'Japan, Communist China and Export Controls in Asia, 1948–52', *Diplomatic History*, vol. 10 (Winter), pp. 75–89.

Yasuhara, Yoko (1991) 'Myth of Free Trade: The Origins of COCOM, 1945–50', *Japanese Journal of American Studies*, vol. 4, pp. 127–48.

Young, John W. (1985) 'Chuchill's "No" to Europe: The Rejection of European Union by Churchill's Post-war Government, 1951–52', *Historical Journal*, vol. 28, no. 4, pp. 923–37.

Young, John W. (1986) 'Churchill, the Russians and the Western Alliance: The Three Power Conference at Bermuda, December 1953', *English Historical Review*, vol. 101 (October), pp. 889–912.

Young, John W. (1988) 'Churchill's Bid for Peace with Moscow, 1954', *History*, vol. 73, pp. 425–48.

Young, John W. (1996) 'Winston Churchill's Peacetime Administration and the Relaxation of East–West Trade Controls, 1953–54', *Diplomacy and Statecraft*, vol. 7 (March), pp. 125–40.

Unpublished dissertations and theses

Førland, Tor Egil (1991) Cold 'Economic Warfare: The Creation and Prime of CoCom 1948–54', D. Phil. thesis, history, University of Oslo.

Yasuhara, Yoko (1984) 'Myth of Free Trade: COCOM and CHINCOM, 1945–52', PhD dissertation, history, University of Wisconsin-Madison.

Index